# Praise for
## *Have a Great Week, Love!*

"A father wrote, a son collected, and voilà, here are Pop's letters. They reveal a patriarch who was devoted to family and embraced life with affection."

—Valerie Kreutzer,
Author of *A Girl Named Maria*

"John Dickson's third book, *Have a Great Week, Love!*, is a heartfelt and humorous collection of missives penned by a loving and witty father to his lucky and appreciative family over three decades."

—Kevin O'Hara,
Author of *Last of the Donkey Pilgrims*

"What a great read! My wife and I both enjoyed it. As I read it, I couldn't help but remember growing up in the eighties when writing letters back and forth in school was the norm that brought out the innocence and truths of adolescence. It was the effort put into writing that made it mean more than a text message from today."

—Nathan Aguinaga, Retired US Army Master Sergeant,
Five-Time Author at Koehler Books

"Pop's personality comes right through. Early on I felt like I could see him and hear him, even though I never met him. I was (pleasantly) surprised by his optimism, positive attitude in all things, and love for his family—especially that someone of that generation, with that upbringing, was so comfortable expressing his feelings. Pretty great. His love for his wife was apparent, and again, it was somewhat surprising that he (mostly) refrained from joking about her, as some husbands might, and was very clear in expressing his love. Wow."

—Jim Nealon,
Author of *Confederacy of Fenians*

# Have a Great Week, Love!

## TWENTY-NINE YEARS OF POP'S WEEKLY LETTERS

*Have a Great Week, Love! Twenty-Nine Years of Pop's Weekly Letters*
by Don Dickson, edited by John Dickson

ISBN 979-8-88824-125-7

Published by

 köehlerbooks ™

3705 Shore Drive
Virginia Beach, VA 23455
800-435-4811
www.koehlerbooks.com

# Have A Great Week, Love!

TWENTY-NINE YEARS OF
POP'S WEEKLY LETTERS

## Don Dickson

EDITED BY
JOHN DICKSON

VIRGINIA BEACH
CAPE CHARLES

The included letter excerpts have not been edited per the *Chicago Manual of Style* to maintain authenticity.

# Table of Contents

Introduction ........................................................................................................1

Family Matters ....................................................................................................9

Ann.....................................................................................................................40

The Shop ............................................................................................................50

The Next Generation.........................................................................................64

Brooklyn Days....................................................................................................75

The End of a Paintbrush....................................................................................80

Which Side Are You On?....................................................................................94

Going Back and Giving Back ..........................................................................105

Furry Friends....................................................................................................119

Nature Notes ....................................................................................................129

The Working Life..............................................................................................142

Digging .............................................................................................................153

The Woodie, Ah the Woodie ...........................................................................165

On the Road .....................................................................................................169

Celebrate ..........................................................................................................188

The Left Side of the Brain...............................................................................197

Friends, Along the Way....................................................................................212

Spag's ................................................................................................................245

Medical Notes..................................................................................................250

A Good Citizen.................................................................................................269

Much Ado About Nothing...............................................................................279

# Introduction

When I returned to work after Pop's funeral in December 2000, a colleague expressed her sorrow. How are you supposed to respond? I didn't hesitate; it just blurted out. "I wish you had known him." At that moment, I wished everyone had known him. Is it too far to say he was a great man? Probably, but for our family, he was at least a great guy, a good father, and an even better grandfather.

The church was filled for his memorial, a service he expressly asked not to have. "Too bad," my mother said after he passed. "You're not here. It's my decision." People wanted to say goodbye.

Tasked with one of the Bible readings at the service, I took advantage of my time at the pulpit to read a short, personal farewell, with my mother's permission. I just didn't think the pastor, while a good man who knew my father well enough, would get it right. As I read, I realized that I knew the people in the pews mostly through the letters he wrote to his children every week for the past thirty years. We each received a copy of the same letter; in the early years, they were barely legible due to the carbon paper, and later, he copied them on a Xerox machine during his weekly trip to town.

The origin of these letters is clouded by memory. I seem to remember they grew out of a minor family crisis, when his five children were out of the house, away at school, or recently graduated. We were supposed to go to an engagement party for my oldest brother David and his fiancée Paula, but we weren't told about the trip ahead of time. One of us objected, pleading upcoming deadlines for school papers. My parents went alone, and the letters started as a way to improve communication in the family.

Each week, without fail, the letter would arrive in our mailboxes.

There were gaps only when they traveled, but longer letters followed on their return home. How do you fill up a page of news each week? It was easy when there were major life events, births and deaths, new jobs, and travel and moves. But most of it was the mundane. One of his favorites was what he called the triple-header: a haircut, a trip to the dump, and shopping at Spag's, all in one week.

But they were mostly about love. Love for those who received these letters, his children and later his grandchildren. We all looked forward to the stories and anecdotes about our cousins and to see if we had made the letter! But also, the affection for his neighbors and friends and pets and classmates, for his college, for his life in a small town in northeastern Connecticut. Most of all, love for his wife, Georganna, with whom he shared fifty-plus years.

The last words I heard Pop speak were about our mother, his wife. He had come down with a bad cold; then he fell down the stairs and broke ribs and perhaps his collarbone. He couldn't cough because of the pain, and his cold quickly turned to pneumonia. An oxygen mask covered his face, making him sweaty. So, I sat on the edge of his hospital bed, wiping his forehead. His breathing strained, as if he had been running a marathon for three days, this man who lived with the constraints of heart disease after a crippling heart attack twenty-five years earlier.

The doctors had already told us he wouldn't pull through. I found it hard to believe; he was a creature of his generation, who grew up in the depression and went to war. Driven was his default gear. He had been on a mission ever since childhood in Brooklyn, where his father was out of work for years and his mother died of cancer when he was a senior in high school. With the help of a mentor at Seamen's Savings Bank, whom he met in his after-school job, he applied to Princeton once he got out of the Coast Guard. The GI Bill, the mentor's blank check that he never cashed, and a series of part-time jobs financed this opportunity. He wasn't just driven; he was in a hurry. When he graduated from Princeton after three years, his new wife and baby were by his side.

A job offer came from Procter & Gamble, and they left for Cincinnati, where four more children were born and where he joined that company's famed business ethos and learned all about marketing. After fifteen years, he picked up and moved his family to New Jersey and worked for Warner Lambert. Another company switch—to RCA—meant relocating twice more, to Indiana and then back to the suburbs of New York.

He traveled for his job. Back then, airlines gave people plaques for miles flown, and he had a bunch of them. When he was home, he worked, mostly on the dilapidated houses he had bought at bargain prices. There's one memory of him shoveling out our driveway, easily over 400 feet long, so he could get to work.

Pop also took his role as father seriously. Saturdays, we were expected to work. Sunday dinners included competitions on geography and current events or the dreaded grilling we expected about the sermon that morning. We took road trips, across country in all directions, camping in the national parks, visiting the world's fairs, meeting my mother's Kansas cousins. Imagine packing coats and ties for the boys for church while we were camping.

What does a man who is this driven do after he's lost his corporate job in his mid-fifties and suffered a near-fatal heart attack? Pop slowed down. He stepped off the frustratingly unreliable commuter train and moved to Connecticut's quiet corner, opened an antique shop with our mother, gardened, took naps, and puttered. His doctor told him to pick the lane with the longest line of cars whenever he approached a toll booth.

Gasping for air on his hospital bed, he looked up at me and asked, "Where's Georganna?" Minutes later, a nurse came in and gave him some morphine to relieve his discomfort. I don't think he regained consciousness. Within a couple of hours, he passed away.

A few years later, I started a project to digitize all the letters. Reading through them again, I realized there were excerpts of family history or town happenings or stories he had read in the paper or anecdotes about nothing in particular, each conveyed with a sense of humor or a poignant twist. Then, I knew that this would be how I could fill my wish that people know him.

A father's love. Love was how he ended each letter. "Have a great week! LOVE!!!"

# Instructions

*"Never read a book to the end, nor even in sequence,
and without skipping."*

**—Fernando Pessoa,** *The Book of Disquiet*

A word on the text. My job as editor was really one of selecting, culling through the roughly 1,500 letters to identify those that might be of most interest. Except for minor changes, like commas outside of quotation marks, I have left my father's words to speak for themselves. This means, of course, that there are a few phrases that sound jarring to us in our times. You will be able to see by the context that he meant no disrespect. I have penned a short introductory paragraph on each chapter. The artwork is courtesy of family members, his grandchildren, a niece, a friend, and me.

The chapters follow themes, recurring threads in the letters over the almost thirty years. The initial chapter serves as an introduction to the family and major events, to provide background to names and places. After that, the chapters cover various aspects of family, events, life in the "Quiet Corner," reflections, wit, and advice. This is not a book that has to be read from cover to cover, but it can be picked up and opened to any page, with a money-back guarantee that you, the reader, will pause and ponder, remember, smile, and enjoy. That part about the money-back, by the way, was figurative.

# Who's Who

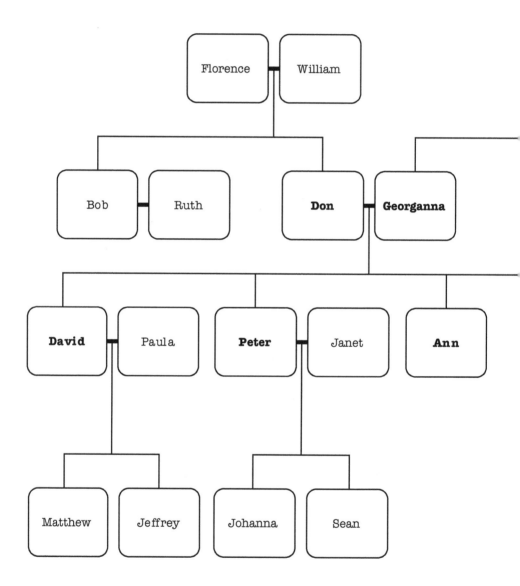

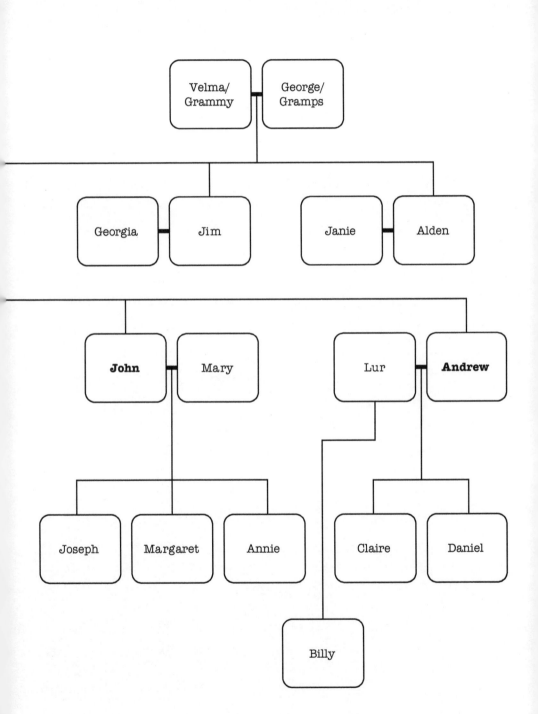

# Family Matters

**"Of course, there are a few leaves on the ground. Anybody for raking? As Ann says, the family that leaves together stays together."**

*Like many in the baby-boom generation, we had a large family. Our parents met in the spring of 1946 in the library at Princeton University, where our father was studying under the GI Bill. Our mother had taken a part-time job at the circulation desk, during her spring break, home from her college, Carleton. They married a year later, and nine months later, David was born. He was followed by Peter, and then Ann. A year later, I joined the crew, and then Andrew rounded out the total to a healthy seven. We grew up in Cincinnati, Chester, New Jersey, and Indianapolis. By the time my parents moved to Wilton, Connecticut, they were empty nesters, with all their children away at school or out on their own. That's where these letters start.*

*Mom* by John Dickson

Dear Wonderful Workers,

I'm only kidding, as you know, for you really didn't work during your visits home, except to saw wood, creosote trees, steam wallpaper, rake leaves, wash dishes, iron sheets, clean ponds, move logs, etc. But it was simply great to hear your laughter, wild music, late snoring and all those other great sounds of a busy home. *(04-12-71)*

Ah – what a week! Imagine a Father who has a son reach 21 and an invitation from a daughter for Father's Weekend all in one week. That was the week that was. *(04-25-71)*

We watched Channel 13 and saw a re-play of last week's Princeton-Harvard game. Peter was very prominent in the action, and the announcer and the commentator had some fine words about Peter's goal tending. Also, at the end of the game, the camera zoomed in on Pop and Peter. Imagine, celebrities in the family! *(11-19-72)*

In case you all aren't aware of it, Andrew's grades are up – and that is great news! We also got Peter's and John's grades and they are both sensational. What a smart bunch! (Must be their Mother!) *(02-20-73)*

The surprise of the week came last evening when I looked out the window and saw Peter winding his way through our new garden. He had finished his comprehensive exam in the afternoon and came home for a 'break.' We had a fine chat and dinner. These are the kind of surprises that we like! *(05-21-73)*

David called twice on Thursday to tell us about his possible promotion and move. He was in Hartford, the home office, to learn about a transfer to Albany. He asked his Pop for advice - – and Pop was cautiously neutral. In these great decisions, the major help from parents comes from asking the right questions, not from pronouncing the right answers. *(06-24-73)*

Then we drove home via Far Hills, picking up Mrs. Casendino. We also picked up a virtual truckload of apples and vegetables. This is 'Apple Pie Week'! *(09-17-73)*

You should see Ann's quilt! (Hi, Ann!) It's sitting on Johnny's 'bench' and it's a colorful combination of a thousand (maybe a hundred) blue, pink and yellow squares. She has a pillow to match and it's very attractive. *(09-23-73)*

On Monday night, Mom, John, Andrew and I went to Shea to see the Mets play Houston. Fortunately, the Mets won, but unfortunately it was in the bottom of the 9th, and we had left early in the 9th 'to beat the rush.' It'll take some time before Pop lives that one down. *(09-03-74)*

For we have sensational news. David and Paula called on Friday evening to tell us that they will become parents next Spring. Do you know how Pop waits for Spring! Well, we're really going to have a Welcome Spring party in '75. Ain't that great, great news! Take good care of yourself, Paula! *(10-14-74)*

On Saturday I drove down to Princeton for a meeting and had the pleasure of seeing Peter and John briefly for a sandwich and beer. Peter was accepted into George Washington Law School and Andrew into Ripon, so they were two rather happy Dicksons this week. *(03-17-75)*

The big news, of course, was the announcement from Peter and Janet about May 24th! Mom talked to them again by phone last evening, and they are coming to Wilton this Sunday along with Janet's parents. The announcement was made shortly after they arrived on Thursday evening for a short visit. *(03-31-75)*

Pop spent this weekend on a great variety of work projects and so did Mom – but who cares to hear about work. We want you all to know that we sure do love what we're doing and the only "more – greater" thing would be to see you – here or there. *(09-28-75)*

Gramps called about 11 p. m., in the middle of a heart attack, and we got the Fairfield police to pick him up, and we raced to the Norwalk Hospital for some long hours of waiting. He responded well to the medicine and seemed to be coming along OK, but Mom's visit today was not too encouraging. Needless to say, the family's schedule has been kind of screwy. *(10-14-75)*

A reaction two weeks after [*losing his job*] – how busy can one be? The past week was a 'jammed pack' week, but I guess things are getting done.
Some great letters last week . . . John wrote to "Ma and Pa Dickson" and Peter to Meadow Rock Industries, New England Division. . . . Ann sent me a postcard of NYC with Bye-Bye Big Apple written on it. *(12-07-75)*

One thing is for sure. Life ain't dull around here. On Saturday morning, while sanding in the early hours in the basement, I heard a noise at the back door, came up and bumped into Ann, who had driven overnight from Cincinnati with a girlfriend, Debbie. They are here for a three-day visit. *(04-05-76)*

The big news of last week was the decision by John to accept an offer from the Peace Corps for two years in Gabon, Africa. He called one evening for a long chat, and then on Friday. Pop drove down for a further chat, only to find that John had already made his decision. And Mom and I think it is a good one. *(04-05-76)*

But there's only one thing to write about. John. At 5PM today, John boarded Delta Flight 103, bound for Atlanta, and beyond. He had the world's bulkiest duffel jammed with an absolute ton of stuff, including a deflated soccer ball, stuck in at the last moment. He had a typewriter. He had a red knapsack with books and things. He had a guitar – the only guitar case in the world, or in Africa at least, that has Alaska Airlines stickers and a check tag from the Princeton Club of N.Y. He also had moisty eyes – and so did his father. *(07-07-76)*

This is obviously no surprise, but autumn is moving in. Leaves are turning and falling, the wheelbarrow has a load of pumpkins, and the sun is setting earlier. We are busy here, we are happy here, and we are bursting with love. Problems? A couple. But love wins! *(09-19-76)*

David, Paula and Matthew arrived yesterday, and are here for the coming week. They are going to spend the days house hunting in the Hartford area. They did their first exploring today, and just wearily drove in. Mom was a most reluctant sitter for Andrew (I did it. I keep saying Andrew for Matthew, and now I typed it. Sorry Matthew. Sorry, Andrew.) *(10-10-76)*

We sold a house – a great house. We bought a house – a great house. It all began last Monday. We had been carrying on conversations with a nice couple called the Liebler's from Briarcliff, N. Y. who very much wanted this house. But we were too nervous to· "count on it." But on Monday, their lawyer talked to Mr. Adams and things looked pretty sure. So, Mom and I left in the afternoon for New Hampshire and some concentrated searching. Three dates had been set up and we were to see about ten homes and farms on Tuesday, beginning at 8 A.M. About 5 P. M. we wearily headed home, with a large amount of disappointment. We reluctantly agreed that our fall-back spot, in Arlington, Vermont would have to be picked up, although it had some serious drawbacks. As we approached Sturbridge, Mass., Mom casually suggested that we might not want to drive all the way home.

We needed gas, and Pop had been dreaming of a dry martini – and so we splurged on a comfortable room at the Inn. We left early Wednesday, and decided to wander the back roads, rather than jump on the Interstate. As we drove through Pomfret Conn., we saw OUR HOUSE. It's hard to believe, but it is the same house that we talked about from an ad in Antiques magazine last spring. *(10-31-76)*

I guess this is the last letter from here. Next week, Pomfret Center! *(11-26-76)*

Can a farm move? Yes. On December 1, the new address for Meadow Rock Farm and the Dicksons is RFD#1, Pomfret Center, Conn. There is a meadow (a long, rolling one that once was a golf course) and there are certainly rocks, so the Meadow Rock sign will now be on State Road 169, in the nice old town of Pomfret Center, in northeastern Connecticut. *(12-01-76)*

The big news of the week was that David and Paula seem to have chosen a new home. It's in Marlborough, Conn., and a relatively easy commute for David. And, so the long search is over, and they were a mighty relieved pair this weekend. *(01-17-77)*

We have a nice bouquet of Valentine flowers on the table, and Thank You – Ann! We talked a few times last week with Ann who is quite bubbly bout her new job. She's working hard, but enjoying it. *(02-13-77)*

It was quite a week. It started off spectacularly with a telephone call from John [*in Gabon*]. It was 8 A.M., and we all got on the phone. John had received all the recent letters, except the one that I wrote from the hospital telling him what had happened – so he was understandably puzzled. He sounded great, and it was a few minutes of excitement here. *(08-07-77)*

It is my plan to send Mom to Las Vegas. After what she did to me in gin rummy last week, it is obvious that it is more than luck – she is a true card shark. It was humiliating. *(12-18-77)*

Andrew kept this place going for the last couple weeks, so that we could enjoy ourselves – a much appreciated use of part of his vacation. Among the things he did to keep from going wacky from boredom was a watercolor of the old wheelbarrow and it is sensational. We need the help of all of you to keep inspiring Andrew to continue with his painting and sketching work. *(01-13-78)*

When you come here the next time, we must schedule an organ concert by Mom. She has been practicing, and it sounds pretty good. She also made a batch of bread M-M-M-M! And she sewed and needlepointed. And she clobbered me at our newest game – backgammon. She is good – or else I must be bad, awful bad. *(01-22-78)*

We were in Ripon from Friday noon to Monday noon, and it was pleasant from start to finish. We saw a lot of Andrew, naturally, and while the pace was leisurely, we did do a lot of things. But the highlights were the comments about Andrew! The stern and old-fashioned Dean of the College said that Andrew was "a fine, decent, friendly gentleman" and he obviously meant it. Andrew's History advisor normally has a reception at his home one evening for his history seniors, but this year asked only Mom and I to join Andrew for a visit after one of the concerts. And the President had some great words about Andrew's soccer and lacrosse exploits. Now can you imagine our grins and pride? *(05-22-79)*

Yesterday was Gramps' funeral. For the benefit of John and Andrew, I detail a little of what happened during the past week.
On Tuesday, while at lunch in Westport, Gramps had a heart attack, a very bad one. It was immediate and he just keeled over while in

the middle of a sentence. He never regained consciousness. He was given first aid at the restaurant, and then rushed to the hospital, but he was essentially gone when he arrived. He was hooked up to various machines, which gave him life support. Mom went down and stayed for a couple days of waiting, but when the doctor said that it might be two or three weeks before the extent of the damage was known, she came home. On Friday, Gramps died. He was 80, and, considering the fact that the attack had caused brain damage and had probably blinded him, I guess we have to say that his death was somewhat merciful. *(08-21-79)*

When Andrew went back, he obviously took a bunch of his stuff. He also asked me if he could take a few tapes. I expected that he would want David Bowie, Led Zepplin and such stuff, but do you know that he grabbed my Glenn Miller, Artie Shaw, Tommy Dorsey tapes? Where have we gone wrong? *(10-09-79)*

John is home. John is home. John is home. That's the big news for this letter! He called on Thursday afternoon from the Boston airport, and Mom and I scrambled up to greet him. It is very, very good to have him home. He has been getting himself organized for job searching and getting reacquainted with Charlie and Pomfret Center. Among the jobs to be done was a refurbishing of his clothing, and so he and I went up to Worcester on Friday to buy some suits and other essentials. *(11-05-79)*

'Tis the last day of the year. And it seems like a good time for Mom and I to thank each of you for all the fine things you did for us during this past year – all the calls, letters, visits, gifts and all of the help that you gave us. We know that there were probably many times when you would just as well be doing other things in other places, but we are mighty grateful for each bit of attention, care and love that came our way. Many thanks. *(12-31-79)*

Today begins the 35<sup>th</sup> year of the Great Romance. Yes, 34 years ago yesterday was the first date – an Abbott and Costello movie. I remember coming back to Pyne Hall afterward, and Leighton Laughlin saying to me something like "you're hooked." I said no, but he was right. Thank goodness. *(04-07-80)*

We went out for supper on Peter's birthday – a part of Pop's philosophy that a birthday is as much a celebration for Mom as for the birthday child. *(04-28-80)*

The BIG news this week comes from Marlborough! David and Paula called to announce that they are expecting. Great news! The event had just been confirmed by the doctor, so, there is much time ahead. But we are all very happy to hear such good news. *(06-02-80)*

Yesterday began with Pop attempting pancakes for everybody and they were a mixed success. Or a mixed failure. I need more practice. *(10-13-80)*

Actually, it was generally slow and quiet here all week. There was some excitement one evening when I said my customary "good night" to Jessica Savitch of NBC news, and then added, "I love you, Jessica." (It's a sign of aging when you start talking to the TV set). But Mom gently suggested that I hadn't said "I love you" to her that day – a point which I stoutly rejected. The excitement has died down, but I have learned my lesson. I LOVE YOU, MOMMA! *(11-10-80)*

April 6! April 6! A day in history! For on this date 35 years ago, Mom and I had our first date – a movie with Abbott and Costello. I don't remember the plot, but I remember the plot since then – LOVE! *(04-06-81)*

Peter called to ask some questions of the old master about wallpapering. He was taking the plunge and had some technical questions, which are kind of hard to talk about over the phone. Hope it worked out without too much difficulty, Peter. *(10-19-81)*

John and Mary were here for a few hours on Wednesday, with the primary mission to return the van that they had used for their move. Generous Pop had turned over the van with a tire that wasn't too good, and it blew with the load of furniture, and John had the pleasure of buying a new tire. We had a long discussion about the fairness of such a transaction. Pop lost. *(11-16-81)*

We had a birthday party for Matthew here yesterday, and one of his presents was a bell for his bike . . . and so the bike was a busy item yesterday. Also, Matthew helped me paint a fence . . . an important step in passing along important projects to future generations. *(05-17-82)*

Well, we're all back in the real world again.
But the happiness we shared at The Point [*thirty-fifth wedding anniversary family reunion in the Adirondacks*] seems to me to be one more reminder of the value of an occasional pause to celebrate some of life's events – big and small. And so, if there's a message from our time together, that message is to keep trying to do those things that give us a chance to collect our memories and think about how they might make us happier tomorrow morning, or better yet, this morning. What you did for us was tremendous. We will celebrate it each day for a long time to come. *(06-28-82)*

Uncle Gil is incredible. Sometimes I wish I had a recording machine to take down his stories about trips and about his life during the depression. He and Aunt Flo went up to Michigan and bought a farm with no plumbing and no central heating and eked out a living selling crops from the small acreage they had. *(08-16-82)*

THE BIG NEWS IS, OF COURSE, THE ARRIVAL OF JOSEPH!!! Our very best wishes to John and Mary and our thoughts and prayers are with you on this joyful day. *(12-28-82)*

The highlight has to be the first visit of Joseph to this place. He and John and Mary arrived late Friday afternoon, just as the first few snowflakes were coming down. And he is one wonderful little boy. As you might imagine, he spent a fair amount of time in his grandmother's arms. *(02-14-83)*

And then to Uncle Gil's. At 84 he is spry and lots of fun. I sense he is lonely. He is a non-stop talker, but it is fascinating to hear his tales of earlier years. He worked as a chauffeur in the 20's, driving a Pierce Arrow for a wealthy family for five years to Florida, Canada and other spots – all on bad roads I gathered. *(03-08-82)*

The enclosed check is for your brother. One of them has yours. This is clearly a bribe. A bribe to get you to write a letter. Have a good time and spread the gossip. *(03-14-83)*

Yesterday's Sports section of the NY Times had a headline: DICKSON MOVING UP, AND FAST. Hope that applies to each of you. *(05-02-83)*

Thursday was Uncle Bob's 65th birthday and I chatted with him on the phone on this important date. Since he will be retiring [*from a career as a minister in the Reformed Church of America to the country house*] in Pennsylvania, Mom and I sent him a dungaree jacket and trousers, work gloves, a bandanna, a dungaree shirt and a corn cob pipe. I have never seen Uncle Bob in any of those work uniforms, and I look forward to seeing him model the items on the job. *(05-23-83)*

Last night after supper, a car left carrying some weary folk to New Hampshire, and then one left for Marlborough with some weary folk, leaving two weary people here. We were all pooped after a busy weekend, but we hope everyone was also as happy as we were. Thank you for coming.

The weekend included swimming at Mashmoquet, a visit to the Woodstock Fair, some fishing at Bigelow Hollow, plenty of eating, not enough sleeping, constant chatter and a good amount of children watching. *(09-05-83)*

WELCOME, JOHANNA ANN!!!!!!!!!!!!!!!!!!!!!!!!!!!!!!!!!!!!!!!!!!!!!!!!!!!
Have a great week! LOVE!!!! [*the entire letter*] *(10-03-83)*

It's fun to get calls from Washington. Mom called last night to relate one more 'progress–things are getting better' report. She had seen Johanna and was so glad to describe all the emotion of seeing a bright little girl. Peter and Janet had held her during the day and so normalcy seems to be taking over, Thank God . . .

David and I had also had a short fishing trip to the Adirondacks last week. It was absolutely beautiful up there (near the Point) with warm sunshine and autumn colors. We scrambled home after Mom's phone call on Saturday morning, but we had had some good hours. David caught one and Pop was zilched. *(10-05-83)*

The BIG call of the week came from John, who relayed the happy news that he had been accepted by the Foreign Service. The assignment will be in the U.S. Information Service and starts with a training program in Washington on June 11. We all know how much John wanted this job and how hard he worked for it – and we are very pleased. Congratulations, John! *(03-12-84)*

The BIG news of last week came from a phone call from John – who said they were expecting again in January! That's great news. John also talked about the complications of where and when of his eventual assignment. As of now it is to Lagos, Nigeria and he would be going sometime around Thanksgiving. *(07-16-84)*

The Second Annual Marathon with Matthew ended here yesterday afternoon. I believe it was a success. First, because we had a chance to spend so much time with some of you, and, second, because as we were approaching Marlborough yesterday, Matthew asked where we were going 'next year.' *(07-24-84)*

On Monday, we were visited by a couple from Illinois who are some sort of relative of Uncle Gil's. They were here for four hours, four long hours, and I do believe she talked for almost the entire time. Near the end of the ordeal, I began to think with horror that they may have planned to stay all night. *(09-17-84)*

On Friday evening, the John Joline's were here for supper. John was headmaster at Darrow, and so David and Paula joined us for an evening of talk of old times. One of the brightest moments came when it was learned that both the Dicksons and the Jolines had gone to the same place for honeymoons in 1947 and even used the same cabin. I found our honeymoon scrapbook and in it were some other papers, including the bill from Princeton Hospital for David's birth. The per day charge was $9.00 and the delivery room charge was $12.00. How times have changed. *(10-22-84)*

Do you remember the great group photo that was taken when we were all together here last fall? Well, we are putting it in Kodak's Family Album which will be placed at the Statue of Liberty when it is re-dedicated. And so, for years to come, we can go to the Statue and see our happy faces. *(01-28-85; see follow-up 04-28-96)*

WELCOME SEAN DONALD DICKSON!!!!!
We got the wonderful news from Peter on Tuesday morning, and Mom has since talked with Janet. All is well and we are so happy

with the whole story. Congratulations to Peter and Janet. *(05-20-85)*

Uncle Gil has been sending me coupons for gin, and I have needled him about my need for many more coupons. Last week, he sent me a recipe for making gin – something he had saved from prohibition days. *(04-14-86)*

Mom had some medical appointments and news. The diagnosis is adult chronic asthma. It is controllable but not curable. She is on various medicines and breathing devices. We do not know how long it has taken to develop to this stage, but there are some hints that it has been coming for some time. The cause is elusive, and she and the doctors have been trying to pinpoint possible allergy problems – but without specific success. *(07-07-86)*

A heavy rain in the late afternoon resulted in the usual large puddle on the other side of the small bridge on the road. A small car came down the hill at too fast a speed and hit the puddle, lost control and slammed into the cemetery wall. A truck driver ran here, and Mom called an ambulance. It was slow in coming, but when it did come, it came en masse. We had ambulances, fire engines, troopers, volunteers, etc. And a helicopter. It landed in the field and took the young woman to Hartford. One lesson is not to speed in a driving rain and eat pizza at the same time. *(08-11-86)*

John, Mary and little friends were here from Wednesday to Friday, and we welcomed Ann's first visit to these rooms. She was a fine little girl. She has quite a crop of hair. When they left on Friday, I don't think they could have squeezed anything more in their car. And, as they were leaving, Joseph got stung by a wasp on his fanny, and we all heard a new kind of scream. It wasn't very funny for Joseph, and he quickly recovered. *(08-03-87)*

It's a little quiet here this morning. Ah! but the rooms are filled with echoes of laughter, screams, tears, and of course, quite a few coughs, sniffles and sneezes. Mom is up this morning after a day buried under the covers trying to shake the cold. I'm not much better.

And it all ended so quickly. But I hope you all enjoyed it as much as we did. I can now walk a straight line from one room to another without hitting trucks, dolls, games, books etc. *(02-29-88)*

It was a busy week – with one very emotional moment. When we watched David and Paula drive from here on Tuesday morning (they had spent the night here), we were happy, so happy, to see them off together for a new home – all together. But it was surely sad, after all these fine years of picnics, pinochle, dinners, celebrations, etc, to know that one era was ending and another was starting . . . *(08-21-88)*

It has to be a Great Week when we get the chance to talk to four guys named David, Peter, John and Andrew. Many thanks for your Thanksgiving messages. Thanksgiving was a little (a lot?) unusual for us. . . . It was the first Thanksgiving when we were alone. Mom prepared a small version of a dinner and we did enjoy a quiet afternoon. *(11-27-89)*

I have a calendar on my desk with a daily message. Today's is most appropriate: "The greatest gift a father can give his children is to love their mother." *(06-17-90)*

We bounce back.

From last week's low point, we have had one of the happiest weeks ever. John and Mary and crew have left for a week in Pittsfield, and we have so much to remember. Such as bikes, scooters, wagons, the barefoot trio, baseball, tennis soccer, crayoning, drawing (Margaret drew a famous picture of a dog – a male dog), John learning to tie a bow tie, John's early morning jogging 'around the block', a church service with three very quiet and wonderful children, and so many hours of just plain enjoying. And food. We had a hamburger cookout last night, and one night Mary's brother Danny, wife Mary and new son (one year), came for a steak cookout. Danny brought peas from his garden; and mine are just beginning to look like peas – very late this year. Although, Joseph, Margaret and Annie did find a few today. Yes, it was one of those weeks. We hope yours was good, too. Someday, when you are in the happy situation we are, you will appreciate how much this kind of week means. We wish you well. *(07-01-90)*

There are so many things to say about Wisconsin [*family reunion in Door County*]. Each of us has our own memories, and I don't want to intrude on those, but I do want to send along a couple thoughts. First, the grandchildren were spectacular. They were so wonderful to us and to each other. The love and affection we encountered was so natural that Mom and I talked about it on the long ride home. A special note should be made for Billy, who survived a bunch of new adults and new children with ease. That's a compliment to Billy and to everyone else. *(07-22-90)*

Among the historic dates of last week were the anniversary of the day that Ann left us, and of Pop's heart attack. *(06-16-91)*

This could/should be a one sentence Letter, and it would say "We have been to one of the happiest events Ever." Ever. [*Andrew and Lur's wedding*]
But there are some things to be added:
—It was great to see all of the cousins together – and we greeted a new one – Billy.
—Andrew and Lur's friends were a most spectacular group. They came from so many places to enjoy the celebration of their marriage. The affection they all had for these two Ripon classmates was very evident.
—Watching 40 or so kids run, chase, scream, splash, etc. was almost

as exciting as the wedding.

—Weren't Johanna and Billy impressive in their roles as flower girl and ring bearer?

—Every time we turned around, Mrs. Casendino was doing 'something.' Ann called her a Rent-a-Mom, and Mrs. Casendino sure reveled in her role with her 'sons.'

—Who can forget Mom and Mrs. Knaak lighting the candles to open the ceremony? *(07-10-91)*

We had a fine day in Rhode Island. Peter divided his time between the beach, the phone and a table filled with papers as he worked on his big case. Mom stayed in the shady porch of the house while the rest of us walked, read or splashed in the water. In the evening, Peter fixed a great pasta supper. John was the leader of games and walks with the kids. Or was one of them. *(07-21-91)*

Then, on Monday morning, we took off with Johanna and Sean for the Eastern shore of Maryland. We took a ferry boat ride on the oldest running route (1693), swam in the motel pool, picnicked, went to the Maritime museum, and played in the park in Oxford Md. It all went well, except for one thought . . . Johanna and Sean said that "Pop snored!" Do *you* believe that? *(08-25-91)*

15 years. 15 good years. That's how long we have been in this old place. We remember Ann's comment (overheard) in a telephone conversation that "Mom and Pop have really done it this time." I guess the place looked pretty bad – but it now seems very comfy. It is great to come around the bend in the road and see it, waiting for us. And for you. *(12-08-91)*

Mom and I talked to a group after church today about our experiences in South Africa. Christ Church has been making (thanks to Mom) an annual gift to a girls school near Durban. *(05-31-92)*

It was an event-full week. One of the events was Pop's birthday, and I thank you for the calls, gifts and cards. I have some spectacular books, and now have another incentive to stay awake longer at night – to read these fine books. From one of you I got a paint bucket, a paint roller, brushes, a scraper, a drop cloth, and a Sherwin Williams ice chest filled with paint rollers. I also had that glorious happiness to talk with each of you. And for all of that, MANY THANKS! *(06-14-92)*

One of the things we all did was to watch a tape of Jimmy Stewart in Harvey – a gift for our Anniversary. One of you has a good memory, for that is the play that Mom and I went to on the day that I proposed to Georganna Dean. *(07-05-92)*

Uncle Jim came home from the hospital ahead of schedule and that is good news. I wrote him a get well letter, and included a Clinton/Gore bumper sticker, and that will probably set his recovery back some. He has promised to leave the country if Clinton is elected. Other Dean news is that Rell has announced that she is pregnant. *(09-20-92)*

On the way, I stopped to see Uncle Jim, and he has graduated from a walker to a cane. And the Clinton/Gore sticker hadn't set his recovery back. *(09-27-92)*

Can this marriage be saved? That is the title of the most popular magazine series. Mom wants to buy a leaf blower. I don't. I will let you know the brand name of the machine. *(10-25-92)*

First of all, Thank You! From your comfortable and orderly homes you came here to sleep on couches, wait in line for bathrooms, work like mess sergeants to put together banquets, and do the cleanup, and still seem to enjoy your time here. And then a long ride home. You are all award winners. But the real awards should go to the

children who played together and helped so wonderfully. Mom and I hope that each of you will someday enjoy the same kind of joy with your own children and grandchildren. You made this a very special Christmas and New Year.
Yesterday would have been Ann's 40th birthday. *(01-03-93)*

We talked to Margaret, and we learned that what she wanted for her birthday was snow and 'scabs.' It seems that Joseph, Margaret and Annie all have chicken pox, and they (New ribbon!) are all anxious for the scabs to appear, signaling the end of the darned thing. *(01-11-93)*

John brought a bunch of pictures of our Princeton weekend, their Christmas celebration, the week here with snow and Joe's birthday. It may be a sign of age, but we look at these pictures again and again. *(01-31-93)*

Valentine's Day has been a great event. Thank you for the cards and calls. It's a sign of something, but I no longer give Mom slinky black nightgowns. This year it is an oversized Snoopy card. *(02-14-93)*

Andrew wrote and talked about the work on their basement. He also quoted from a newsletter from Billy's school . . . "For weeks the third grade class has been studying human history. Finally, when asked on a quiz to name the three major races of the world, one boy wrote (1) The Bossten Marython, (2) the Kintuci Durby, and (2) the Indian Apples 500." *(03-19-93)*

IMPORTANT! READ THE CARD FIRST! THEN CALL THE MYSTERY NUMBER!
Great News, Ain't It! (Lur's pregnant.) *(02-20-94)*

Speaking of romance, Mom, as a Justice of the Peace, is going to marry a couple on June 24. They stopped by yesterday to make the arrangements. *(04-10-94)*

We all know the BIG NEWS OF LAST WEEK! Welcome Claire Theresa! I was working outside when Mom came running out of the house with the news that she had had a call from the Delivery Room only an hour after Claire's arrival. And from two excited parents. And to two excited grandparents. Mom left in ten minutes to book her tickets for Chicago. She leaves on Wednesday for a week of helping. *(10-23-94)*

Ah! But here's happier news. We spent some great hours in Princeton with two families from Silver Spring. Mom and I arrived Friday afternoon, ran some errands, and the two cars from Maryland came for supper. On Saturday morning, we had long, long breakfasts, and then rambled around before meeting for a tailgate lunch. It was especially fun to watch some girls (named Dickson) in their Tiger cheerleader outfits. *(11-16-94)*

It was such a glorious Thanksgiving weekend. How does one measure such fine days? By the number of empty cans and bottles? No. By the number of trash bags jammed into the rubbish cans? No. By the number of towels going through the washer? No. Well, my judgment is that there is no numerical measurement. How to add up pictures of grandchildren at puzzles and card games, at grandchildren in an endless parade of carrying leaves (and each other) in the garden cart, at scenes of John, Mary and David working for hours to move leaves from one place to another (despite the pleas of Pop to STOP), at the joys of sitting down to a vast display of Mom's cooking successes, particularly at the Thanksgiving banquet, at the joys of just plain chatter in the kitchen, before the big fireplace, and in countless other moments. And so forth. It was so great. *(11-28-94)*

Our prime message has been to thank each of *you* for the joys of the past week. It ain't easy sleeping in cramped spaces, waiting in line for a shower, preparing and cleaning up for huge meals, and generally living in endless noise and confusion. It's a hassle, and we know it, and it all makes us all the more thankful that *you* do it. We love *you*. And as one anonymous on-looker said: "The Dickson males are not at their best when loading cars." *(01-01-95)*

There is truly only one story about last week . . . and that involves Mom. As of this moment on Monday morning, you are all up-to-date by virtue of phone calls over the weekend. By the time you get this, we will hopefully have talked again, and hopefully with some better news. The report from the hospital lab confirms that there is something growing in the chest area that is causing the terrible coughing. *(01-16-95)*

On a happier note, we talked to Margaret on her birthday. And we thank you all for the calls, letters and cards relating to Mom's situation and to a bunch of thank-yous for the Christmas visits. I think the thank you notes should have come from 233 Pomfret Street, for you have no idea how much we love to have you here. *(01-16-95)*

There are two clippings. One is for an ad for a ranch in Idaho. During my younger and more stupid days, I thought we should buy a ranch in Idaho. And so, after the Seattle Fair, we went to Twin Peaks – and learned that a meal can consist of three types of potatoes. We left – and found Elkhorn. *(03-12-95)*

The BIG news of the week came from Peter, who went public with his decision to have a new law affiliation in Princeton. He has spent many months arriving at the decision, and we wish him well. They have been house hunting in Princeton and nearby. As always, these are wrenching moments, and Peter said that Johanna was most affected. Happily, new friends await her. *(04-09-95)*

A special week because it has been a special weekend. John and Mary and good friends arrived here yesterday, and we have enjoyed so many good moments together. Including an Easter egg hunt, which took John one-half-hour to put together, and Joe, Margaret and Annie only ten minutes to complete. *(04-16-95)*

I suspect, or hope, that the participants in the Princeton (lacrosse) weekend have filled everyone in on the events of that time. It was one of those times when parents sort of slide along on cloud nine. At least this time it was not my idea. It was David's – a great one. He and the Hobart delegation were good sports as Hobart lost a tough one. And, of course, Pop's athletic efforts were directed at chasing $100 bill across the road. Someday *you* will be in our 'shoes.' We both hope that your reunions and celebrations will be as joyous to *you* as those of the past weeks have been to us. *(05-15-95)*

I am sitting at the typewriter in the 'back room,' and next to me is a photo montage of Mom and me leaving the Chapel, hand in hand, of a Christmas morning with all of you at Cunningham Road, of all of you on a sled in Indiana, of David and Peter and a Jaguar in Far Hills, of David and Paula's wedding, of Rex Ranch. And of so many more memories. Some days, I just look at these wonderful pictures. *(06-11-95)*

Speaking of birthdays, October brings one for Janet on the 12th, Claire on the 19th, and Billy on the 24th. *(10-01-95)*

I had lunch with Rosemary Paquette on Monday, and with Jim Dean on Tuesday. Before I left for Old Lyme to see Jim, Mom read my horoscope for the day and it advised "to avoid controversial discussions," which I did, and we had a fine lunch. *(11-19-95)*

I've just come back from a walk around Rectory Pond. A good walk, but not as good as yesterday. Why not? Because, yesterday I had Joe, Margaret, Annie and John as companions. They arrived yesterday afternoon (Mary stayed in Pittsfield with her family), and in the short time of their visit we walked, we picked out a Christmas tree at the Aicher's (the tree is smaller this year), we did a lot of eating and talking and laughing. This afternoon, there was a football game going on at one end of the house, and a Fawlty Tower tape at the other end, and I can still hear Joe's laughter. *(12-17-95)*

And *now* for a few memories. The tree – very wide, but not as tall; we didn't see the living room rug for three days; after Joe opened his 104th package, I lost count; Jeffrey became a vice-president for Logs; he also worked on a film project and sighted some deer for that project; American Girl dolls and furniture; Billy had short hair, because of 'basketball'; lots of hours on the hills of the golf course with sleds and skis; Claire with wide eyes and walking all over the place; Joe's birthday on the 28th – the same date as the anniversary of Pop asking Mom to marry him!; jig *saw* puzzles; books, books and more books; games of cards and Monopoly; hide and seek; the job assignment list from John; Pop left his credit card in a liquor store; the various *crews* chopping the ice in the driveway; the VCR movies; Matthew buried in a big science book; Paula, Janet, Mary and Lur putting together huge meals; and that brings me to the subject of food . . . it seems like one long meal and it *was* so great; and finally, the many hours of chatting and laughing.
And rubbish. The man picks it up tomorrow morning. I think I should warn him. *(01-01-96)*

The weather has involved all our lives. We talked to Andrew, and he talked about the unreal bitter cold. But in the chat, Mom heard Claire say "Hi," and that would melt almost anything. John and Mary were in Princeton, and Peter had challenged (for a price) Sean and Joe to shovel the driveway – which they did. *(02-04-96)*

Our trip started off with Pop without his glasses. I just couldn't find them. But on our way to Hartford, I remembered where they were, and we returned home. Neither of us spoke about the memory of when David told us as we approached Indiana that he had left his duffle in Indian Hill. And we had a drive to Canada ahead of us. But I broke the ice and said that this sort of thing does happen, doesn't it? On Friday night, we had a fine fish dinner with Peter and Janet and were impressed with Johanna and Sean's knowledge of state capitals as we played a dinner game. *(03-03-96)*

I finished a book by Bill Bradley – a great story that covers a diverse set of subjects. On the subject of basketball, Aunt Dorothy called from her winter spot in Phoenix, and spoke about the exciting basketball game by Princeton. And then she said, is it 8 o'clock there? and Mom said, No it is 12 o'clock. Midnight. *(03-17-96)*

Peter called, to report that a house called Cobblestone on Jefferson Road in Princeton was for sale for $675,000. This was the home that Mom lived in when we first met. Her folks purchased it for $29,000, and with more land. But Pop remembers it as being so close to the Princeton theater when we walked to town, and so far (as we hugged) as we walked home. And further as I walked back to the campus alone. *(04-14-96)*

We had a wonderful call from Johanna. Her class (and school) had visited Ellis Island, and the computer image called up the name Dickson, and there on the screen was a picture of many Dicksons in front of the maple tree. Some years ago, as part of a Kodak promotion, I sent in this picture – and there it was, on Ellis Island! *(04-28-96)*

On the subject of children, there was a Class Note in the Princeton Alumni Weekly that Dr. Stan Garber had died. Dr. Garber was the OB for Peter, John, Ann and Andrew. He is also the guy who asked

Pop to come to the door of the operating room (after I had driven the place crazy) and handed me Peter just after delivery. I fainted. *(05-12-96)*

Wotta Day! Wotta Day! It was at least a #9, maybe even a #10. I had breakfast on the porch this morning and wore a sweater. *(07-21-96)*

MOM'S 70th BIRTHDAY!!
Such a Great Weekend! From Dundee, from Fairport, from Silver Spring, and from Princeton, they came. And last night, in a wonderful and noisy get-together at a Marriott and a TGIF (will they surely remember us!), we celebrated with a hoped-for surprise, the milestone birthday for Mom. And today, in a l-o-n-g breakfast, and in a pool-side gathering, we talked, talked and talked.
These things don't just happen. They take planning, many telephone calls, some lying . . . but they mean so much. Mom and I hope that your future lives include events where your children surround *you* with so much love. And cameras, jokes, noise, and their children. Good luck.
We've been home a few hours, and Mom somehow hasn't opened the great new laptop computer. I'm surprised. Technology will finally enter this old house. It's a wonderful gift! *(07-28-96)*

The trip was so good. Coming home was so good. The high points were the visits in Fairport and Dundee. In Fairport, we visited Matthew just before he took off for Australia. He plans a trip to New Zealand at the end of his studies, and Mom and I gave him our memories of a wonderful visit there. It should be noted that on the refrigerator door was an award to Jeffrey for The Most Improved Student in Spanish. There are all sorts of awards, but to me, Most Improved is The Best. *(09-29-96)*

It was Claire's birthday! We got a long letter from Andrew, and talked to him a couple times. And we got pictures! Billy's soccer team is undefeated, and in one game, the opposing coach yelled to his team "do not let Billy out of your sights." Billy scored two goals. *(10-20-96)*

And on Thanksgiving Day, we had a phone call from Matthew from Brisbane Australia. He sounded so great. What a treat! *(12-01-96)*

Speaking of New Year's, it was 50 years ago that after a party at Will Ludwig's in Brooklyn, and a trip back to Princeton, that I crashed my father's beloved Packard when I was returning it to him. Snow and ice. *(01-05-97)*

BULLETIN: Debbie just called and said that Uncle Bob had had a stroke. He is in the hospital, is stable, and we are looking at our calendar for a trip there. We will keep you posted. *(03-16-97)*

Lancaster was at the center of our lives last week. Despite some predictions of heavy snow, which never materialized, we drove down and were there for parts of three days. Uncle Bob's condition is obviously serious, but he does seem to have the use of his arms, legs, fingers, and that's a blessing. The problems now are speech and swallowing. The therapist was there, and it was an unsuccessful visit, but she was still encouraging. The day we left, he gave us a glimmer of recognition and a slight smile. Aunt Ruth has reported more, and she has been upbeat. *(03-09-97)*

I gave a cheer when I thought I had finished the photo project . . . only to find another few hundred pictures. I am almost finished. As I look at the pictures, I have a feeling that life is a succession of touch football games and birthday cakes. *(03-24-97)*

Speaking of enthusiasm, I must talk about Trinity Episcopal Church in Princeton. Pop, ever eager to rush home, was persuaded to join the Peter Dicksons at church. Also persuaded by a gentle nudge from Mom. It was an hour of unbelievable joy, music and appreciation. It was Senior Youth Day, and they did everything in the Service, except those parts that a Bishop would not allow. Maybe. If there is truly a Good News, that church resonated with it today. One of my greatest moments in a church. (4-20-97)

Mom and I are now special members of a Carleton Society. After so many years of supporting Princeton, we now have honored Carleton. But both of us are ambivalent about these 'Societys.' We have always found that anonymous giving was the best, and joining a group was not in our style. *(05-26-97)*

The ride from Princeton to Pomfret Center was the same length, but it seemed to go quicker. Perhaps it was because we talked so much about time together with all of you, about the Chapel service, about the Dedication, about the happy meals together, about the great Quilt, about the Book of Letters, about the collection of words and pictures from the Weekly Letters, and about EVERYTHING! The passenger in the car read those Letters and the collection. Not once, but more than once. [*Following the 50th wedding anniversary celebration*] *(06-29-97)*

Pictures! Pictures! We got a zillion pictures from Peter of the weekend in Princeton. Please pass the handkerchiefs. They are so great. We are having copies made for each of you. Actually, there are a couple that I wanted to hold back for blackmail purposes, but Mom talked me out of it. *(07-20-97)*

This is a Great Letter. Because on Saturday afternoon I stepped into Uncle Bob's house in Lancaster and he greeted me with "I'm glad you're here!" in a clear and loud voice. It brought tears to my eyes. He has made so much progress, and yes, there is much to go. But he keeps trying, and Aunt Ruth keeps pressing. I will remember that welcome forever. *(10-29-97)*

It was a white Christmas, probably thanks to Margaret. After arriving here, she put a sign in the window asking for snow, and we really got it the next day. Plus sleet, freezing rain and hail. And various flurries kept it white. The snow didn't stop some brave people from racing around in a touch football game. Among the results was a sore back for Andrew. The 28th was a special day. We celebrated Joe's birthday, and Mom and I celebrated the anniversary of a Proposal at the Graduate School in Princeton. Mom says she got frostbite waiting for me to pop the question. *(12-31-97)*

A tragedy. One of our wedding presents was a set of four cocktail glasses embossed with wild birds. One survived these many years, but one evening the last one fell from a too-precarious perch on a chair on to the tile floor. The martini in it didn't survive, either. *(02-08-98)*

WELCOME DANIEL ANDREW DICKSON! SUCH GREAT NEWS! Andrew called us early this morning, and it was a wonderful way to be welcomed back to Pomfret. We have spent the last two weeks in Lima [*Peru*], and we awoke to learn that there was a great new name, Daniel! And we love it. *(03-01-98)*

On Sunday morning, after a telephone chat with Paul Nelson and watching the Weather Channel forecast of bad weather between Rochester and Boston, we decided to spend another night in Rochester. There were various reasons, but the clincher was when Mom said, "If you go in the car, you go alone." Decision made. *(03-23-98)*

The big news, to us, is that Joe and family have decided (99% sure) that he will accept the Pomfret School 'invitation.' We are thrilled.

But there's also a message here. We are sure that it was a tough decision in Lima. Someday, hopefully, you will be grandparents, (what a wonderful word!). You will have opinions about schools, courses, games, clothes, haircuts, friends, rooms, meals, etc. But, for grandparents, silence is the magic word.

Our concern, naturally, has been that we became an ingredient in the Lima decision, for we 'live down the road.' We do want to be thought of in the many decisions that are ahead, but we know that you know that the real votes belong to you and your children. *(04-13-98)*

Well, we met Daniel! And we helped celebrate his second (monthly) birthday. And we met Andrew, Lur, Billy and Claire. A great reunion. *(05-05-98)*

And it was a big birthday for Pop. But, each one is Big. And I have a thought or two about birthdays and celebrations. All of you are very creative and thoughtful. It says a lot about you. I ask you to think what it means to open packages with shirts, books, safari trousers, a Princeton Lacrosse cap, a case of Pasta, a picture of grandchildren, a Civil War framed print of Camp Princeton, a Tiger that roars, and (from Mom) a key chain with a Peruvian silver dollar dated 1923. Think of that list. The variety says a lot. And it all fits. *(06-14-98)*

And, of course it was Father's Day! I remember hearing John advise his children that this day was the most important of the year. Well, You all made it a great one for me. Thank you for your gifts, cards and calls. *(06-23-98)*

Mom pulled out some old albums. One involved Split Rock Lodge – six nights in a cabin with great meals (she kept the menus) for $207. And David's birth at Princeton Hospital for $200, also for six days. *(07-5-98)*

Also, Bill Kline called about breakfast. Some years ago, in Arizona, I suggested to Bill that I would buy him breakfast, but when the bill came, I found that I had no wallet. He has never let me forget it. *(10-18-98)*

First, Aunt Ruth. True grit is a good description. Legally blind and with health crises of her own, she manages to steer and control Uncle Bob. It is not easy to do, nor to watch.

The common wisdom is that there will be no change six months after a stroke. But, for Uncle Bob, there is. There are new words and new responses. Hard to hear and hard to understand because his voice box has been damaged. As his abilities grow, so do his frustrations. For example, driving a car with Uncle Bob as your front seat passenger is a new experience. He can't instruct, but he is very emotional about which turn to take.

When I see Uncle Bob and Aunt Ruth, I think of all the families trying to cope with physical limitations. Incidentally, I should mention that Debbie calls every night. *(11-22-98)*

I got a haircut. Finally, says Mom. *(01-11-99)*

It was a normal week. Mom did the crossword puzzles daily in the NY Times, the Norwich Bulletin and Friday's Wall Street Journal. *(05-23-99)*

Where to start? How about a grand birthday party in Rhode Island? It was Annie's turn. Johanna and Sean joined them after their arrival by train. And the Boyles from Stonington were there, plus Marge (Mary's Maid of Honor and Lou). A happy, happy time. *(07-16-00)*

Then on Friday, David and Paula arrived, followed by the clan from Dundee on Saturday at Providence Airport. And then, Peter and Janet. Our Saturday dinner was a great event with the adults at a festive table in the dining room, and the 'children' dining on the porch. Not surprisingly, Claire and Danny were the center of the cousins' attention. Such a glorious time. And I announced that the Garden at the renovated Audubon Center would be sponsored by Mom and me and identified as "Ann's Garden." *(07-16-00)*

# Ann

**"This is Ann's big week."**

*Our sister, Ann, was born with a heart defect. One of the walls separating her ventricles leaked, so the clean blood ready to be pumped out mixed with the used blood coming back to the heart. Nowadays, such a problem is easily correctible; but in 1953, it was unclear just how long she would live. Mom and Pop decided early on that she would lead as normal a life as she was able to. That meant schools, playgrounds, friends, chores, vacations, college, jobs, boyfriends. It also meant waiting for her to catch her breath as we walked; or it meant extended periods in hospitals with either illness or attempts to correct the issue. And, finally, it meant a serious degrading in the quality of her life and a courageous decision she made to undergo open heart surgery, a risky procedure that she had to have known might not succeed but with the realization that the path she was on would lead to an incapacitated life.*

*Mouse Ears* by John Dickson

40

On Saturday, Ann and Pop began the father's Weekend with a stirring tennis match at Dobbs. Then I inspected her absolutely great art exhibit at the Library. Imagine a "one-man show" during father's Weekend! We came home to 550 for the afternoon, and then back to school for a wonderful French dinner and then the dance. As usual, Pop was the most unbelievable dancer – doing all sorts or tangos, hops, etc. *(04-25-71)*

We also had a chat with Ann (and a letter, too!) last week. She was getting ready for her big med. boards on Saturday. We tried to call on Sunday evening, but no answer. Guess Ann was celebrating. *(05-08-73)*

We also got a nice note from Ann – mostly about course plans and changes. Unfortunately, Ann has also had a health problem or two, and we spent some time on the telephone this weekend. Today she goes to see Dr. Kaplan again, and we hope for a good phone report this evening. *(07-16-73)*

The major event of the week was not a totally happy one – although it all worked out OK. Early Wednesday, Ann was taken from the UC [*University of Cincinnati*] Infirmary where she had been for about a week with a 'virus' to the Children's Hospital Intensive Care Unit. She stayed there for a couple days and now seems to be on the road to recovery. Mom went out on Wednesday and came back on Saturday. *(11-05-73)*

Well, last Thursday I dropped Mom and Andrew at JFK, and they flew off to Tucson and thence down to Amado and the Rex Ranch with Ann, whom they met at the Tucson airport. I talked to them yesterday, and they were already sore from bouncing on the horses. They also said it was 86°, sunny and gorgeous. They all have sunburns. Ann said she was beet red – and I am green, green with envy. *(03-18-74)*

Ann was accepted into the Master's Program at U.C. which is a great event. She's also getting organized into her new apartment and is busy at summer school. *(06-24-74)*

Ann called today from the camp that she's working at as part of her courses. It is a camp session for cerebral palsied adults, and it must be quite a sight and quite a remarkable project. She described a square dance in wheelchairs and a soccer game that was also played in chairs. *(09-09-74)*

Ann called to tell us she was back in Porkopolis, after a fine and happy visit with Jim [*boyfriend*] in Pittsburgh. *(01-05-75)*

Ann called last week to give us the exciting news that she had earned a study grant which will reduce the cost of her Master's program. Earned with a capital "E" is what it's all about, too, for she really plugged to get it. Congratulations, baby. *(02-03-75)*

The big news this week is from Cincinnati. Ann called on Saturday to tell us that the doctors have finally concluded what to do and when to do an operation. It is scheduled for about a week after she gets her degree (about June 20), and she has proposed that it be done in Cincinnati rather than Boston, New York or some other exotic place. In a couple round-robin phone calls we all agreed to the wisdom. The timing and location. She will have some preparatory work done during Spring vacation, also in Cincinnati. She was very excited (in a subdued way), and we are, too. It means a chance to correct a situation that has been diminishing her energies and endurance. *(03-10-75)*

Pop went to the Midwest one day last week, and managed to spend a few hours in Cincinnati. This included a supper with Ann at her famous 'garlic' restaurant. It took me at least two days to recover. We also talked to Ann twice, on Friday and Sunday. The prospect of the June operation has dimmed somewhat due to some things that turned up in the tests at Children's last week. Dr. Kaplan is doing some checking around the country with other doctors, but the situation is a little uncertain at this moment. *(04-07-75)*

I picked Ann up Tuesday evening and we drove out to Disneyland. We had a sensational room on the top floor of the hotel, overlooking the 'yacht basin.' We were there two nights and one day, and it was for me one of the greatest 'holidays' ever. I ate too much, slept too little and walked a million miles – but oh what enjoyment. The Disney people were so good, and the Park is hard to describe. It's beautiful, large, comfortable and there's just too much to do and see. Ann dragged Pop on to the Matterhorn ride, and I survived! Another highlight was Pop getting his picture taken with Minnie Mouse! *(04-28-75)*

Yesterday I was in Cincinnati for Ann's 'Masters' ceremony. It was in the football stadium and absolutely jammed. The procession took one half hour. There were 5,300 graduates (not all there). It was amazing how smoothly it all went. It had personality, dignity, and even some good-natured fun. I was very impressed. We've got some pictures of Ann in her cap and gown. She goes to Columbia, Missouri this week for a job interview. Good luck, Ann. *(06-16-75)*

Please don't write/call Ann, for she gets upset at publication of such news, but she is back in the hospital with a new and puzzling problem. We think you should know of such things, and we'll keep you posted, of course. I may try to visit Cincinnati this week. ("Things look better. I talked to the doctor today." *Handwritten.*) *(09-15-75)*

Ann has a job! It sounds kind of tough, and she was a little pooped at the end of the first day, but it involves teaching severely retarded children in a private home. She was excited, and so were we, whom she called the other evening. It's also six days per week, but only five hours per day. Hope it works out, Ann. *(02-07-77)*

Ann has cut back on her job – the commute back and forth to Kentucky was getting a little too much. An understandable decision. *(08-22-77)*

Ann called with the news that she has a part time job working with truant girls in Newport KY. *(12-11-77)*

Ann arrived at the Hartford airport on Thursday afternoon loaded down with Christmas bundles AND looking so sensational in a new, short hair-do. And new glasses. She's here for a short visit this time, for she has her tonsils out on the 28th. *(12-25-77)*

We drove to Marlborough for Matthew's third birthday party, and a great treat it was. We had thick, juicy hamburgers, chocolate cake and ice cream and tons of presents. Well, Matthew had the presents, and the rest of us had the goodies. It was a clear, warm evening, and grand party. Ann was there, having arrived from Cincy on Sunday, and she is here now. She is in Pomfret Center for a "vacation" before the doctors take over on June 15th. *(05-23-78)*

This is Ann's big week. She checks into the hospital on Tuesday, and the surgeons do their thing on Thursday. Mom leaves here tomorrow at 7 A.M. from Hartford for an indefinite stay in good old Cincy. I am sure the telephone lines will be buzzing as we hear of the progress on Thursday and the days afterward . . .
Ann, we will all be in your corner this week. We'll be thinking of you through the minutes and the hours. During those tough moments, we want you to know that we are sending messages and they come from Matthew, Andrew, John, Peter and Janet, David and Paula, and Mom and Pop.

Have a great week! Have a good week, Ann. LOVE!!! *(06-12-78)*

[*Ann passed away on the operating table, the doctor saying her organs were too weak to withstand the trauma of the surgery.*]

We've spent a fair amount of time doing various kinds of needle work. Some of them are items that we found in Ann's collection, and are finishing. Mom is working on a rug and I've worked on a Mickey Mouse picture. When Ann and I were in Disneyland we both had pictures taken with Minnie Mouse, and I think she was planning the needlepoint as a present and reminder. *(09-05-78)*

We got a nice letter from Mrs. Kaplan, and I quote in part: "Until about 3 years ago, I used to exercise every night and to help the monotony I would play a record. At the time I stopped (pure laziness) I was exercising to music from The Sting. To one particular tune I had made up a dance in honor of a wonderful resident – Sam Dalinsky who was killed by a hit and run driver. Ann thought the world of this young man, as we all did, and his death was a great loss to her. I've started exercising again, and without thinking, put on The Sting. I thought of Sam and had a strange feeling that he and Ann were together having fun up there." *(09-10-78)*

When I was in New York, I bought some tapes – the first ever, after my years of "collecting" RCA tapes. One was of Richard Tucker, a famed tenor from the Met, and I thought it was totally opera. I was therefore surprised to hear "Sunrise, Sunset," a song from the Fiddler on the Roof that is almost guaranteed to bring a tear to a father's eye. Further, for our 25th, Ann gave Mom and I funds and instructions to go see the show in NYC. Unfortunately, we didn't make it. And so, there were some sentimental moments here yesterday. *(04-23-79)*

It's been a dreary day here, and a little sad, of course, but Mom and

I keep reminding ourselves of many bright things, past and present. One bright event was the planting on Friday of Ann's tree. It is a splendid dogwood about twelve feet high and sits on the grass area in front of the bay window. It is really a beauty. *(05-13-79)*

I also spent a good amount of time in my "office" – a spot under the huge trees near the garden. I have set up Ann's old rocker, a portable radio, and some small pieces of furniture that need sanding and scraping. *(08-06-79)*

Gramps had asked that all memorials [*when he passed away*] be sent to Children's in Cincinnati in memory of Ann, which touched us deeply. *(08-21-79)*

One of the items Mom brought home from Gramps' place was a metal frame with pictures of you folks. One picture is of Ann at her graduation in Cincinnati, and it's one of the best pictures ever of Ann. It was a windy day and she is holding her cap with one of the happiest smiles. I remember that day, and it was a proud and happy one. *(08-27-79)*

Among the other projects of the week was to paint Ann's rocker. I well remember sitting in the rocker in her high rise room at U.C., and now it is freshly painted and in my basement shop. *(12-17-79)*

Speaking of Ann, we finally got up the courage to go through the stuff we brought back from Cincinnati, knowing that some of it should be thrown away. It was a very tough afternoon, but reading her notes, and going through the endless hospital bills, it is clear that she had pains and problems that took their toll. You can almost feel the tears on some of the pages. *(02-11-80)*

And then we watched The Sting on TV. I remember Ann trying to coax me to go see it, and I finally did and thoroughly enjoyed it. And did again last night. *(04-21-80)*

This was a weekend of memories – and some tears. The flowers in the church yesterday were quite nice, although rather formal – not the wildflowers that Ann liked so much. It's also strange that a service that I have listened to for years and years can somehow seem different on a particular Sunday and hit kind of hard. *(06-16-80)*

These June days are important for what they are – and for what they have been. On this day, June 15, there is so much to remember. It would serve each of us well to pause and think of Ann and her courage, particularly on those days when life does not seem to us to be treating us too kindly. *(06-15-81)*

We went into NYC and after dinner in a noisy madhouse called the first saloon in New York (it was good) we saw Fiddler on the Roof at Lincoln Center. And so, many years afterward we celebrated Ann's gift to us on our 25th. It was a super show. *(07-20-81)*

Tuesday morning I was in Cincinnati for a visit to Children's. It's a selfish thought on my part, but I wanted to give our annual gift in person. Mrs. Kaplan said that they bought an infant defibrillator (sp?) with past gifts from all of us. I then spent some time in Indian Hill – a place full of memories. The visit to the churchyard is still very hard for Pop to manage. An afternoon chat with Mr. Tucker was fun. *(11-23-81)*

The bulletin from Indian Hill Church has the following: 'The flowers this morning are given to the Glory of God and in memory of Ann Gordon Dickson and her grandmother, Velma Dean, from the Dickson family.' *(01-31-83)*

The old rocker that was a fixture in the 'office' has finally gone. It collapsed from rot. It was a sad departure for it was one of Ann's prize possessions. *(09-05-83)*

On Saturday evening, we had dinner at the Grotto. Do you remember the time we went there and Ann ordered chicken that took forever? Not one of Pop's finest hours. *(02-24-86)*

It was on June 15 in 1978 that Ann left us. Sometimes it seems a long time ago, and sometimes it seems so recent. *(06-15-87)*

Mary left with the heaviest suitcase ever. It reminded me of trying to pick up Ann's suitcase when she was in Los Angeles, and then I learned that she had packed her sewing machine plus a bunch of books. *(08-04-91)*

The attic work continues, and I am now working on my hands and knees cleaning the area under the eaves. We also went through some of Ann's papers with the plan to 'weed them out.' It turned out to be too emotional – and it is now all back in the attic. *(01-11-93)*

Wintertime projects include cleaning out attics and basements. Today, I grabbed some bags from the attic, and decided to clean them out. They were Ann's, and included hundreds of letters and notes and stuff that she had collected. One of them was a place mat from Ivar's Seafood Restaurant in Seattle where John informed us that fish made his ears 'wiggle.' I soon realized that I had tears streaming down, and decided that someone else at some other time would handle Ann's letters. They are back in the attic. *(02-12-95)*

The garden, ah yes, the garden. I spent many hours this week on my hands and knees (in prayer? – maybe) but I pulled up a few hundred pea plants, with deep roots, but dying from the top. I then planted lima beans, which the varmints seem to ignore (I just saw one). Speaking of limas, I have a good memory of a meal in Cunningham Road, where we served Donald Duck lima beans to an unenthusiastic group. And Ann said, "I don't care whose name is on the package, I don't like them." *(07-07-96)*

January 2 was Ann's 44th birthday. I have often wondered if she should had gone through with that high-risk operation, but then I remember Dr. Sam Kaplan saying that the required autopsy showed that she was a prime candidate for a major stroke . . . and that is what Ann feared most. *(01-05-97)*

When we were closing down Ann's apartment, Mom took down a poster from the fridge that said, "Before you kiss a prince you must first kiss a lot of toads." Mom found it in the attic. Some tears. *(10/03/00)*

# The Shop

**"We've put in one of those driveway bells that they have in gas stations, so that we can hear cars drive in."**

*Maybe it was because they couldn't afford furniture when they first got married. They always bought distressed furniture and sanded, stained, and polished them, becoming quite expert in the process. At the same time, my mother turned her hobby of knitting hats and mittens and sweaters for her children and decorating her own homes into a social and then charitable venture. The combination of antiques and crafts evolved into a dream for a post-corporate life, in a bucolic setting. At first, Pop's letters informed us of these hobbies, filling up the page with references to how they were spending their empty-nest time. Then, he tracked their decision to turn the whole venture into a business, their own "Mom and Pop business," which they jokingly referred to as Meadow Rock Farm Inc. We knew it simply as the shop. It was never clear if they made any money, but that may not have been the point.*

The Gas Pump by Margaret Dickson

Mom went to the Yankee Fair at the Congregational Church on Saturday – and came home empty-handed! The antiques have gone up into the stratosphere, with chairs going for $1,500 and highboys for $7,000. This gives Pop renewed incentive (which he needs) to keep sanding away at the unfinished pieces that I have in the basement. Each morning last week I inched away at the dough-box and I guess it will be Christmas before it's ready for a finish coat. *(08-20-73)*

Mom's shop opened officially last week. I think the merchandise is even better this year than last, and they had some good sales. Mom sold six of her hand-sewn wreaths. The girls also put a Christmas pinecone wreath on the fence between the driveways to let everybody know 'they're open' and it's a real double-take when you drive by. *(09-30-74)*

Yesterday was a busy day of unloading, cataloguing, and storing the many items that were purchased. Actually, Mom has already sold a couple at enormous profits. She's worse than an Arab oil sheik. *(11-13-74)*

Last week was also a busy, busy week. Especially for Mom. To give you an idea of how busy the shop has been, Mom told me last night that in the past four weeks they have cleared a 'profit' of about $1,000. This will be divided among UNICEF, a hospital for crippled children in New Britain, the Southbury Training School and the Children's Medical Center in Norwalk. Pop continues to be the main supplier of pine-cone wreaths, and I guess they've sold about 50 to date. *(12-09-74)*

Mom spent a good part of the weekend at the sewing machine making ties. She also spent some time with Mrs. Vartabedian on Saturday in the shop. Mrs. Vartabedian's antique orientals [*rugs*] are now in the shop, and do they look sensational. Mom and I look wistfully at them, but we have agreed that the kitchen floor has priority. *(02-10-75)*

On Wednesday, Mom and I travelled across the Hudson to do some antiquing and found plenty of stuff – a lot of furniture in the rough. We ran out of money and space in the car about the same time. *(05-03-75)*

Yesterday was Mom's Darien 'show,' and while she sold some stuff, she was disappointed that she didn't sell one of the big pieces. So was I, for I loaded the wagon on Saturday night, unloaded it at the show, and then repeated the process in the evening. Afterwards we went to the Vartabedians for dinner where the three 'partners' discussed business while the husbands (with RCA, IBM and Chase) discussed gardens, grass, and other major domestic issues. *(09-10-75)*

The wreath sales are also slow. Perhaps it's the weather. Yesterday I put a sign out front and put about a dozen 'on display' on a big piece of plywood at the ice-house. I sold two, which was helpful. I told Mom that I'd take her out to dinner this week with the profits. *(12-14-75)*

Mom spent a lot of time on pillows, and she has them at various consignment shops (and they are selling!). Yesterday, she and Mrs. Anderson spent a long day at the New Rochelle antique show, and with disappointing results. We moved two wagons full of furniture and stuff, and none of the furniture sold. They did sell a fair amount of small stuff, but I'm afraid it wasn't too profitable for them. *(02-23-76)*

On Friday we had an interesting visit from an antique appraiser who looked at the tavern [*an actual Colonial tavern, outbuilding, next to the house*], and told me it wasn't worth much, if anything. Baloney, I say to him. *(03-15-76)*

At long last, we began some of the framing work of the Harper's prints. We picked out about a dozen old frames, and have had mats made from them, and the shop now has some rather handsome prints. *(09-07-76)*

We had been to Portsmouth, NH and came home loaded with acquisitions. Actually, we went to three auctions last week, on Monday, Thursday and Friday. The Friday one was in Pittsfield, Mass., and was great. Unfortunately, there were some dealers from Texas and Arizona who bought heavily, and we missed some items we badly wanted. *(04-04-77)*

Mom and I went up to New Hampshire on Wednesday for an evening auction and came back with a van full, including a Civil War trunk with a folding cot inside. The strangest contraption I've ever seen. *(05-02-77)*

We've put in one of those driveway bells that they have in gas stations, so that we can hear cars drive in. Makes life a little easier. [*There was an actual old gas pump next to the shop that used to serve the golf carts when the house was a clubhouse for a golf course.*] *(09-26-77)*

We have lots of ideas about things we would like to do, but are proceeding slowly until we see how this antique business develops. It is somewhat slow, but we have to remind ourselves that the sales are much higher than our original estimates, and that we knew it would take a long time to develop. Actually, our big problem is space, for we have too much stuff and not enough room. Pop has a basement full of stuff, and I'm working on it, but there's really no place to put the finished product. *(11-20-77)*

I finished an old wood box, stained it this morning, and will begin the varnish work tomorrow. I also did some sanding and scraping on a table and tool chest. Yesterday, Andrew and David struggled with the big old cupboard from the shop to the basement. I began working on it this morning, and I think it is going to come out great – but it's going to take a lo-o-o-ng time. *(01-15-78)*

I finished the big cupboard last week, and now I'm like the guy who built a boat in his basement – for I can't get it out. *(02-12-78)*

We had a couple fine sales from the shop and thus experienced our best week in a long, long time. That's good for morale. One day while Mom was touring around, a gal came in who looked vaguely familiar. When she left, I noticed her license plate was Ella – we had had a visit from the Governor. [*Ella Grasso*]. *(03-05-78)*

Mom had another good week in the shop. Just a few sales, but each one reasonably good – and they add up nicely. Pop is now the bench king of this part of the world. I bought ten broken benches in lengths of 6 to 12 feet, and I hope to be able to construct 7 or 6 good ones. I'm still working away on the one in the basement, but I'm getting close to finishing up on that endless job. *(03-19-78)*

We had picked up a few things en route to the auction, and picked up some more afterwards. Two of the pieces were welcomed by Pop with only slight enthusiasm, but Mom was adamant. She was nice enough not to crow too loudly, when she sold them both the following day – at a handsome profit. *(08-28-78)*

Yesterday Mom spent the day on the Thompson Village Green at an outdoor antique show. The day was beautiful but chilly. Actually, in the early hours yesterday when we were setting up her booth, it was just plain cold. Unfortunately, despite all the work and time, she was zapped – meaning no sales. It is truly a peculiar business – to have sensational sale at a show one week, and zero the next. *(10-01-78)*

On Wednesday, Mom drove to Swansea, Mass., to pick up a dining room table (reproduction) which now graces our dining room. She also picked up two cupboards, one of which is in the dining room and the other is in the shop. As we were unloading them yesterday, I heard David mutter: "I thought you said you were not going to buy any more heavy cupboards." *(10-29-78)*

I procrastinated yesterday about writing the Weekly Letter, and now I know why. For last night, super saleswoman Mom made the biggest sale we have ever had – and so I can bring you this hot news immediately! She sold the big desk and a table to a couple that was in and out of here all weekend. He came by yesterday and clinched the deal. And so, congratulations, Mom. *(02-27-79)*

The shop business is booming – we are about four or five times ahead of last year. A couple big sales-plus a good Greenwich show (last year's was poor) have helped things along. One of the big items that I bought at last week's auction was sold in Greenwich, and that's what is known as turnover. *(03-05-79)*

Mom had better sell a few items, because Pop bought a bundle of expensive things at an auction in Cohoes, N.Y. (near Albany) on Saturday. The auction was to settle the estate of an old man who for thirty or forty years went to auctions, bought and stored the things in every room in his house and in barns and garages. He had a hoard of about 4,000 things. Some items had the original price tags, of a few dollars, and they went for hundreds of dollars. He specialized in Shaker things, and the prices were astronomical. For example, he had about forty rockers, some of which went for a thousand dollars. *(03-12-79)*

Shop sales were good last month, and we were ahead of last year again. Sales weren't helped by Pop putting out the Closed sign by mistake one day. Mom couldn't figure out why nobody even stopped, until she went out in the evening to bring in the sign. *(04-02-79)*

Mom began last week with a trip to Boston on Monday to do some shopping for the church Christmas shop. As you know, the church shop will be using part of our new space come late October. And Mom is on the committee to stock it. *(09-03-79)*

The mantle that Pop worked on for a million hours and refinished was sold to a man who plans to paint it. We gulped and went through with the sale, but when a guy buys something he owns it and can do with it what he wants. I just wish he hadn't told us of his plan. Oh well, on to the next job. *(12-02-79)*

Mom went to a meeting of her tourist council group one day, and because she is such a career person, we excused her from the kitchen and took her to Chuck's Steak House for dinner. Her "career" is doing very well – and the shop has broken all sorts of records this month. As her repair and refinishing man, I completed a small table and made some progress on a small cabinet. I also drove down to Greenwich on Saturday to deliver one of her bigger sales. *(12-17-79)*

On Friday, Mom and I headed for Oneonta, NY, which is in the mountains between Albany and Binghamton. We expected to see some snow there, but it was only a light covering. But, it was c-o-1-d. We went to an auction of country primitives on Saturday, and we think we have an idea why our stuff has been selling so well lately, namely that we are underpriced. The stuff at the auction went for astronomical prices. *(02-04-79)*

We are busy at the needlepoint and quilting. I scraped away at the inside of an old chest, and found the front page of the Manchester Guardian, dated 1844. *(02-19-80)*

Mom left on Friday morning for Greenwich, to set up for the "big show" on Saturday and Sunday. Apparently, she also had a quiet weekend. I talked to her last night, and she also sold zilch. It's disappointing not to sell anything, but it's more so considering all the work to set up and take down the stuff, plus all the standing around waiting for a sale. As we talked last night, we agreed that we would "re-assess" this idea of shows. Sometimes they work and sometimes they don't. But we have a nice place here, and we don't need to do the darned things, so why go through the hassle. She has a couple more this month, and perhaps that will be about it. *(03-10-80)*

I refinished a small corner cupboard last week, and the result was so disappointing that I'm afraid that I am going to have to do it again. *(05-12-80)*

I spent a fair amount of time beginning to finish a pewter cupboard that we bought in Middletown. As I began to take it apart to get at some of the tough places, I find that it is a "put-together" cupboard. I've been had again. It will work out alright, but we thought we had quite an original piece. *(06-02-80)*

She [*Mom*] also celebrated by making the biggest sale of Meadow Rock Farm Antiques' history. She sold more in one sale today than we have sold in three months. The recession is over! *(07-28-80)*

Who says you can't teach an old dog new tricks? I read an article about a different way to refinish furniture, tried it last week and the results are super. And so, the big schoolmaster's desk has been completed, and John helped to carry it to the shop yesterday. *(01-19-81)*

Mom had gone to an auction, and when she came back, she spent a long, long time flying a kite with Matthew. Since the auction was just up the road, we had a lot of traffic here – but Pop made no sale. But the first car in after Mom arrived home bought a chest and some other things. Now we know who the super seller is. *(04-13-81)*

I made degrees of progress on various pieces of furniture, but nothing emerged totally completed. It is most pleasant now to be able to do some of this work outside. It is also distracting, as I watch the birds hop around, the grass turn green, and the bulbs inch their way up. *(03-31-81)*

We did much searching for antiques [*while in Scotland*]. Mom bought every candlestick she could find. Pomfret Center will now have its own Candlestick Park. *(11-06-81)*

The Unicorn Shop opened here last week with a mighty successful grand opening. There was a traffic jam here, with cars parked along the road. Sales were excellent, and the shop is off to a good start. The proceeds this year go to the local Battered Women's program and to the St. Jude Ranch for abused children in Nevada. *(11-23-81)*

Buying things for the shop is a bit risky now. We made two 3-dollar sales last week – the first sales since early February. And so, rather than having monthly volumes in the four-figure range, we are now at six bucks for March. We gather the antique business is in trouble everywhere, but we seem to be setting the wrong kind of record. *(03-29-82)*

Mom went to an auction at an old farmhouse on Saturday and came home with a couple crocks that she had coveted. One has a mark of "Pomfret Landing" on it, and you can bet that it is not going to end up in the shop. *(07-12-82)*

And then on Saturday, I drove to Darien for an antique toy auction. It was quite an educational experience. The prices were staggering. I can understand some of the prices for real antiques – but Mickey Mouse toys, tootsie toy cars, teddy bears were all bringing prices in the hundreds. I got a few items, including an old Lionel train – which

I need like a hole in the head. *(08-23-82)*

Shop sales were good last week. Reaganomics is working! *(09-13-82)*

Yesterday, Mom sold a cupboard, and the other day sold a pair of expensive quilts. We may be heading for our best month of the year. We had a retired couple here yesterday from Idaho who were lots of fun – and she ran a fishing tackle business and gave me one of her lures. Maybe I should go to Idaho to try and catch a fish. *(10-25-82)*

Pop made a trip to New Hampshire to an antique auction at an old farmhouse and came home with a large farm cart and a plant stand. They just squeezed into the van. The cart now sits outside the shop with a display of Indian corn. *(09-05-83)*

I went to an auction of political items on Tuesday and picked up some Lincoln stuff. It was interesting to note that some items of RM Nixon, with expected bids of $100 received bids of 25 cents or nothing. *(11-15-83)*

Pop left early on Friday for a five-hour drive to Port Henry, NY for what promised to be a good two-day antique auction. Port Henry is north of Ticonderoga and is the pits. I surveyed the merchandise and turned around and drove the five hours home. The sequel to this sad story is that the next morning the van had a flat tire. Now the question (never to be answered) is: would I have had the flat in Port Henry or en route home later? *(04-16-84)*

On Friday, I took off for an auction in Binghamton, NY. I began to sense that there were fumes in the van and decided to open all the windows and vents to increase the circulation of air. It did but I had forgotten that the van had a ton of dust from hauling bricks and junk to the dump. As a consequence, I was covered with dust for the trip. I only made a couple purchases, and when I was loading a cupboard into the van, a man came along and offered me a profit of 50%. I took it. *(08-20-84)*

December was a poor month, and we missed a couple nice sales that might have changed our fortunes. We are used to having a wife or a husband turn down a proposed purchase, but we have never had a child, a five-year-old girl, talk her mother out of a purchase. *(01-01-85)*

On Saturday, I drove three hours to Henniker, NH for an auction, looked at the stuff for five minutes, and then drove three hours home. My advertising experience has not helped at all in judging the glowing descriptions by auctioneer ads. *(09-09-85)*

We had a bus break down in front of the house one rainy afternoon, and the driver came in to use the phone and to complain about the cranky old people who were in the bus. I suggested that he send them into the shop – and they all trooped in, but we made only one small sale. It was interesting to hear the chatter – about half were genuinely cranky and the other half treated it as a lark and adventure. There's a lesson there. *(10-07-85)*

I began work on a chest of drawers that needs refinishing, but to my horror when I took off the top old finish of shellac, I found a layer of plaster type substance. It is the very dickens to remove, but now that I am committed, there is no direction but to go ahead with it. I've been refinishing furniture for a long time, but never have seen this stuff. *(01-06-86)*

Many hours were spent getting figures ready for the tax man. We lost a few bucks on the shop last year, but the figures keep getting better. However, Macy's is still secure as the champ retailer. *(01-12-86)*

The Dope of the Week Award goes to Pop. On Friday, I drove to Oneonta, NY for a supposed Saturday auction. But I was a week too early. I then drove back 4½ hours, again in driving rain. And pretty pooped at that. *(03-17-86)*

Then to Philadelphia for a Friday evening and Saturday morning toy auction at which we bought nothing. We had high hopes and we were willing to spend a few bucks, but I'm not sure I could face myself (nor you) if I spent a few thousand bucks for a toy. *(10-07-86)*

Shop sales continue their disappointing pattern. We had a couple call last week and ask us to hold two big pieces and it would have been a nice sale. But they came, got into an argument with one another, and left without buying anything. There was also a couple who had recently moved from Cincinnati, and the conversation revealed that his best friend was a teacher at Indian Hill – Mr. Terwilliger! *(05-25-87)*

Shop sales for January were quite good. And so we are off to a reasonably good start in a year when the future of the shop is still undecided. Actually, last year's sales, helped by a strong December, were the second best in our 'history.' *(02-01-88)*

We have a saga of an antique sale. A couple weeks ago, a couple from California bought a table and asked if it could be shipped. So we wrapped it, took it to Flying Tigers only to discover that they had changed the formula for charges, and instead of 20 bucks, it turned out to be 160 bucks. So we shipped it via Greyhound. But all during the week, we got phone calls asking for other items to be shipped – which we did – and to send pictures of still more. And then, the husband called and said he didn't like the bench, and he was sending it back. Kind of a looney deal. *(05-23-88)*

We took a day off and drove up to Hudson, Mass. to visit the man that provides us with all the shore birds. We watched him take a block of wood and in just minutes have a bird all ready for painting. . . . We spent a lot of time putting together figures on the shop business for last year, for tax purposes, and it is no surprise that we lost money in '88. *(01-09-89)*

We are really enjoying the No-Shop life. The freedom is really wonderful, and it's a pleasure on a weekend like this to not be standing around in the shop all afternoon. *(05-29-89)*

I went to an auction yesterday in New Hampshire. Can you remember the many times that I have mentioned going to auctions and coming home empty-handed because of the high prices? Well, yesterday was different – the prices were all quite low. Unhappily, the stuff was ours. The auctioneer with such a reputation for getting high prices had an off day or an off-audience, and the result was that the stuff from our shop went for such bargains that we really lost our shirt. Thank goodness, it's all over. *(06-27-89)*

The full details of our antique auction debacle arrived with the item-by-item material. We could cry. One Shaker item worth hundreds was sold for ten dollars – and there were other examples of stuff we really should have kept. *(07-03-89)*

An article in an antique journal describes the auction by the government of Seamen's Bank's collection of toy banks. I doubt that Mr. Thayer [*Pop's mentor from his high school job at Seamen's Savings Bank*] ever thought his collecting would turn up such a fortune. They went for almost $800,000. When I worked at the bank, new accounts of $5 or more received a small ceramic sailor bank. They went for almost $2,000 each. *(06-03-91)*

She [*Mom*] and Mrs. McCobb and Mrs. Rauh had a very successful tag sale yesterday out of the old shop room. It was packed with stuff from basements and attics. The weather was great, and so there were many tourists, too. After the sale, a motorcycle came in – and it was Danny Boyle [*Mary's brother*]. I wanted to go for a ride with him, but Mom reminded me of her pre-wedding threat to leave me if I ever got on a motorcycle. I decided to stay grounded. *(10-09-94)*

# The Next Generation

**"Some day when you are hopefully grandparents, you will know the joy of seeing youngsters as they start their lives, and to watch them change and grow. It is a renewing process, and it means much to us and to all the grandparents in the world."**

*The refrigerator in the kitchen was covered with magnets, cartoons, postcards, photos, and artwork from all the grandchildren. Tucked away on the side, in the neat cursive handwriting of a third grader, was a paragraph from a school assignment: who is your hero? Our daughter picked Pop to write about, mentioning how he has a garden and takes her blueberry picking and has a nice dog—all the important stuff for a third grader. He would surely have been the choice of each of his ten grandchildren.*

*Picket Fence* by Margaret Dickson

David and Paula dropped by on Friday (Good Friday), and Mom had a surprise for Matthew – a red tricycle. Mom has been aching to buy one for a long time. Grandchildren are so good to grandmothers. *(03-26-78)*

Last week was, as all you guys know, Valentine's Day. Mom got a very special card from Matthew, saying in his own handwriting, "I Love You, Matthew!" Of such thoughts are great days made. *(02-19-80)*

Mr. Frank, David and Matthew came out for a visit on New Year's Day. Matthew brought some of his new Star Wars items. If I could have anticipated his interest in that subject, I think I would have invested in the movie company. *(01-05-81)*

A special time for a special letter for a special person ••• Jeffrey Andrew Dickson ••• who arrived on January 7!!!! Everybody is well! Jeffrey checked in at 6 lb. 4 oz on a snowy morning. It was snowing so hard early that morning that David called the state police to check out on road conditions, and they advised, and they called the ambulance. And so, in they went to the hospital in style, and shortly thereafter – along came Jeffrey! *(01-10-81)*

Without question, the major news of the last week has been Jeffrey's first steps. All else must yield to such an historic event. *(09-07-81)*

And then Mom went out to the shop and left me with Jeffrey, I remember the famous stare-down as we watched each other alone in the house. *(11-30-81)*

The enclosed Diary is by Matthew Dickson, who was with us last week, for a very enjoyable visit. He was a very good boy. Can we have him again? *(04-19-82)*

And in Washington, we had a great supper put together by Mary and Mrs. Boyle and an evening of watching Joseph watch his cousin and surprisingly, not watch his new sister too much. *(01-22-85)*

We have had a friend here all week – Jeffrey. And we have had many, many good times. However, Pop, Mac and Sandy all conspired to play with Jeffrey too long in the snow for a couple days and he came down with a bad cold – but all is better now. We built forts and threw snowballs at the dogs for too many hours. And in the area in front of the barn where we have a large ice patch, he played 'hockey' which was mostly sliding and falling down. *(02-11-85)*

We had many good hours (and a few bad minutes) with the boys. One of the benefits of a large house is the ability to separate boys when tensions mount. As we learned with David and Peter in Cunningham Road. *(02-25-85)*

Tomorrow is Johanna's birthday and Mom sent an unusual gift. Mom's grandmother had given Grammy a small ring, and Grammy gave it to Mom, and Mom gave it to Ann – and now it goes to Johanna. Happy Birthday? (09-30-85)

As you might expect. Most of the time and attention of everyone the past few days has been for Johanna and Sean. Johanna is a busy little girl and growing up so quickly. Sean is a charmer who has an unbeatable smile. He really 'breaks' into a smile. *(12-02-85)*

Then I stopped in Marlborough to pick up Matthew and Jeffrey for a visit here. On the drive home, I heard a whispering conversation and finally asked what was going on. What was going on was a discovery by Jeffrey that "Pop has hair in his ears." *(04-21-86)*

John and Mary look fine – and Joseph and Margaret have certainly grown. We already found out this morning that Joseph's love for cars and trucks still flourishes and that Margaret truly loves dogs. Mac is in for a lot of affection. *(05-19-86)*

Yesterday, in church, Paul Elmen gave a homily about children. He amazes me with his ability to pull quotations from poets, authors, scriptures, etc. One of his quotes was very appropriate – "Every child has the right to the age in which he finds himself." *(06-02-86)*

Janet called – they will all be here from Dec 24-28. She also alerted us to the fact that Sean is "into everything." We're ready. *(12-08-86)*

Whew! What a week! A glorious one. Ann Dame Dickson arrived home on Wednesday, in good shape, after a shaky start that had us concerned. But all is well. Also, David came out and joined us and Uncle Gil for a picnic supper and service at the church. John, Joseph and Margaret arrived on Saturday to give Mary "some breathing room" in Pittsfield. To give Mom some respite from the kitchen, we went to Hank's for supper. *(07-21-87)*

The big news for me, at least, last week was the Fifth Annual Marathon with Matthew. . . . We swam, sort of, in the Lake (very rocky) and visited the museum, ate ice cream endlessly, and enjoyed living like millionaires. . . . We took the trip up Mt. Washington (not in my car – thank goodness), and that is an experience I would just as soon not repeat. It was also 40 degrees at the summit (in the clouds) and the wind was blowing at 42mph. I was staggered by the number of hikers and campers with small children, some of whom looked no more than four or five. And when we stopped at the Hiking Club headquarters in the valley, there were couples heading out, many with small children strapped to their backs, for overnight camping. At least in some of our own escapades in the West, we had a car as a 'headquarters.' *(08-27-87)*

On Wednesday, John and Mary went to New Hampshire for a wedding (Charlie – John's best man), and so Mom and I had the joy of babysitting. It was marked by Joseph coming into our dark room at 3am sobbing . . . and the reason was he 'had forgot to brush his teeth.' *(01-04-88)*

Among the other highlights were two trips to the dump! This has got to be the only place in America where children cry because they are not going to the dump in the van. *(02-29-88)*

I received a greeting from Johanna and Sean last Saturday that must rate as the high point of the week. It was at Reunions, and the two of them raced across a quadrangle shouting Pop! Pop! And Where is Mac? *(06-06-88)*

Among the sentimental events of the week was washing the windows on the Woodie. Why sentimental? Because, I scrubbed away all the finger and palm prints and the nose smudges of such friends as Joseph, Margaret, Sean and Johanna. *(09-12-88)*

Mom has been virtually running a cottage industry in knitting sweaters for grandchildren. They are beautiful, and if I had the courage to wear a sweater with ducks, pigs and chickens, or trucks, I would ask to be included on the list. *(05-01-89)*

We talked to five grandchildren last week! Actually, I am sorry to report that I hung up on one of the calls. I picked up the phone and heard this voice and figured it was a child playing with a phone. . . . It was a child alright; it was Johanna and she was calling to tell us that she was about to move into Ann's old four poster bed. *(09-10-89)*

The quote of the week belongs to Sean, who after walking too long at the zoo said: "My feet are getting crowded." *(09-16-90)*

We are Home! After a long and busy weekend, highlighted by the Great Getaway with Johanna and Sean. We now also know why older folks cannot and should not have young children. Whew!

But we had a wonderful time . . . saw many people and many places. First stop was the Strasburg Steam Railway trip; next to the Landis Valley Farm Museum. Since there had been a ton of rain, the farm was loaded with puddles, and I don't think Sean missed one of them. *(10-16-90)*

Among the highlights of the week that we remember are: The endless hide and seek games. Particularly the one when Johanna answered 'Upstairs' when Billy and Sean asked in the living room, "Where are you?" *(12-30-90)*

We brought Johanna and Margaret home with us, and about 20 minutes after we left, Johanna said that she had to go to the bathroom. So, we stopped – but no bathroom. I asked Margaret whether she wanted to go, and she said yes, but that she was afraid if she went to the bathroom, she would throw up. It was a nervous ride home, but we made it. All of us. *(07-21-91)*

I tried to get the machine to reproduce a note that Jeffrey left with us last week (plus a secret note that we did find, Jeffrey). But the words are: "Dear Grandma, Pop and Mack. I had time of my life these past few days. It was the prime of my life and tell my regards to Uncle Gill I hope he feels better. Whoof whoof to Mack. Grandma keep up the good cookin. Pop I can sense you will see the Buck this year. till next time love Jeff always be I hope a Dickson." *(12-08-91)*

I must make note of Joe's letter. He thanked us for a Christmas present – a dictiananary. A big word, and John said that Joe had used the book, but somehow went astray. *(01-15-92)*

Among the things that Matthew received for his Eagle Scout ceremony were letters and cards from Presidents Clinton, Bush, Reagan, Carter and Ford, plus many from Senators and Cabinet members. Most were obviously printed, but some had personal signatures. *(06-21-93)*

We sent some Civil War stuff to Jeffrey for his class work. We also had chats around the circuit relating to the timing of a possible Gettysburg 'retreat' for sons and grandsons. *(04-17-94)*

Hooray! Mom is home. She was full of talk about what a wonderful little girl Claire is. Sleeping four and five hours at a stretch, and by now you should have received the pictures from Andrew. Finally, from Dundee, I am so proud to report that Billy made the Super Honor Roll! *(11-06-94)*

This Christmas celebration was so special because of the presence of Claire. She was so good. And the center of attention. Especially from her girl cousins. And her grandparents. *(01-01-95)*

BIG NEWS! Claire is walking! Andrew called with that great news. *(09-04-95)*

I remember a box of Halloween cookies from Silver Spring; and Sean's greetings at breakfasts of "What time did you get up?" *(10-30-95)*

Someday, you will be grandparents. You will be settled in your ways and routine, and suddenly (but with great expectations) a 'bunch' will take over your kitchen, your bedrooms, your bathrooms, your refrigerator, your freezers, your floors, your closets, and your peace and quiet.

My advice? Hope for it. People write books and make films about the joys of family life. Mom and I have just lived one week of it. The language has yet to arrive to put it into words.

At various times, we heard admonitions about it's 'too much.' Perhaps. But think back to your own camping trips, pack trips, canoe trips, weekend breakaways etc. Of course, there's a 'too much' point. But also think of the times and events that preceded that point. Would *you* want to lose those? Of course not. *(01-01-96)*

Peter and I and the girls went up to Spag's on Saturday. On the way home, we stopped at a Dunkin Donuts, and a Worcester cop came in and gave the girls pins naming them Junior Police. They promptly came home and 'arrested' Joe and Sean. *(04-08-96)*

Birthday news! Sean's birthday was Tuesday, and we talked to him as he was opening presents. One present (from ?) was a Pomfret School shirt. He had had a party at school. Also, Matthew's BIG 21 is on the 22nd. Finally, there was a small item in the paper about a boy who was asked how old he was, and he said 3. And when will you be 4? When I am finished with 3, he said. Good answer. *(05-19-96)*

Two thoughts: Yes, it was a super week. Yes, it is quiet.
I won't go through a travelogue, because the enclosed Diary of various authors should tell a story. But I can add some thoughts about bikes, roller blades, a wagon, movies, swimming at the Nelsons and at the Park (tadpoles!), reading old Weekly Letters, old Photo Albums, UNO, Monopoly, Solitaire, the overnight in the Camper, and so much running and laughing.
It was also the week of the 49th Anniversary. And Mom and I awoke to a huge banner made by children. We also celebrated by a dinner at Hank's. And we thank you all for your cards and calls. *(06-23-96)*

Enclosed is a copy of an essay that Margaret wrote [*who is your hero?*]. I am flattered. We heard Joe play the drums, Margaret on the piano, and Annie with her new flute. *(10-29-96)*

We found a school notebook that Margaret left here on a visit. I peaked, and read a few of the pages. This is a very creative writer. I was tempted to read further, but I also think that this is a very private writer. Margaret, how wonderful! *(07-21-96)*

One of the joys of going to the mailbox is opening a letter from a small person. We got a letter from Annie last week. Annie, do you *know* that Grandma and I read and re-read these letters? Thanks so much. *(06-08-97)*

Last week brought us many things. First, there were letters from Margaret and Annie [*from their new home in Lima, Peru*]. Margaret's letter was in six different colors! She mentioned trips to the beach and a bunch of bugs. And she closed with "Please come down and visit." That is surely our hope! Annie said she was so lonely. I am certain that won't last long. *(08-17-97)*

I painted some fences. That says something about how far behind I am in my projects. But, many times I have had 'volunteers' from Silver Spring. Where are they? *(09-01-97)*

An e-mail from Jeffrey told us about homecoming in Fairport, which he helped organize. A busy time. He is also on the student council. Jeffrey, Grandma and I are so proud of your work, and we eagerly read your e-mail messages. Keep it up! *(10-12-97)*

I just talked to Joe on the phone. What a thrill for Pop! He has been busy, he likes the food, classes start tomorrow, and he is 89 on the football team – a wide receiver. I went up [*to Pomfret School*] yesterday to watch practice, but with 50 guys running around, I couldn't make out Joe. But, tomorrow, I'll look for 89. *(09-13-98)*

A highlight of the week happened at the Providence airport, where

Joe, Mom and I met John. He is here for a week in Washington for a meeting, and then back to Pomfret for a week of projects and time with Joe. Speaking of Joe, we watched him catch the kickoff and run it back many yards. I started saying 20 yards, but I am now up to 60 yards. *(10-12-98)*

Jeff has received acceptances from two colleges, but not his top choices. His e-mail included the following quote by Lily Tomlin: "I always wanted to be somebody, but I should have been more specific." *(12-28-98)*

Johanna gave me a large print of a picture that she had taken and developed. It shows Pop on the front porch [*photo on the cover of the book*]. *(02-09-99)*

Mom had a chat with David and learned that Jeffrey had chosen Wooster College of Ohio. We have heard great things about Wooster, and we congratulate Jeff for his choice. *(05-03-99)*

The phone rang. And a small voice said "Happy Father's Day." And an older voice said "How are you, Claire?" Add the small voice said "Fantastic!" May you all look forward to such joyous moments. *(06-20-99)*

We had a call from Jeffrey as he was about to depart from Fairport. And then an e-mail expressing his wonders about the first lonely days at college. He also listed his courses. I envy the chance to do that kind of studying. *(08-29-99)*

And today is Johanna's birthday. I vividly remember that day. David and I were fishing in the Catskills when we got the message that there was a 'birthing problem.' David said "I don't feel like more fishing. Let's go home." And we did. But a happy ending. Look at Johanna today. Happy Birthday! *(10/03/00)*

Think back on your week. Imagine the pride we have in seeing college friends, in having the visit of a son, in watching a grandson compete and be with us for so many hours. Count your blessings! *(10/22/00)*

# Brooklyn Days

**"He brought some of his movie films of our camping trips and church excursions. You can imagine the hooting and hollering."**

*Like many in his generation, Pop didn't talk much of his youth. Living through the Depression and then a world war was better left in the forgotten distance. Almost thirty years of letters, but very few mentions of growing up. We would hear snippets here and there, mostly from our mother: his father out of work through the Depression; his mother dying of cancer while he was in high school; the Coast Guard, hardly anything. And then, once in a while, he would blurt out something. Once, he told Mary that the first time he ate an egg was in the service. No wonder he preferred to avoid the topic with his children. He'd rather talk about the "hooting and hollering" than those tough times.*

*Boy Scout* by John Dickson

Sunday brought some company in the form of very old friends of Pop's. I have known Al and Lillian Lemaire since I was twelve, and maybe before. But Al and I joined the Boy Scouts together, and sort of have kept in touch with each other for all these years. They live down in Wallingford, and they came up for supper and an evening of you-know-what. We also called the third member of the "gang," Will Ludwig, down in Philadelphia. Old friends are something special. *(02-27-79)*

En route [*to David and Paula's*], we stopped at an antique shop, and Pop bought a sea print by Gordon Grant (signed). He used to do work for Seamen's Bank, and Grandpa Dickson also did his tax work for many years. *(02-03-81)*

And then, on Saturday evening, we went down to Wallingford to see Pop's old friends, Al Lemaire and Will Ludwig. We were in a Sunday School and Boy Scout Troop over forty years ago. Will in those days was our official photographer, and he brought some of his movie films of our camping trips and church excursions. You can imagine the hooting and hollering. I haven't seen Will in about twenty years. *(04-06-81)*

Yesterday was my mother's birthday and sad to say I don't remember too much of those days, except that she was sick for a long time. She had been a schoolteacher in a bad section of Brooklyn, and I remember her saying one day that one of her students had gone to the electric chair on that day. Her father was a house painter (do you suppose that's where I got the painting passion?) and her grandfather was an iron worker brought here by John Erricson to work on the Monitor. Her name was Florence Dorothea Holm, and the old pictures show that she was a beauty. *(03-29-82)*

This is my mother's birthday. She died when she was 49, and I am sure that her life had its happy moments, but all I can really remember were the final few years when she was wracked by the most horrible pain and illness. Sad. *(03-28-83)*

On the boat ride, we saw the Coast Guard training ship Danmark (one of the tall ships), and Pop remembered his terror at having to climb the rigging when I was at the Academy. *(08-01-83)*

There was a report on television the other night about the mining of Corinto Bay in Nicaragua, and I showed Mom a snapshot from my album of a street scene in Corinto during the war. Two different worlds. *(05-14-84)*

We salute the inventor of the air conditioner – whoever he was and wherever he may be. We have survived, particularly Mom, because of the stream of cool and dry air that has flowed from these important machines. It has been said that this is the worst heat wave since 1936, and I wondered where I was then, and I know. I was living in my grandfather's house in downtown Brooklyn with a bedroom on the third floor – and it was fiendish. As it is now. *(08-14-88)*

When in Manheim, we took a side trip to visit my old pal Will Ludwig (he and I joined the Scouts 55 years ago). When backing out of his driveway, I hit his mailbox, and put a gash in the rear of the camper. Phooey. *(03-02-90)*

The attic work is finished! While up there, I glanced at some of the boxes with old stuff. I offer two examples. One is a letter I wrote when I was 8 . . . "Dear Mother, I have to thank you for the nice Keds. For they are so nice. Yours Truly From Donald P. Dickson." The other is a telegram from Scout camp. I had signed up for a month, but my Mother wrote, and said they could not afford more than two weeks. I scurried around and got a job as a dishwasher in the mess hall, and sent the following telegram "Staying Have Job Don't Worry Send

Wash Will Write – Donald." I was thrifty even then – ten words for 25 cents. *(01-17-93)*

In 1940, I went to work at Seamen's Bank on Wall Street as a Page, really an errand boy for the officers. My 'teacher,' and Page, was Dick Burnard. We became close friends. And before I went into the Service, Dick and I took a bike ride and got as far as Wilmington, Del. With balloon-tired bikes, blanket rolls (before sleeping bags) we went down Route 1 and then up the Jersey Shore for two weeks. Sleeping mostly in town and state parks. After the war, he came to Princeton once, and then we lost touch. AND this week, I got a letter from Dick. After 40 years! He had gotten my address from the Princeton manual. *(11-24-96)*

When I lived with *my* grandfather at 177 South Oxford Street, it was a street of rooming houses and by-passed lodgings. An ad in the Times the other day said that the house at 133 had sold for $446,000. *(09-05-99)*

A lesson re-learned: I had hesitated visiting Lillian Lemaire, widow of my Scout pal Al, because of the emotional triggers. But my better self decided to do a lunch with her on my way to Lancaster. Good decision. Emotional, yes. But helpful, yes. *(09-19-99)*

We went to a funeral service for a woman who had been ill for a long time. She and her husband had a habit of singing the old hymns. So it was quite a songfest. One of the hymns was The Old Rugged Cross, and it brought back many memories. In the '30's there was a daily program sponsored by Ivory Soap called the Gospel Singer . . . Edward McHugh, and that hymn was his theme song. My mother would stop everything and listen to his booming voice sing the old hymns. *(01-18-00)*

Uncle Bob. Rest in peace.

Bob and I grew up as Depression boys. In one of the great sacrifices of parenthood, my Mother (especially) and Father passed up the option of a new wage earner (my father was out of work for at least five years) and sent him to Rutgers on a church scholarship.

And there he met Ruth.

Part of the Depression experience was being forced to move into my grandfather's house to the 3rd floor servants' quarters. He was a tyrant, and I think his attitude toward Bob and me helped us to generate a special love for grandchildren. *(10-29-00)*

# The End of a Paintbrush

**"The marriage has once again survived that most traumatic of all decisions – picking wallpaper."**

*Pop had a list ready. Every day. On Saturdays and vacation days as we grew up, he left us a list on the breakfast table with chores for the day: pick up sticks, rake leaves, mow the lawn, trim the hedges, fix the fence, and for my older brothers, paint the house. He even kept a list of items to include in the weekly letter. No doubt he made a list as soon as he got to the office. He needed a list for all the chores around the big houses they seemed to prefer, ones in serious disrepair. These houses were wrecks on closing day, of the "everywhere you look" variety. There was always something that needed fixing, cleaning, clipping, overhauling, or updating. One image stays with me because it happened so often throughout his life. After our Saturday morning of work, he would call it quits. For us. He, though, returned to work, typically at one end of a paintbrush, listening to the Metropolitan Opera on the radio. Could that have been his heaven?*

*Paint* by John Dickson

80

The grass is starting to grow – good grief. At this point I neither have equipment ready – nor anybody to run it. Anybody want to volunteer? *(04-19-71)*

This was the weekend of the "big plant." On Friday (Pop took the day off), Pop dug up 500 bushes at the Hoyt Nursery and brought them here for transplanting. By 4:00 p.m., when I was too tired to move, I only had 200 trees planted, and was somewhat discouraged. But friends and sons to the rescue! On Saturday (when 600 more bushes were delivered!) John, Andrew, Mr. Ferguson, Doug and Dick Ferguson and 2 high school boys from New Canaan all started early, and by 1:00 p.m. we had transplanted 900 more! And so the back field now has the beginnings of a nursery business. *(05-12-72)*

The house is just about all painted, I am happy to report. I took Thursday and Friday off and really concentrated on the project, and except for an hour or two of trim work, and putting up a few shutters, it is now done-finished-all over.

The place looks pretty good. The ice house and the tavern are all painted, the lawn is in excellent shape (thanks to Andrew), Ann has been painting the front fence, and we've begun to tackle the bush trimming jobs. The project list is still a mile long, but there are visible signs of progress. *(08-20-72)*

Speaking of needlepoint, we are on the 4th square of our mammoth rug job (with Pop doing the background). You'll be hearing about it for a long time. *(11-19-72)*

Saturday was a very, very tough work day. David, Peter, Andrew and I put new shingles on half of the stable roof, and it was some job. The heat must have been 100° on the roof, too hot to touch, and the shingles were melting as we put them down. I don't think I'll ever get my fingernails clean again. *(07-02-73)*

I finished the barn painting (except for some trim), helped by Andrew who steadied the ladder during some of the more risky reaching work. *(08-14-73)*

The major project of the long weekend was trees – and we took down seven of the red pines. They are now mostly cut up and in a huge pile in the back field ready for burning. Also, Andrew and I worked on the Meadow Rock National Forest, which is the area near the gazebo. It really looks great. *(09-03-73)*

Pop paid the price this morning for his early-hour working in the basement. I conked my skull on a pipe and bit my lip – and I'm now a bloody mess. And obviously it looks just great. *(10-29-73)*

The chimney was fixed on Friday, so now we are back in 'roaring fire' business [*after the chimney fire of the great ice storm of 1973*]. It sure feels (and looks) great to have the logs aglow. The floor work didn't begin, although it was scheduled. *(01-20-74)*

Andrew and I took 6 pine trees down on Saturday morning, and we decided to start a project to build a log cabin or lean-to down at the pond. We therefore did not saw up the pines, but left them, pending some decisions on length of log needed. Volunteers for log cabin work will be welcomed. *(02-18-74)*

We decided to get a new ceiling in the library, because it had the very inappropriate tiles. Well, on Friday, the men came, and Mom asked them to see what was under the old ceiling. Under it is the most spectacular beam ceiling – and the side beams must be 12"x18". And so, all the plaster came down, and it also revealed wide, wide floorboards from the bedroom upstairs. So, I guess we are going to take the library back to its original 1712 situation. *(02-25-74)*

Andrew, Mike and I moved some of the pine tree sections down to the pond area, in preparation for the log cabin work. We've decided on nine and twelve foot lengths – and the darned logs are therefore quite heavy. I haven't figured how we are going to raise them when we start building the cabin. Anybody have any experience building pyramids? *(03-11-74)*

Yesterday Mom said it was a good thing that most of my jobs take place where people can't see me. For during a steady rain I worked in the garden and planted corn, squash and gourds. After about four hours of wet and muddy work I came in drenched, tired, dirty but with a good sense of accomplishment. *(05-13-74)*

First of all, has anybody seen Andrew? This has been the 1-o-n-g-e-s-t weekend, because I had to do so many chores that Andrew always volunteered for. I've pushed the wagon back and forth, cut grass, picked up thousands of apples, carried wood, picked vegetables by the ton and have been general errand boy and handyman for the gal that runs this place. *(09-22-74)*

I spent the weekend at the end of a paint brush. Yes, we finally started the library painting project. The walls are an off-white and the woodwork is an old red. When Mom first suggested red, I was apprehensive, but it is really a great color and complements the floor (now finished) and the paneling (not yet finished). *(01-13-75)*

Pop took Thursday afternoon off, and John and I took down 15 of the red pines. The chain saw worked perfectly, and John tugged them down from a large rope tied to the back of the tractor. *(03-31-75)*

John and I also did a marathon job of putting stakes along the stone wall on the lower part of the lower field. On a very hot day we put in 90 seven-foot stakes and then strung them with barbed wire. To finish off that pleasant day, I put another coat of tar on the stable roof (after John and I repaired it). *(05-19-75)*

The rug is being worked on. It will be ready for the nation's tricentennial. *(02-08-76)*

Andrew, the Locke [*large lawn mower*], the rake, the little mower, the tractor and manure wagon etc. have all been asking for you. Poppa is caught in a real dilemma. I don't like to cut the grass; but the furnace is surely not running when the Locke is running. *(08-29-76)*

These are busy times. The house sale still seems to be on track, and we are beginning to do the packing job. Yesterday, I worked on books, records, closets and miscellaneous and I must have packed about fifty cartons. They are standing in a line in the basement – all ready to go. *(11-07-76)*

POMFRET CENTER!!!!
We're in!
Sort of. Some of the rooms are simply stacked with furniture and cartons, with an aisle here and there. And in so many others, it's just like camping out – or camping in. And there is dust everywhere. And I suspect this will be our way of life for some time to come.
But are we happy? You can bet your boots we are. Mom hasn't come down from Cloud 9, and now she's even joyously greeting the snow which is falling rather steadily outside. She's doing the dishes by hand in an ancient sink, and she has to take clothes to the laundromat, and the clutter is enormous, but she is still bouncing around with joy. She has a talent, and you guys know this, for seeing the "big picture," while I concentrate on the dumb old things like painting, carrying,

etc. Seriously, all is well. *(12-04-76)*

Have you ever been so happy you could burst? That's us. Yes, we country pumpkins in Pomfret Center are bursting with happy-ness. And dust. And mess. And confusion. But we love it. *(12-12-76)*

I don't know what happened to the quiet world we were supposed to "retire to." But these days are mighty busy days. For Mom, unfortunately, it's a never-ending struggle against the dust that surrounds us. . . . One of our problems (for morale, anyway) is that we have three or four rooms "started" and nothing finished. *(01-10-77)*

Since Tuesday we have been putting in long days trying to complete a room or two. The downstairs powder room is now finished, as is most of the dressing room upstairs. We miscalculated on our wallpaper needs, and I have a few more strips to put up. It looks great. The guest room has been painted, and the wallpaper should be finished today. Also, part of our bedroom and the upstairs hall has been papered. It is slow but satisfying work. *(02-22-77)*

We have one less barn. After much debate and much sorrow, we finally decided that the bigger of the two barns near the house had to come down. And down it came – in one day. The workmen first took the roof off, then pulled the rafters down, then took out all the wooden pegs, and one good pull with a rope and the framework just settled down to the ground. The barns will "rise again," for we intend to use many of the beams and the siding in our kitchen and in the renovation of the big barn for the antique shop. But it looks kind of sad now. *(03-13-77)*

The only real reminder of summer (besides the temperature) is the doggoned grass, which is growing at a fantastic rate. In addition, Andrew, the belt broke yesterday on the mower. Mom and I have had an interesting arrangement. She starts the mower, and I run it. *(08-28-77)*

Among the projects here has been the painting of the shutters, which is always one of Pop's favorite jobs. I don't have the usual big production line, and so progress is slow. Also, I've had to scrape so much off the old shutters, that it is taking three coats of new paint. *(09-26-77)*

The other needle project here is the doggoned rug. I have all the squares attached and now have to figure out a way to put a border on – no small job because the squares haven't exactly lined up properly. I think this whole thing deserves an award as the boondoggle of the year. *(03-19-78)*

The marriage has once again survived that most traumatic of all decisions – picking wallpaper. I lost – no more eagles. But the back room is now ready for papering (hope to start tomorrow), and soon after that we'll tackle the little bathroom (plaid paper!). And then the upstairs bath. We spent a good part of the week painting woodwork and getting ready. *(04-09-78)*

The doggoned grass is growing, and the maddening mower situation still exists. After getting it fixed last fall, and then having a spring "tune-up," it went fifty feet and conked out. There ain't no justice. Particularly since I can no longer play "the terrible-tempered Mr. Bang." I have to sweetly tell Mom that the mower won't work – and no more. *(05-15-78)*

Pop had a list ready. Most of the jobs were lifting and moving jobs. No fun. But Peter planted ten fruit trees in our new "orchard" between the antique barn and the shed. We planted pear, cherry and apple trees. We also planted an apple tree next to the screened porch. *(05-30-78)*

After waiting weeks for the crew to come cut the grass, one of them arrived yesterday morning to advise us that they would not do it this year. Poppa isn't supposed to get angry, but it took a lot of control not to pick up the guy and throw him off the place. And so, David pushed the little mower and Paula raked, and considerable progress was made. Today, I signed up another guy who promises to be here soon. *(05-13-79)*

We had a visit from a chimney sweep, complete with brooms and stovepipe hat. He cleaned the chimney that uses the library wood stove. *(09-03-79)*

I've come up with a system of walking that has somewhat of a purpose. But it's like the Chinese building a dam with shovels. I walk up to the back corner of the property where the old elm was cut down and cut into small pieces, and I carry a log back. I've got many, many trips to come. *(10-22-79)*

The needlepoint is finished! Mom just took a couple of pictures of it, and it looks sensational. We figured there are about 181,000 stitches in it – and about two years of work. *(03-24-80)*

After endless delays (over months and years) I finally tackled the binding of The Rug, and surprisingly it has gone quite easy and looks good – providing you don't look too close. I've also started to do the center section of the church things, and have also (for relief) started on some needlework strips for the luggage racks. *(02-25-80)*

I'm back to sawing wood for the stoves, and while I go at it slowly, it is still good exercise – and besides, it gets me outside. *(01-26-81)*

Nothing came out of Pop's workshop since I am still working on the bench for a replacement for the front porch. I am going to paint it but still must get the old paint off and that includes 38 spindles. *(06-01-81)*

Peter 'volunteered' for one of the unhappy jobs that pops up here – cleaning the loft in the barn. It isn't exactly sparkle city now, but it is much, much cleaner and some new bales of hay have been added to add a more pleasant odor. Incidentally, the bats have been less noticeable of late, but yesterday a customer in the shop pointed to one that was swooping around. Pop got it. *(08-10-81)*

One of my outstanding events was to paint the workshop floor in the basement, leaving my glasses on the other side of the room. *(02-14-82)*

There was some barn painting done and for the first time, I trimmed the evergreens – a job normally done by one of the 'helpers.' Where are you guys? *(07-19-82)*

First, I no longer believe in ESP. I tried and tried mentally to let you all know that a load of firewood had been delivered and that you should come and help me heave it into the barn. And so, I did a dumb thing. On Monday, with the temperatures in the 90's and on Tuesday, in the rain, I moved six ton of wood. I think I was wetter in the heat than in the rain. But it's in. *(07-26-82)*

Mom had the traumatic job of undoing a sweater that she had been knitting. It was sad to see all of that work undone but she said it just wasn't working out. For my part, I have just about finished the belt and it sure looks super. *(03-21-83)*

The house painters were here last week, and I expect will finish up in a day or two. Pop had most of the shutters finished, but will complete the last ones today. I'm anxious that the painters put them back up, rather than me. (07-11-83)

Did you all hear me last week? I stepped off a ladder into a bucket of paint – and the cry could be heard for miles. *(07-25-83)*

We have had some early conversations with the architect and are putting together some ideas. It is meant to be a large room behind the library, with the entry to come from a door from what is now the dining room. *(02-21-84)*

The chimney is almost finished. We hope. The scaffolding is still up, but hopefully it can come down this week. Then we can get back to work on the inside. It has taken three months to build this darned chimney. *(08-13-84)*

If you can visualize the greenhouse building, you can see a section over the glass that can't be reached by ladder. It was handled by going to the roof, leaning over and painting upside down. All of this accompanied by a nervous Mom (as well as a nervous Pop). *(07-29-85)*

I spent a fair amount of time at the end of paint brushes. I finally did the high part of the barn building. Strangely, I could not reach the high points although I believe I was using the same ladder as the last time. And so, I had to borrow another ladder and completed the job, with Mom sitting on the bottom rung and keeping it steady while I flailed away at the top. Thank goodness, it's done. *(08-17-85)*

The work on the front of the house is moving ahead. I am the go-fer for the project, and this means visits to the lumber yard for loads of lumber, etc. It also means I am the cleanup man, taking debris to the dump. *(07-29-86)*

I washed all the windows in the shop. Nobody has noticed yet. *(08-17-86)*

A large part of our routine these days involves the addition. The slate has been all laid down and looks great. And the painting work continues. First, the wood needs sanding, then two coats of shellac (to hide the knots), then re-sanding, then a primer – and finally the finish coat. Or coats. We are at the primer stage. And the ceilings are finished. *(09-22-86)*

Last week was a good one in terms of productivity. For one thing, the van passed the emission test – almost a miracle. For another, some broken hardware on a drape in the back room was repaired – it has needed fixing for about a year, and it took me ten minutes to do the job. *(08-31-87)*

Uncle Bob once called me D. Paint Dickson – and it has certainly been true lately. The basement floor is finished, as well as the basement stairway. And I am slowly making progress on the new interior shutters. It takes me about six hours per window. *(02-24-91)*

Leaves. Leaves. I have started on the annual project of mulching the leaves with the small mower. But one problem has been that I could not get it started. I put in a new spark plug, and tried for a couple days to start it. Do you know what happened? Mom went over, took one pull, and the machine started. I still love her. *(10-20-91)*

Department of "I'll get around to it someday." When we moved here, I put a big batch of ties in a carton promising that I would sort them out someday. Well, 14 years later, I have done it. Since I wear a tie only once a week at best, I really didn't sort them, I just threw them away. Finally. *(11-19-90)*

I have also been washing windows. Big deal. *(09-20-92)*

I know this isn't important to *you*, but you can't imagine the thrill of having the grass mower start on the second pull, after a winter in the barn. *(06-06-93)*

Leaves, leaves, leaves. Better than snow, snow, snow. I suspect all marriages have their on-going 'debates.' Here, we debate about the leaves. I say let them be. Mom says let's get at them. Further, there is a debate within the debate . . . a rake vs. a leaf blower. Well, Mom bought a leaf blower. She uses it, I use a rake. All of this gives rise to my bumper sticker, The Family that Leaves Together, Stays Together. (10-24-93)

In anticipation of a house painting in mid-month, I am painting shutters on an assembly line in the garage. I have painted shutters in Indian Hill (84 windows!), Far Hills and Wilton. But Pomfret Center is the first place that I have done it in the daytime. My former jobs were in the basement before I went to work. And I always ask myself the same question – why do I bother doing the backs of the shutters? *(08-07-94)*

Speaking of mowers – when we moved here, I bought a rather expensive unit, which gave me endless trouble, mostly under the warranty. But then, I bought a cheap Sears unit. It has sat in the garden room since last fall, and it did take a few pulls . . . but it started! *(10-22-96)*

One of the challenges has been to paint that part of the greenhouse building over the glass. Usually, I have climbed on the roof, leaned down and painted upside down. The last time it was done, John did it. But I looked around, and no John. And when I got on the roof, my body rebelled with a series of charley horses. I got the message. And that night, I got another message. Use a roller on a pole! It worked reasonably well. *(08-18-96)*

Trick of the Week: I was painting the white trim on the porch, and was getting up from a sitting position, when I stumbled and sprawled the width of the porch. AND, although I had a brush in one hand and can of paint in the other, not a drop got on the floor. However, I don't think I did my recovering back any good, and my knee has suddenly bothered me. *(06-01-97)*

My Job List has had one item for many weeks . . . paint the garage. The rear, that is. My procrastination was based upon two thoughts – who cares about the rear of a building, and second, it will be a tough job. Well, I did it, and it was the most unpleasant painting job of all. Heat, humidity, bugs, wasps, poison ivy, etc. It needs a second coat, but it ain't going to get it. *(08-17-97)*

I am working on a new needlepoint project. It involves Noah's Ark. Very appropriate, for we have been deluged by rain these past few days. *(11-09-97)*

Speaking of flowers, we tried to find some daffodils to bring to David. To symbolize the daffodils that I picked and took to Mom in the Princeton Hospital the 'morning after'. *[David's birth in 1948]* *(03-23-98)*

And for about a month I have a job list that included cleaning up the bat stuff in the barn. After a month of procrastinating, I did it. In an hour. *(07-12-98)*

Another event was that Pop finally got some paint brushes in his hand and painted the bench from the porch, and then the porch itself. I may have mentioned this before, but this is the first year that I can remember that I haven't painted some or all parts of barns. Any volunteers? *(07-19-98)*

We had a night of wind and rain. But we also had left a large carton of those pesky plastic 'peanuts' on the bench on the porch. They were all over the driveway and grass. Fun. *(11-15-98)*

The annual chore of scraping and painting the floor of the porch has been finished. It was helped along via the use of that great invention – the garden kneeler, and by Mom's suggestion last year to use a roller on a pole rather the old brush method. I also painted some deck chairs. AND I got a haircut! *(05-23-99)*

I also bought an ice scraper for the windshield. I haven't been able to find the old one. But I couldn't fit the new scraper into the pocket in the door panel. Why? The old one was stuck in the panel. *(11-14-00)*

# Which Side Are You On?

**"Election Day was a busy time here, for our house was the Democratic Town 'headquarters.'"**

*We grew up in a politically involved and aware household. At Sunday dinner, we waited for two questions. The first one we dreaded: what was the sermon about? The second one was a bit of a competition: name the Supreme Court justices. Or the Senators from our state. Or the eleven cities in the world with more than a population of a million that begin with the letter "M." Both parents started out as Republicans, and I'd like to think they moved left down the political spectrum because of their involved and aware children. Thus, it was no surprise that, in the weekly letters, we often read about their political involvement at the local level and their feisty awareness at the national level. It's a time capsule now to look back and see what issues and people engaged them over the final decades of the twentieth century.*

*The Flag at the Front Door* by Annie Dickson

The preacher, incidentally, at St. Matthews was Rev. Michael Allen of the Yale Divinity School, who described what it was like to be in Hanoi last Christmas. *(02-27-72)*

Today was the Silent Service at St. Matthew's, to pray for the end of the bombing and the success of the peace talks. It was a very moving experience. The clergy were in black vestments, the service began with the ritual for the Burial of the Dead, and instead of a sermon there were spontaneous prayers from the congregation. If prayers can end this awful mess, this morning at St. Matthews should help. *(01-07-73)*

On Friday evening, Uncle All and Jay were here for dinner and then to watch the announcement of a new VP's name. We had a secret ballot, and Andrew picked Mr. Ford. So, everyone was surprised but Andrew. *(10-14-73)*

We're into November, and it is starting off chilly. We've been working on projects to reduce the oil consumption at 550, and we could use a 'mild' winter. The back of the house is 'shut off.' And it was rather cool back there last night. But we'll warm it up for you when you come home. *(11-05-73)*

Gramps, Uncle All and Mrs. Pratt stopped for a drink on Saturday evening, and then Gramps stayed for dinner. We had, of course, one of our tumultuous dinner conversations with Gramps defending the oil industry. He sure picks unpopular causes. *(01-28-74)*

Another reason for staying home is that the gasoline situation is really getting terrible. Mom got some on Wednesday after 3 hours in line. What a colossal waste of time, but there's no alternative. *(02-03-74)*

We had a terrific weekend, but it was complicated and confused by the doggoned gasoline problem. Life has certainly become an involved one. On Friday evening, partly because of the weather but mostly because of the gas shortage, we decided against going to Fathers' Day at Lawrenceville. On Saturday, we vacillated back and forth, and finally made the "go" decision. We had almost a full tank in the Jeep, topped it off with some gas borrowed from Uncle All, and put a 5 gallon can in the car (an illegal step). Then, with Mike and Steve from Hutchinson [*Kansas cousins*] with us, we took off. We were able to buy $1 at three different stations on the turnpike – and made it back and forth satisfactorily. *(02-11-74)*

On Tuesday, Mom and I went down to Essex for a 'half-way house', dinner with Uncle Jim and Aunt Georgia. Uncle Jim had had a luncheon with Prime Minister Thatcher of England and was also full of his various conservative views and I was full of my various liberal views. And so it went. *(12-24-79)*

Among the week's other major events was the decision to change my political registration from Independent to Democratic. It really had nothing to do with great national issues, but rather as a protest against some dumb, even ugly, machinations by the local Republicans. *(01-25-82)*

Quote of the week: "We don't have to worry about endangered species; why we can't even get rid of the cockroach." Answer at the bottom of the page. [*James Watt*] *(04-19-82)*

Mom and I (and Mrs. C) went to the Town Meeting on the nuclear freeze which passed by about six to one. The evening was hampered by a couple of obstructionists who tried every technical move possible to keep the vote from happening. Their message was that we should not be telling the President how to run his job. Somewhere I missed a turn (or they did) in civic lessons in public school. *(05-17-82)*

One evening last week, a delegation from the Democratic party in town came to ask me to run for Selectman. Of course, I declined, but it was good for ego. I wish I were younger and in better health to be able to try for such a job. *(07-18-83)*

Mom switched her party registration last week from ? to ? *(03-12-84)*

Political statement of the week: The Journal had an article about the duplication of War Colleges, and it included the happy thought (to we taxpayers) that there are, "81 holes of golf, eight swimming pools, four recreational lakes (two with cottages), three riding stables, a marina, a yacht club, three aero clubs (with government supplied airplanes), plus bowling alleys, handball courts, tennis courts, woodworking shops, post exchanges and commissaries." *(02-18-85)*

I wrote a letter to the Editor of the New York Times commenting on the plans for the Statue of Liberty celebrations. In a brazen but probably honest statement, the head of the committee said the invitations to the aircraft carrier which will be in the harbor would be limited to the normal list of rich people. All other tickets will be by lottery. To get on the carrier, you must fork over $10,000. *(03-24-86)*

Do you recall my note about writing a letter to the Editor of the Times, commenting on the article about some of the invitations to the 4th of July celebration at the Statue of Liberty being limited to a certain group of rich individuals who could afford the $10,000 price tag? Well, we had much laughter here one day when a fancy package arrived with an invitation for Pop. As we suspected, it came from Mr. Dooley [*a friend from Pop's marketing life*] who is on the Staff. *(03-31-86)*

Mom has a good idea for the surplus of cows that we are currently killing. She suggests that we tell the nations that are buying our guns, planes and missiles that they have to buy so many cows for each purchase of military stuff. *(04-28-86)*

First was a Town Meeting to consider the idea of setting up a fund to help farmers stay in business and avoid selling prime land to developers. A paradox was pointed out that the Federal Government is paying five dairy farms in Pomfret to go out of business while the town is thinking of raising taxes to keep farmers in business. *(05-12-86)*

We went to a Town Meeting where we decided such critical subjects as a new dump truck, a pension plan issue, regional bus service and plans for a town dump. *(09-29-86)*

I read a series of articles in the New Yorker about the homeless and their children. It's a story of New York City and contains examples of just about every sin known to man . . . greed, stupidity, cheating, lying. It's an outrageous story about bureaucratic bungling and profiteering on the backs of some lost souls. *(02-08-88)*

The big social event of last week was the Democratic 'our House to the White House' party on Thursday evening. The idea, well-organized, was to have friends and neighbors in to watch the acceptance speeches. I am told there were about 6,000 of such affairs across the country. We had about 40 people in for a potluck supper and raised over $500 for the campaign. They provided posters, stickers, balloons, ribbons, and Mom really had this place decorated with flags, flowers and such. And also a ton of food. *(07-25-88)*

I closed out the New Year by doing something I had wanted to do for a long time. I let one of my conservative 'friends' have it with both barrels – after he blamed the deficit on Truman, Johnson, Kennedy and Carter. Guess who is missing from that list? It wasn't much of a friendship – but it sure ain't one now. *(01-02-89)*

Here's an interesting quote: "The autocratic monarchies were like great ships that sailed majestically on, until they struck a reef and sank forever, whereas democracy is like a raft – it never sinks. But damn it, your feet are always in the water." *(05-01-89)*

The Wall Street Journal, my source of all things from the 'other side,' had editorials last week against Federal Child Care, the Clean Air Bill and the Disabled Workers bill. They are a real fun bunch. *(10-29-89)*

It was a week of various meetings, too. We went to a Hearing on the proposed Town budget (taxes are bound to go up, since the State, as many others have had to do, has cut back on the dollars sent to the towns – but more services have been mandated). Read my lips is a fine theory – but the burden keeps getting pushed to the localities. *(04-12-90)*

Mom is also the Big News of the week. She won the election to the Library Board. Further, John, Mary and Pop provided the three-vote margin that made her a victor over a man who had been absolutely nasty about her role as a Democrat. Well, there may have been another three votes that did it, but it is nice to think that we all helped Mom. Election Day was a busy time here, for our house was the Democratic Town 'headquarters,' and all day there were people running in and out with voting sheets, etc. Our candidate, the Selectman, won by a landslide, and for the first time in 40 years, the top two slots are owned by Democrats. *(11-12-89)*

Uncle All continues to be the champion writer of Letters to the Editor. The most recent was to the Christian Science Monitor when he wrote about Bush's veto of a bill funding abortions with the comment: "Our national leadership worries more about financial losses than the mental and physical well-being of legitimate victims. Our national priorities are backward." This is Uncle All? It sure is. *(12-10-89)*

Signs of the times: I passed a long, long convoy of Army trucks painted in sand-like colors yesterday. And each night we hear the roar of those huge airplanes (cargo) that are based in Chicopee [*MA*] and pass over here on their way somewhere. *(12-16-90)*

We spent many hours watching the television on the Kuwait subject. The vote in this house was divided – and I suspect that is the mood of the country. Let's hope for the best. And that is peace. *(01-13-91)*

We have had the radio on all day trying to get some news from the Gulf. We pray that it will end soon. *(02-24-91)*

When I wrote last week that 'we prayed that the Gulf War ended soon,' little did we expect such a sudden and happy ending. *(03-04-91)*

I revisited the town of Greenville, Miss where many years ago I spent a week on a voter registration drive. It was a terrible place then; now it is larger, but still terrible. We drove around some of the black neighborhoods. Never again. *(03-25-91)*

I spent a day with a pal touring high schools here and in Mass. to talk to college guidance counselors. It was quite depressing. Do you want to play football? – $200, please. Do you want to play in the band? – $50 please. The school libraries are open ten hours each week; advanced placement courses have been cancelled; class sizes have been increased to 35; and technical courses have been cancelled. This because of budget problems. A very sad story. *(10-20-91)*

For other events this past week, I went to a fine dinner at the Rauh's, a Development Committee meeting at the Pomfret School, too much time working on the leaves, and a party at the MacLeans where I finally let one of my far-right 'friends' have it for her endless complaints and attacks on teachers and the local school system. It felt good to get it out of my system. *(10-27-91)*

It was sort of a quiet week, although Mom went to a Democratic Town Meeting where there was some fireworks. Small town politics can be just as bad as big town stuff. And possibly more personal. *(05-03-92)*

A sign of the times . . . Mr. Republican and Mr. Conservative (the same guy), Harvard '27, told me after church that he was fed up with George Bush. "And he comes from such a good family." *(05-17-92)*

Mom the Activist! She read in the paper that the granddaughter and major owner of L.L. Bean was running for Congress on a platform of no gun control, no pro-choice and no a few other things that Mom believes in. So, she sent her catalog back with a stern note. *(08-02-92)*

A Woman of Principle! One of Uncle Gil's stocks was in a cigarette company, and finally, finally, the stock was transferred to Mom. She promptly sold it. *(10-18-92)*

Our dining room was headquarters for the town, wherein we tabulate the voting lists so that get-out-the vote-calls can be made before the polls close. However, 91% voted, and telephoning was not needed. Mr. Perot had big margins in this area, even taking some towns. You may not believe this, but Pop stayed up till 11PM savoring the results. *(11-08-92)*

Mom has a favorite new bumper sticker that says: "I'll be happy when our schools have all the money they need, and the Navy has to have bake sales to get a new battleship." *(02-28-93)*

Mom had a Library Board meeting, and I went to a Study Center to discuss the idea of gay rights. *(02-28-93)*

We also went to a town meeting relating to a tax proposal for a planned unit of housing for the elderly. It's amazing how the word 'tax' seems to bring out the strangest statements. Speakers would extol the idea and the need for such housing, but then quickly say they didn't want to pay for it. It passed. *(11-16-93)*

Bill Clinton called and congratulated Mom for her purchases (a new washer/dryer) and her efforts to jump start the economy. *(12-05-93)*

Pomfret had a road study which showed the town needed 1.2 million to fix the roads. In the last budget fight, the anti-tax folks reduced the road budget to $50,000. A familiar story. *(08-07-94)*

I suspect that on Tuesday night we went to one of the few Democratic victory parties in the nation. Actually, this state was the only one in the nation in which the legislature added more Democratic seats. An interesting figure: more people voted in Greenwich than voted in Hartford. *(11-13-94)*

Mom went to a Democratic Town meeting, at which the Board of Education, under John Rauh's leadership, presented their three-year budget. John has done a sensational job, under difficult conditions. An interesting comment came from one of the Board members who said that the prior meeting with the Republican Town Committee concentrated on tax implications, while the Democrats mostly talked about education matters.
Speaking of politics, I got a Christmas card from Newt Gingrich. The envelope was postmarked Hutchinson, Kansas, and I suspect Bill Kline is passing along some revenge for the various Bill Clinton messages that I have sent him. *(12-18-94)*

It's hard to believe, but one of Congress' plans include closing Antietam Battlefield Park. It is the site of the bloodiest day and hour of the Civil War. I know that I am a 'special interest,' but I wonder at the values of our leaders who press for a billion-dollar bomber that the Pentagon doesn't want. End of message. *(07-09-95)*

This week's soap box. The National Parks. We belong to an association for the Parks, and this month's magazine makes rather grim reading. There are proposals to close Antietam and Harper's Ferry (by Congress); to open the Shenandoah to development, for mining in Yellowstone, for more and larger cruise ships in Glacier Bay, and to flood a canyon in Utah, opposed by 80% of Utahans, but proposed by its two Senators and two Representatives. Further, the Mojave Desert Park, passed by the last Congress over the objections of California miners and ranchers had its appropriation reduced from 1.7 million dollars to one dollar.
Speaking of Congress, 88% of the members of Congress who voted to weaken water standards in 1994 had bottled water delivered to their Capitol Hill offices. *(09-24-95)*

This is the time of year when the mail brings the annual reports of corporations. And it is the time when Mom strongly registers her message on the proxy forms of MORE WOMEN! The reactions are about the same, namely silence or a form letter of no consequence. But last year one company wrote and asked us to submit names. Smart. *(03-24-97)*

We had the Old Goats meeting here on Monday. Mom put together a great lunch. After the economic report, with all of its never-ending good news, I said that "if George Bush were president, there would be a sing-along for his performance. How come nobody says anything about Bill Clinton?" Silence. *(07-20-97)*

Another (e-mail) was from Matthew, and I have copied a part of it for you all. It is said that Education was a big issue in the recent election, and I am learning that it deserves to be. Matthew is obviously in the front-line trenches, and it is discouraging to read about a wealthy nation in a time of economic boom not able to support (nor willing) the kind of investment in education that we clearly need. *(11-15-98)*

We hear about teacher salaries and the inevitable complaints at Town Meetings (Conn. is the highest). But figures from last week had Conn. at the top of the nation in reading and writing scores. *(03-07-99)*

Election news. We were somewhat disappointed about the primaries. Interestingly, Pomfret voted overwhelmingly for Bradley and McCain. Pomfret? *(03-12-00)*

I got a mailing from the Adirondack Council, which we support with a modest gift. Some years ago, at a Princeton function, an elderly Tiger stood up and gave a great speech about acid rain and the Adirondacks. He was interrupted by the moderator who said that it was interesting, but not on the agenda. The Tiger responded that "he didn't give a damn about the agenda, but Princetonians should be aware of the acid rain problem." He got a great ovation. *(04-02-00)*

Another Annual Report came from Fidelco, a seeing eye dog training operation. A couple in Pomfret for years have begun the initial home training of the puppies. One man near Hartford started all of this about 30 years ago, financed it for many years, and today it is a thriving institution. Making a difference! *(4-10-00)*

# Going Back and Giving Back

**"The Chapel – a rather important place in this happy marriage."**

*Princeton changed Pop's life. A child of the Depression, who enlisted in the Coast Guard after high school, he ended up at this elite private university. Thanks to the GI Bill, and to the kindness of his first boss, Thornton Thayer, who was the bank manager at Seamen's Savings Bank where Pop had an after-school job before the war. We all knew Mr. Thayer as the man who gave Pop a blank check as he departed for Princeton; he never cashed it. He graduated in three years, held down dozens of jobs, met his future wife in the library; they had their first child right before he graduated. He worked so many jobs at Princeton that when he started at Procter & Gamble after graduation, he said he took a pay cut. And, he gave back to the place that changed everything. His letters to us chronicled his love affair with Princeton.*

*Princeton Tie* by John Dickson

Pop is having a ton of fun working on his 25th Reunion. Since the old Class of '49 graduated at 16 different times, our theme is 'Re-doing our Senior Year – all together this time.' Therefore, we are going to participate as "Seniors" in the University Convocation on September 16th, and Pop reads the Scriptures in the Chapel – in cap and gown. *(08-20-73)*

Today was Pop's Princeton day, and it was a great and emotional charge. Peter, Ann, John and Andrew were at the Chapel with Mom, and it all went very well. Afterward, Mom and I had luncheon with President Bowen and the Trustees. *(09-17-73)*

Speaking of Reunions, one event that has been added to the schedule is the awarding of the University's annual Alumni Award to Pop. The notice came last week and is certainly the icing to a glorious year for '49. *(05-13-74)*

I dropped Ann at the airport a little while ago, and so the exodus is about over. It was so great to have everyone in Princeton, and your father deeply appreciates the effort that all of you made to come to the 25th. I know it was loads more fun for Pop than it was for you. I'll come to your 25th.
So it's back to life as usual. But the memories of sitting in the tent, and listening to the great music, and the champagne 'graduation' party for Ann, and the P-rade, and the reception, and the award, and the dinners, and the dancing, and seeing old friends again will be around for a long time. And you all made it better. More better! *(06-10-74)*

On Wednesday I went to Princeton for lunch and a series of meetings and then to dinner with Mr. Ruckleshaus (of White House fame). He addressed the freshman class on the Honor Code and it was an impressive affair. When he was being introduced and the mention was made of his refusal to fire Archibald Cox during the Saturday night 'massacre' the kids went wild with applause. After the meeting, I met John and we had a couple beers together. *(09-15-75)*

Friday morning, Pop went to Princeton for a presentation before the Board of Trustees. It was very impressive and in the great old room at Nassau Hall. After a meeting in Cherry Hill, I returned to Princeton to pick up Mom for a dinner with the Trustees. Earlier I had bumped into Governor Byrne (a Trustee) and he asked us to stay at Morven, the Governor's Mansion. We did, and felt very important, with troopers carrying luggage etc. *(10-27-75)*

The Princeton dinner in St. Louis was great – the 100th Anniversary of the Club. Pop sat at the head table with Pres. Bowen, 3 other college Presidents, the Governor (a Tiger) and the Attorney General (a Tiger). *(02-01-76)*

Pop went to Princeton on Wednesday for a lunch, an afternoon meeting with Bill Bowen, and a full evening with the freshman class and the explanation of the honor system. This year's speaker was Bill Bradley, who did an outstanding job. He was very serious and touched upon characters in literature who had reflected upon the honesty and integrity of their own lives – mostly as aged men. It was a moving talk, and the kids reacted with a great cheer at the end. After a beer party in the gym (remember last year's, John?) I staggered home, arriving in Wilton at 1 AM. *(09-12-76)*

Sunday was the baccalaureate service at which Father Hesburgh of Notre Dame preached. Interestingly, one of his subjects was Albert Schweitzer and his work in Africa, right near where John is. If you want to have a good understanding of how much happens in one year, think of all the events and changes since Mom and I sat in the same chapel at John's graduation. *(06-07-77)*

*[A week later, he had a massive heart attack.]*

Pop went to NYC on Wednesday for a meeting and a luncheon. It was the first time I had been in the Club since the "event," and I was very cautious. I stayed overnight, and after a luncheon meeting on Thursday, drove down to Princeton for a meeting and dinner with Pres. Bowen. Then Pop was the host at the Honor Meeting for the freshman Class, which is always a very stimulating and exciting evening. And it was this year, too. Quite a gang of kids. *(09-19-77)*

For Pop, the weather was an inconvenience, more than anything else. I was traveling with Pres. Bowen of Princeton and we toured some cities in the Midwest and southwest. Too many cities . . . but it was a good trip. Bill does an absolutely sensational job and it's a pleasure to travel with a guy who enjoys his job and enjoys life so much. I haven't laughed so much in a long time. . . .
As a sidelight, Bill had breakfast in Dallas with Ross Perot, the skillionaire that wanted a little more information on why Princeton had turned down his son – and was completely satisfied and even a little more respectful of the place that had ignored his obvious wealth. *(01-29-78)*

We had a quiet week. Very quiet. I guess the most excitement involved the phone bill. Poppa hit the so-called roof, and gave lengthy speeches about financing the Bell System's expansion plan, etc. etc. Momma then proved that many of the calls were about Princeton, legal stuff and so forth. I can't stand facts – particularly in arguments. *(02-19-78)*

The Princeton meeting began at 4PM and went on into the late hours of the night (late for Pop, anyhow). The purpose was to bring a few trustees together with a delegation of Association of Black Princeton Alumni, and it was some meeting. These are impressive guys, and it's not the kind of subject that can be condensed into a few sentences, but suffice to say that these black alumni are doing quite a job for Princeton, and for the black undergraduates now on campus. *(03-26-79)*

The President [*of Ripon College*] is Bernie Adams, who Pop knew at Princeton (Class of '50). He asked Mom and I to join him at his table at one of the dinners [*graduation for Andrew*], he recognized Pop at the Alumni lunch, he sat with us at one of the concerts, and he had us to the faculty reception for honorary degree recipients. So, we were somewhat "honored" ourselves. Incidentally, at his home, he showed his award when he was inducted into the Basketball Hall of Fame. *(05-22-79)*

Pop's Princeton job ended officially last Friday, and it was a good two years. The timing was perfect, for it gave me much to do during the transition from Mr. Businessman to Mr. Dropout. Also, I'm glad I don't face the need for all that driving with the gas problems that we apparently are going to have. But I'll miss some of the good times with some mighty good people. *(07-02-79)*

We both are busy with needles and books. Somebody gave me a book by a recent Harvard graduate called – Harvard Hates America. Thank goodness this particular pain in the neck snob didn't go to Princeton. *(02-11-80)*

I have been concentrating on one of the mantles from Witherspoon Hall, and while a bit tedious, it is fun to clean up the initials carved by dozens of students. It looks like one of those tables down at the Nass. *(04-07-80)*

Mom made one of her famous Princeton ties, which we presented to Bill Bowen [*President*], and he went wild with praise – showing it to half the people in Nassau Hall. He promised Mom that he would decree it as "the official Reunion tie" for all time to come. *(06-09-80)*

Alumni Day was a huge success, but somewhat dampened by the death of our old friend Freddie Fox. For the first time in my memory, the Service of Remembrance (Pop was Chairman) was jammed. I think the Service is one of the finer hours of Princeton activities. *(02-23-81)*

At one of the meetings, Bill Bowen pointed out to the audience that his colorful tie had been made by Georganna Dickson and that he planned to make it his ecumenical Reunion tie for the future. I think you guys know the type of tie that he was wearing. *(06-08-81)*

Our week at Ardsheal House in the Highlands was super. The American couple who run it (Princeton '53) have advertised in the Ivy League Alumni magazines and thus the place was sometimes overrun with Tigers and such. Actually the biggest bore of the whole trip was a Tiger who wouldn't shut up. *(10-06-81)*

On Tuesday, we went up to the Pomfret School for a concert by Yale's Whippenpoofs. Perhaps it's a sign of my old age, and I thought they were a rather immature bunch and the singing was only fair. Are my orange and black colors showing? *(10-25-82)*

The Princeton Alumni Weekly had a cover picture of the Service of Remembrance on Alumni Day, and clearly visible are Mom, Peter, Janet and Pop. *(04-04-83)*

At the luncheon meeting of the Alumni Council in the great hall at the Graduate College (where Pop proposed to Mom!), Pop heard his proposal for a special Maclean Society for 'retired' alumni volunteers adopted and praised. Nice . . . President Bowen visited all the major reunion tents wearing Mom's tie and described at each place the origin of that elegant item. . . . Saturday night we had the Glenn Miller band playing the good old songs, and Pop even took a few turns on the dance floor. And stayed up late – sort of late. *(06-04-84)*

We had a surprise visit on Saturday morning of our friends the Laughlins from Princeton. They were en route from Hyannis to home. It reminded me of the summer right after we were married when Leighton's parents offered us jobs as maid and butler at their home in Hyannisport – which was one of four homes on a piece of land and the neighbors were all Kennedys. Because of summer school, we turned it down, but we've wondered what kind of a summer it would have been. *(09-10-84)*

Quote of the week – from Morehead Kennedy, Princeton '52, when asked how he treated his captors when he was in Iran with the hostages. He replied, "I treated them like stewards at the Club." Only a Princeton man could say that. Awful. *(07-09-85)*

You're about to lose part of your inheritance. Mom and I have decided to make a capital gift to Princeton and to the Library in particular. It will be for a dedicated book fund and seems appropriate, given the role of the Library in our lives. *(06-03-85)*

Do men hug? Yes, they do – especially when you meet an old friend like Mr. Rahr or a special new friend like Dr. Scheidt, both of whom were back for their 25th reunion. *(06-10-85)*

We are dry and warm and so far there are no signs of pneumonia, but for some time last Saturday afternoon, all of these claims seemed dubious. We were at the Princeton-Yale game in Palmer Stadium and sat through three hours of wet and cold rain.
Princeton finally beat Yale although there were some anxious moments. Yale's resurgence in the final quarter plus a broken field

clock heightened the anxiety for nobody knew in the stands how much time we had left to defend the score. But we won. Surprisingly, the stands were rather full. *(11-18-85)*

A breakfast meeting on Saturday morning had me sitting next to Prof. Fitch, a Nobel Prize winner in Physics who gave me some horrifying statistics on the state of basic research in this nation. The US invests less money in basic research [*as a percentage of GDP*] than any country in the western world – and, of course, far less than Japan. The most important advance in physics in the past decade was made by two Americans, who were denied funds in the US, and so did their work in Geneva. *(02-24-86)*

Among the events of the week was the final severance from RCA. We turned over our stock to Princeton's Fund – with the designated purpose of the Chapel – a rather important place in this happy marriage. *(06-09-86)*

Some Princeton notes: a few years ago I gave a lukewarm recommendation to the Admissions Office for Kirk Parrish's daughter. He advised me last week that she had graduated with High Honors and Phi Beta Kappa. *(06-30-86)*

The other major event of the week was the Celebration of the 40th anniversary of Pop's proposal – or more importantly, the anniversary of Mom's acceptance. We both remember that very cold evening up at the Graduate school at Princeton. *(12-29-86)*

This past weekend was reunion weekend at Princeton. . . . Rather than come home on Saturday night, I stayed over and went to dinner at Lambertville on the river with two classmates and their wives. It was all very nice, sitting on a terrace overlooking the river. But it was unpleasant when it came to poor service, which we could have lived with but not with the antics of one of my classmates who became so outraged that he made an ass of himself. It once again proved the old adage that money and brains do not always go together. *(06-08-87)*

When I was first in Princeton at 1903 Hall, there was a guy in a nearby room that 'had it all.' A real golden boy. He stopped here the other day. He is in the real estate business looking for land with possibilities for low-income housing. He spent many years in Europe, and shocked me with the comment that his wife was an Italian Communist – and he leaned that way too. *(10-24-88)*

I didn't go to Reunions this year, but at 2PM when the P-Rade starts, I put on a Princeton Band record. I haven't missed one in many years, but this year just decided to take a breather. *(06-10-90)*

And I spent nine hours on the road on Saturday to and from Princeton to attend a meeting on the Alumni Service Awards. For twenty years, and sixty recipients, including me!, this committee has performed very well. But last June, the award went to a woman named Sally Frank who applied for admission to two male only clubs, was turned down, and she sued. Ten years later, the Supreme Court upheld her view. The Alumni Council gave her an award, to the outrage of many alumni. And so, the Council put together a committee to revise the rules. And Pop, for good or bad, let the committee have it with both barrels that the system was right and proven, given the experience of twenty years. I may not have made or kept some friends. *(02-10-91)*

We spent the weekend in Princeton to celebrate Alumni Day. We attended an Annual Giving dinner, various meetings and lectures, did some shopping, attended the Service of Remembrance and the Service Award luncheon. The award winner this year was Lawrence Rockefeller, who gave a fine acceptance talk. He mentioned that the Award seemed to vindicate his choice by his Classmate as the 'most likely to succeed.' He said that, surprisingly, his brother had also received the same recognition from his classmates. *(02-18-91)*

The Rauh's [*Pomfret neighbors*] nephew, Jimmy, has increased his interest in Princeton, and I am organizing a visit to the campus. His grades are spectacular, and he kept at his studies during the long painful period of his father's tumor. His father must have been quite a guy. After his death, his customers and his employer put together a very large scholarship fund for his children. *(03-04-91)*

The Adventure of the week for me was a trip to Philadelphia. I went to a memorial service for George Denniston, Princeton '27, who died en route to a Princeton football game. I hope your lives are enriched, as mine was, by an older person such as George. He was one of my predecessors at the Alumni Council, and we became good friends. The service was at the First Presbyterian Church in Germantown. It is a huge building in a neighborhood of total black and Hispanic population. It is typical of George that he never fled to the suburbs, but for 70 years worked for this Church, even as its environment changed. The church was packed, and someone said that half the lawyers from Philadelphia were there. I believe it. Mom and I had lunch with George and Martha in August – a fond farewell. As a sidelight, it should be reported that Martha, aged 85, is president of the Pennsylvania Trout Fisherman's club. *(10-27-91)*

I have been interviewing some promising young people for Princeton. The odds are so long, and these youngsters are so eager, that it is tough to go through the process. One interview was in Thompson, with 13% unemployment, and this bright young man dwelled upon the problems of his fellow students who have such bleak prospects. *(01-15-92)*

Uncle All was back for his 40th, and he is the new president of his class. He also was on a panel on . . . women in politics. The oldest man back returned for his 80th reunion. Sometimes it is sad to see old friends who are in wheelchairs or on crutches. My predecessor on the Alumni Council, George Faunce, has had a couple strokes plus some other problems, and he looked pretty bad. *(06-08-92)*

Each year, Princeton sends out a form inviting names for the Wilson Award for Service. I sent in the name of Wendy Kopp, the young woman who started the idea (as her senior thesis) of Teachers in America [*Teach for America*] whereby Seniors commit themselves to two years of teaching in inner city and rural schools, funded by a foundation. I am sure there were other votes besides mine – but she will get the Award! *(11-15-92)*

I interviewed a boy from Bulgaria for Princeton one morning. It is hard to convey the pride that one gets for our country after listening to a person talk about his life under another set of rules. It is also hard to understand how such a system prevailed for so many years. Finally, here was a young man who first learned English a few years ago and scored great grades in high school and in the achievement tests. *(02-07-93)*

There was an obituary in the Alumni Weekly for MacPherson Raymond '40. Mac was Ass't Sec'y of the Alumni Association, and as I was about to graduate, he suggested that I succeed him. It was a tough decision, and life sure would have been different. *(02-14-93)*

I finally got an applicant to be accepted at Princeton. He spent the weekend there, and I am hopeful – but cautious because he has been accepted at some other fine places. His 'thing' is hockey, and I suspect the most persuasive hockey coach will make the decision. This year, I interviewed applicants from Alaska, Bronx, Bulgaria, West Virginia and Seoul, South Korea. All wonderful kids. *(04-18-93)*

I had a couple interviews with Pomfret students who have applied to Princeton. One was with a young man from Bangkok. I have learned separately that he comes from the royal family and from enormous wealth. But he told me that when he was small his mother and father took him to the slums and told him that his role in life was to help such people. And he has done just that. Last year, in London, he met a woman who was sponsoring a relief organization for the Croatians, and he determined that he would do the same here. He set up a network of New England prep schools, raised the funds, collected medicine and food and clothing, arranged for the transportation etc. CNN came here and interviewed him. He is a straight A student, # 1 in the school, and a delightful guy. *(12-19-93)*

The Alumni College: the College was sensational. Absolutely. Three great professors enraptured us on a subject very alien to my own interests and background reading. The general theme was Frontiers and was specifically related to the Great Lakes (both U.S. and Canada) and the Indian, French, English and American experiences from about 1600 to 1830. *(09-21-94)*

Mom was a geology major at Carleton, and she gets an annual report from the department. It is an amazing document of about 50 pages, detailing developments in the department, news of the faculty and alumni, and an up-dated list of alumni. I know of no other such material from a college. The Woodrow Wilson School at Princeton sends out some material, but nothing this detailed. *(08-06-95)*

Peter lent me a book about the Admissions process, and it featured five high school seniors and the Dean at Princeton (called the dean of all deans). It follows them through the business of choosing and applying. It is a great book. The Dean mentions that one of his favorite questions on the application is a free-thinking one, in which he adds, Please don't lose any sleep over this question. One applicant responded with the thought, Please don't lose any sleep over my answers. *(11-12-95)*

I interviewed a young man from Uxbridge High in Uxbridge, Mass. The town is a former mill town, is slowly making a recovery, but is somewhat depressing. But what a candidate! Good grades, good scores – but just on the edge for acceptance. But he is a great pitcher and a southpaw, and the Princeton coach is pressing the Admissions Office. Further, how many candidates can say that they get up at 4AM on weekends to clean stalls at a dairy farm. A wonderful boy. *(01-21-96)*

Speaking of Princeton (I think I was), a few weeks ago the issue of the Alumni Weekly had a cover story of Commencement, with Bill Clinton as the speaker and the recipient of an honorary degree. My comment was that this will bring out some letters. And it sure did. One was from Lawrence Rogers of Indian Hill, who called Bill a thief, a draft-dodger, a womanizer, a cheat, and some other nice things. And asked to be removed from all Princeton records, and mentioned all his ancestors that had gone to Princeton, and also that one ancestor had given the land for the college. I have written a letter to him, and haven't mailed it. *(10-06-96)*

The enclosed material is from the Princeton Alumni Weekly. It has that famous picture of Mom and Pop leaving the Chapel on that historic June day. *(02-11-96)*

Mom gave me a great volume titled Princeton – the first 250 years, and on one page there is a photo of an undergraduate's room in the late 1800's in Witherspoon Hall, and the unmistakable fireplace mantle that now sits in our library. *(06-30-96)*

The other item is from the Princeton Alumni Weekly, and shows Bill Bowen, Harold Shapiro and Bob Goheen leading the P-Rade. But it is Bill's tie that is important. It is Mom's tie, and I hope I can find a color copier. *(07-07-96)*

When Neil Rudenstine accepted the Woodrow Wilson award at Princeton he said that when he arrived as an undergraduate, the teachers might say that "the student not only doesn't know anything, he doesn't even suspect anything." And now he is the president of Harvard. *(05-04-97)*

I have a new project, writing obits for my class. On that subject, I was interested in one in the Times, which included: "Former President American Handbag Association and catcher on 1927 James Madison High baseball team" (Pop's high school). I guess he wrote his own obit, and he sure knew his priorities. *(11-09-98)*

I have decided to retire from interviewing candidates for Princeton. I first started about 45 years ago, and this was my most disappointing season. I interviewed 8 fine youngsters and they included a couple long shots, two legacies, three were top students in their school, and one had almost four years of A's and A+'s and he had an early acceptance from Harvard, but wanted Princeton. One dean said that he was the best student he had seen in 40 years of teaching. The results? No acceptances. *(04-12-99)*

I finished the Princeton mailing, helped along by some rainy days that kept me inside. I wrote (in my poor handwriting) 15-word notes in 700 letters. Incidentally, one of those rainy days brought 5.2 inches of rain. Quite a downpour. *(09-11-99)*

# Furry Friends

**"Charlie and I kept each other company."**

*We always had a dog. Before Charlie and Mac and Sandy in these letters, there had been Henry, Freckles, and, briefly, the biting German Shepherds, Five and Seven. We inherited cats in our New Jersey barns, chasing mice, but they were second-class citizens in Pop's eyes. The cats survived outdoors and had no names, except for two: Squeaky, who hopped on board the van of visitors who later asked to keep her, and then Mr. Cat, who was the only one to make the moves with us to Indiana and Connecticut. Pop barely tolerated the cats, and I don't remember any special affection for any of the dogs before the three who showed up regularly in these letters. They were indeed best friends.*

*Mac* by Sean Dickson

A busy afternoon was spent with Mom doing the Times crossword puzzles and Pop sitting on the dock at the pond watching Charlie try to catch frogs. (He didn't.) *(09-18-72)*

Boy, is it cold! Charlie, Mr. Cat and I just returned from a walk, and Charlie is the only one not anxious to come in near the blazing fire. Charlie saw the skaters on the pond, and I practically had to drag him in by the collar. *(01-07-73)*

The house is so doggoned empty. Charlie follows me around like a lost dog – which he is. And so am I. I'm just kidding – we're fine. Sort of. *(03-18-74)*

I am sorry to report that Mr. Cat finally used up all his lives. After surviving dogs, raccoons, etc., he was done in by the auto. He was hit (we are told) by a speeding car and disappeared into the bushes. I found him Saturday. *(05-03-76)*

Mom and I have been cleaning closets, trunks etc. Today I found Jeff's dog tag. How's that for nostalgia? *(02-08-76)*

One of the week's unusual events was getting rid of the head of a deer or calf that Charlie dragged into the yard. Also unpleasant. I'll be damned if I know where he got it. Charlie is beginning to show his age. He has white whiskers, and his breathing problem has returned, which means another visit to the vet this week. *(11-13-77)*

It was my plan to go up to an auction in New Hampshire yesterday, but I changed my mind because of the weather, and because Charlie had kept me up for a few hours during the night as he tried to hide from the thunder and lightning. *(08-08-78)*

The last item concerns Charlie. Yesterday, in giving him his daily dog bone or biscuit, I noticed how white his whiskers are under his mouth. That would suggest that he's old and decrepit. But, not old enough to not wander out at 9PM and wake me up at 1AM begging to get back in. Good old Charlie. *(01-29-79)*

Just to let you know that life ain't all that dull here, on Monday evening we went to the Blodgett's for a drink to celebrate their dog's birthday. *(04-02-79)*

The major mystery these days involves Charley – and where is he getting his food? He appears to be in good shape, but he hasn't touched his food in a week. If he's found another source, we sure don't know where it is. *(01-07-80)*

But it was quiet here. Charlie and I kept each other company. He did a lot of snoozing, and I did a ton of paperwork and mucho needlepoint. And some reading. And some napping. *(03-10-80)*

I do have some sad news for you. Charlie is in bad shape. He came limping in from the field yesterday morning, and I thought he had banged his paw. But he went downhill during the day and in the evening had what seemed to be a stroke. We brought him into the house, and we both thought he was about to go. But he seemed more alert this morning, but unable to walk and with his head crooked in a strange way. He is now at the vet's and I am not optimistic. *(04-28-80)*

I picked up Charlie on Thursday, much to my surprise, for I never thought he would be released that soon. He is in fair shape. He has a permanent tilt to his head and stumbles a bit going downstairs and has some difficulty walking in a straight line. It was a stroke, and I also suspect it has affected his hearing and seeing on one side. *(05-06-80)*

Furthermore, we couldn't find Charlie, who had been left in the house.

We found him in the basement, in the back room where he had fallen into the dry well trying to hide from an apparent thunderstorm. And so, by flashlight Mom and I hauled him out – no easy feat. The lights come back just as I was climbing into a very warm bedroom. *(07-21-80)*

When we got home, no Charlie. On Sunday morning, we got a call that he was in a house about two miles away, where he had arrived during the storm. The lady of the house awoke from a nap to find Charlie in the house. He is really getting worse about the thunder and lightning. *(08-04-80)*

Unfortunately, Charlie is in bad shape. For three or four days he has been really dragging, has lost much weight, and the outlook seems bleak. Last night at dusk he was sprawled out on the grass, and I went to him and there was hardly a movement and for a second, I thought he was gone. I suppose we should get him to the vet, but if he is going to go, I would just as soon have it happen here rather than in the cement block cage at the vets. *(08-18-80)*

We think we have finally figured out part of Charlie's health situation. He hasn't been eating and getting thinner and thinner. But we learned that an old couple in the apartment have been feeding him scraps, which of course is the worst thing for a dog, especially an old dog. We have to gently put a stop to that. *(11-17-80)*

Also on the medical front is sad news about our old Charlie. He has hardly eaten anything for a couple weeks and is getting really bony. I've taken to virtually hand feeding him. But there is obviously something serious bothering him, and we will get him to the vets this week. It's been amusing, but sad, to watch him take his favorite dog biscuits and bury them in the field and then later search all over for them. He is alert and the tail wags as much, but it has been sad to see him go downhill so fast. *(12-01-80)*

We thought of old Charlie a few times this weekend, for the 4th was not his favorite time because of the firecrackers. We still have some torn screens to remember him by. *(07-06-81)*

We will have new members of the family next week. We journeyed to the puppy farm last Tuesday and purchased a black lab and a yellow lab. They are seven months and three months respectively. We need some names and are counting on ideas from you all. *(06-14-82)*

We have our two puppies – named Mac and Sandy. Mr. Blodgett went with me to pick them up, and it was a wild ride home. These are two strong and sometimes wild dogs. For a while on Friday afternoon, I began to wonder if we hadn't made a mistake. But they are starting to calm down – although mealtime is a vigorous time. *(06-28-82)*

Of course, much time has been spent with the puppies, and I am glad to report that Mac seems to be calming down. He still runs across the lawn like the 7th Cavalry, but he is a little less frantic. And that helps. The Braaten brothers have built a fine dog pen that is attached to the back garage, and opens in to the garage. *(07-06-82)*

What do puppies eat/chew? Rocks, corn, beans, cow dung, branches, cucumbers, benches, tools, weeds, rugs, apples, tree trunks, etc. We spend a fair amount of time checking them just to see what they have in their mouths. *(09-07-82)*

The dogs are fine, but they continue to bound across the driveway, to greet all comers, and this can be disconcerting. So far, they have resisted all attempts to discourage this practice. Actually, we had the same problem with Charlie, but he slowly walked across, rather than the frightening dash of these guys. *(09-27-82)*

The dogs have finally found the road, and we are very concerned.

Last week, a dog similar to Sandy got killed by a car right near our driveway, and the next morning the Nelson's dog went to investigate, and he was killed, too. *(10-04-82)*

The dogs got out of their pen during the night on Saturday, and proceeded to chew on the bench on the front porch, to dig up some of the new bulbs, to drag some of my tools out of the workshops, to chew on an old rug, and to generally create quite a mess. Patience, Pop. *(10-11-82)*

We had the experience of watching what happens when one of the dogs is separated from the other. Sandy did some bad chewing, and so I put him in the pen, and let Mac run free. But Mac wouldn't run – he just sat by the fence. It was a real test when mealtime came, but he ran to the porch, gobbled his food, and ran back. *(01-10-83)*

Also yesterday, the dogs were picked up by the dog warden and it cost me twenty bucks to get them out of the pound. They spent the rest of the day in the pen – where they are now. *(08-29-83)*

One of the projects for the day is to clean up a major mess in the dog's pen. We had them there during our day away, and they somehow got into a roll of insulating material stored in the building, and tore it into shreds. *(05-07-84)*

Andrew has a nice apartment. He also has a kitten that spends much time learning how to fly. *(10-15-84)*

One day, I saw a woodchuck ambling across the lawn and I sent Mac to get him. Unfortunately, there was some question as to who was most frightened. But, when I turned Sandy loose, he knew what to do and did it. One less woodchuck. *(06-17-85)*

Lots of happy reunions this past week and one sad departure. The sad news is that Sandy ran across the road once too often and got hit by a car. We had been trying to train him to stay around without the chain, and we thought we were making progress. And now we have one confused Mac. *(09-02-85)*

We had snow three times last week – only one being a bother – about six inches. The other two I sort of shoveled – helped by Mac. Mac does the exact same thing that Charlie used to do. He sits on the section of snow that is about to be shoveled, and then moves to the next and the next and the next. *(02-17-86)*

For the first time in memory, Mac ran away – he just took off across the road. I fetched him back, but it was a puzzle. Do you suppose he saw Sandy over there? *(04-28-86)*

Question of the week. How does Mac do it? No matter how many cars come in here, he manages to leave his 'mark' on their tires. What kidneys. *(10-26-86)*

One of the nice parts of coming home is the happy greeting from Mac when I pick him up from the kennel. Now that I think of it, he even enjoys going there. *(01-13-87)*

What is the longest hour of the day? For Mac, it starts at 3PM. He gets fed at 4PM, but spends the hour staring at me while I try to hide from him until 4PM. *(02-15-88)*

We also have a great crop of apples, but alas, since I didn't do an adequate job of spraying, they are not too good. But the pears are great and plentiful. Ask Mac. He loves the pears, and it's a race to see who gets it when one falls from the tree. *(09-26-88)*

The Big Drama here last week was all about something quite little – a kitten. When we came home last Sunday night, there was a meowing noise and the headlights on the car picked out a brown and white kitten. It meowed all day Monday and Tuesday as we vowed not to feed it. But on Wednesday, we relented because the skinny thing was obviously in trouble. And so were we. I think it doubled in weight during the next few days, spent most its time sunning and cleaning itself, and frankly was an attractive looking critter.

And it intimidated Mac. He avoided it, but the kitten insisted on friendship. Our next problem was where to keep it at night, and we decided on outside, knowing full well that it was a temporary solution, with the nighttime temperatures in the 30's. But yesterday, the whole thing was resolved, for Mom found a gal at the church who wanted a kitten. Happy ending. *(10-09-89)*

Mac is on half rations – we have to do something about his weight. I should probably join him. *(11-07-89)*

I picked up Mac after 38 days in the kennel. I think he still loves me. *(04-02-90)*

It seems to me that I say this every year, but this year seems to be a particularly bad one for ticks. I take ten or more off Mac every day, and the other day after a walk in the fields, I took nine off of me. No more walks. *(05-06-90)*

Last Monday was the great Memorial Day Parade, with half the town marching and the other half watching. It was also marked by a big skid mark on the road near the bridge, where Mac came mighty close to following Sandy to that great dog heaven. A couple times a year, at least that we are aware of, he runs across the road. *(06-03-90)*

Do you know who had a birthday last week? Mac! Mac was ten years old. He looks great with a beautiful and shiny coat. We started to take afternoon walks up to the golf course, and he runs like a puppy. I thought the recent freezes would make it tick-free, but alas, I picked two of them this morning. Mac has been a great pal – he follows me, watches me, and goes overboard when he hears the word RIDE, as in car. *(11-10-91)*

Mac went to the 'hospital.' He had a lump on his left leg, and it was removed by the vet. He has a long bunch of stitches. And I believe the experience has unnerved him. He absolutely will not stay outside alone, and cries and cries to get in. He is agile, but something is bothering him. *(10-18-93)*

Mac had his annual checkup. Because of the various shots and pills, Mac's checkups cost more than mine. But then, he's so much more handsome than I am. *(03-13-94)*

Sad news. Mac's rear legs are really going fast. He fell down the steps the other day. I fear that a tearful decision is around the bend. *(08-20-94)*

Also, Mac is always at my side during the leaf project. Actually, not at my side, but in front. Be it rake, or broom, or shovel, Mac likes to lay down in front of the work. *(10-30-94)*

Our old pal Mac is having some hard times. He is having trouble jumping into the back of the wagon for a ride. And a ride is on the top of his happiness list. But he just can't make it. I have been lifting him, but at his 75 pounds, my help is limited. *(11-28-94)*

Someday, *you* will be grandparents, and I wish for *you* the thrill of opening a letter from a grandchild. We got a letter from Margaret this week, and I quote one sentence: "Bubba told me to tell *you* to tell Mac he says Hi." *(10-01-95)*

First, some sad news. Mac is gone. He went downhill so fast. His hindquarters just disintegrated. When I took him to the vet, as if to confirm the sad decision, he just fell out of the car into a heap. After I left him, I sat and sobbed in the car. A good and noble friend. *(12-01-95)*

Here are a few items from before Christmas that I couldn't fit in last week: we keep taking an imaginary step over the spot where Mac used to lie. *(01-07-96)*

But painting the green doors and screens is one job that is finished. Lots of trim work. And one sad part. Painting over the scratches that Mac made over the years on the porch door. Again and again, I promised myself that I would break him of the habit – and then I went to the door and let him in. *(08-18-96)*

Mac II? John Rauh stopped by with a black Lab in the car. The dog had been 'dumped' at his house (he already has three Labs). He asked if we wanted to take on a house-broken one year old Lab. A great dog. I said No. And Mom agreed. But a tough decision. *(05-04-97)*

# Nature Notes

**"By golly, it is Spring!"**

*Nothing could beat the arrival of spring and the promise of a summer season. Pop made winter look better by celebrating December 21 since the longer days heralded spring, even if only after the hard winters of New England. His daily walks and chores meant a lot of outdoors time, so he developed a keener eye for the life all around him. His reading chair faced the windows and his bird feeder and the fields beyond. The observations he shared in the weekly dispatch made us simultaneously laugh and long for the outdoors.*

*The View* by Annie Dickson

Savor these days! Savor these days! A glorious weekend – and today was a day of superlatives. Who cares whether I didn't catch a fish – it is wonderful just to stand at the pond and look down that long field with the color from the woods on both sides. *(10-14-73)*

Pop has a friendly owl who flies from tree to tree as I drive with the tractor from about the place where the large roller sits all the way down to the dumping ground. It's now happened about a dozen times over two weekends. *(05-06-74)*

We had a temporary visitor this week, in a baby sparrow hawk, which we tried to nurse along, but to no avail. It died on Thursday evening. It was a beautiful bird, russet-colored feathers, and sharp eyes and beak. *(07-24-77)*

The storm. I guess everyone has read and seen enough by now. But we really got clobbered. I don't know how much snow we got, because the Pomfret Center Weather Station doesn't publish official figures. But Rhode Island said 44 inches in the northwest part of the state, and that's close to us. . . . Happily, the power held. And so, we read books, watched the reports on television, did needlepoint, and a variety of odd jobs. We had no mail for three days. We heard last night that Providence will begin delivering mail Tuesday, for the first time in eight days. It's hard to imagine a city like Boston that has had roadblocks up and no traffic in the city for six days. *(02-12-78)*

If you are an optimist – a real optimist – I think you can see the faint glimmer of green in the fields. This is the week that Spring arrives, and I think it is only logical to begin the search for clues of the great season ahead. We can point to some daffodils coming through on the slope near the barn. Hooray! *(03-19-79)*

Mom says the birds sound "different." Since she is an optimist, I believe she thinks they are chirping about spring. And why not! We are chirping along here – hope you are too. *(03-03-80)*

We have a rabbit under the shop, and a pigeon showed up on Saturday. David took him in a trap and released him on his way home – and yesterday, the pigeon was back, walking under the chairs, in front of Charlie, and generally being a pain in the neck. *(06-16-80)*

On the "nature" front, we once again have swallows trying to get into the barn, we have deer flies (a deer fly is a pest that doesn't attack until he sees you have both hands full), we have deer watching from the upper field (checking the crops?), and Mom and I watched a fight between a blue jay and some sparrows in which the jay literally flew away with one of the sparrows. *(06-30-80)*

B-r-r-r-r! Like everyone else, we have had our share of weather. It is -16 out there right now, and it was -22 yesterday morning, and the pipes in the kitchen froze yesterday, and still are not thawed, despite a hair dryer blowing warm air on them for most of yesterday. And the driveway bell froze and the brakes froze on the station wagon. And we froze. *(01-19-82)*

Nature was busy here last week – and still is. We spent many hours squishing gypsy moth caterpillars, for they have really arrived. *(06-07-82)*

It's a very mild morning here – and we keep wondering when we are going to get hit by some wintry blasts. The current issue of Country Journal has an article about this coming winter, and it describes the forecasts of four different theories – and they all agree that this could be the worst winter of the century. One theory is based on sun spots, another on the Mexican volcano ash, another on sea currents and another on some sort of cycle. And so, I guess we should enjoy this relatively good weather. *(11-22-82)*

A pair of swallows swooped around here all last week, apparently looking for a place to build a nest. Since they spent much time under the porch at the barn, I kept checking the area for the beginnings of a nest. However, they fooled us, and the nest has been started over the window on the porch of the house. And so, every time the door opens, a swallow or two swoops away. They will be nervous wrecks soon – or we will. *(06-06-83)*

Puzzle of the week: where did the rabbit go? Yesterday morning, I trapped a rabbit in the greenhouse. I then debated how to dispose of him – and with some reluctance decided to give the dogs a chance, (kind of hoping the rabbit would escape). But when I opened the door there was no rabbit. *(06-27-83)*

At 3:45 AM on Thursday, I leaned over and drew the comforter over us in bed. I guess that was the official change in seasons. *(09-19-83)*

The surprise of the week was when Mom opened the door to the woodstove in the back room – a bird flew out! I can figure out how a bird can come down a chimney, but I sure can't understand how he can come down the stove pipe. *(03-05-84)*

There are big events – and there are BIG events. Last week, saw a really BIG one. We saw our first robin. He was standing on a branch that was frozen, but he was here. A great sign of things to come. *(03-26-84)*

Nature notes: we have a family of six snakes in the small garden near the greenhouse; I was surprised (and angered) to see that the concrete blocks that I had placed over a hole in the fence had been moved by my adversary – the woodchuck. *(07-30-84)*

August is here in all its glory – hot, humid and hazy. But I try to remember some of those awful February days, and then I feel better. *(08-06-84)*

Good grief! It's dark outside at 5PM. The official search for spring has begun. We've also had a string of cloudy gloomy days and that hasn't helped the brightness. *(10-29-84)*

As I sit under the ash tree at the 'office,' I watch a leaf here and a leaf there – autumn is clearly with us. We had a fire in the fireplace last night. And the chimney sweep was here last week, so we are prepared for what's ahead. Sort of. I had the file out last night of islands in the sun. *(09-23-85)*

A little varmint ran across the driveway yesterday – and it was a mink! He was really frightened, and I hope he found his home before nightfall. *(02-09-87)*

The other day during a walk with Mac, I came across a deer all crunched up and trying to hide on the ground. After a few minutes of staring, another young deer that I had not seen bolted, and the large deer got up and ran across the field. And then I saw that it had a dangling front leg. A sad sight. *(04-04-88)*

Nature note: A spider built a huge web in between the two panes of glass at the kitchen window. A big spider. This morning, it was gone -totally. How does a web disappear? *(09-14-89)*

Do you recall my describing the big buck deer that I saw in the back field? Well, our neighbor called to say he had come across the deer, with his tail and antlers cut off, lying in the snow. *(12-04-89)*

On nature notes, the starlings are once again raising a family in the gas pump. Watching the difficulty they have bringing food to the nest, I have wondered how the heck the little ones ever get out. *(05-21-90)*

We have some sort of animal raising havoc here at night, I don't believe it's a raccoon because the evidence suggests something bigger. One night, it grabbed another animal, and there was some screaming outside. Our neighbor, Mr. Nelson, thinks it is a coyote – for they have been seen in the area. *(06-17-90)*

We have had some weather. First an ice storm and then a snowstorm that was wet and heavy and then quickly froze. The driveway has been an ice-skating rink, but some sun this afternoon has helped a lot. The mailbox got it again. These cowboys in the state trucks have a bad habit of hitting my mailbox. And one of life's ornery chores is to fix a mailbox. It is now fixed, but it sort of leans. *(01-13-91)*

Some nature notes: On my walk on the golf course yesterday, I saw seven or eight bright blue birds – beautiful. Also, we have watched a spider in the space between the window and the storm in the kitchen (how did he get in – plus how did the other things get in?). But we have watched him catch a large fly, a moth, and a large box elder bug – quite a struggle. *(02-04-91)*

Nature notes: I spent some time trying to get a bird (mockingbird?) out of the greenhouse – it was a question of who would be exhausted first. I won. I have determined that deer flies work in squadrons of three – with a backup of three. When you swat one – another fills in so that you are always struggling with three. There is a bird in the field with a song that I interpret as "what did he say? What did he say?" *(06-16-91)*

Mystery of the week: Mom looked out the back window one evening and saw a white duck ambling along the walk beside the stone wall.

Where did he come from? What was he doing here? *(08-04-91)*

Thursday night was a Seder supper at church, followed by a service. That was followed by a heavy snow, and when we arrived home, we found a car on the front lawn. So much for Spring. *(04-19-92)*

There was a lot of screaming by robins one morning last week, and I found that two of the robins from the nest in the greenhouse building had taken their first flight into the greenhouse. I managed to get them out – but they didn't cooperate too well. *(06-08-92)*

Signs of the season: the chimney sweep has been here, I had a fire in the fireplace, and the silage trucks go back and forth, back and forth. I estimate there are ten trucks, and they make four trips an hour, from the dark morning to the dark evening. My guess is 500 trips. *(09-27-92)*

And The Storm. the paper said that we had gotten 26 inches. I did not measure that much, but we got a bunch. After all these years (and dollars) I finally got a chance to use the generator. And I have rather faithfully started it up every other week. Do you think it would start? No. The electrician, who also plows us out, said 'one more try' – and it started. And so, we had current during the long period when the power was out. The tree damage is considerable, and the cowboys with the state plows again managed to tear down the mailbox. An annual event. *(12-13-92)*

This time of year also brings a thing called gnats. And they are vicious. A local remedy is a lotion put out by Avon called Skin So-Soft. It does repel the little monsters, but it also traps them, so that I come in with a forehead and face blotched with bugs. *(05-13-93)*

If I had had a camera, I could have taken a photo to send to the maker of plastic owls. The claim was that the owl would scare off birds and varmints. My photo would have shown a rabbit sitting and nibbling under the owl. *(07-17-93)*

There was one aspect of the storms that kept me busy – feeding the birds. I had a couple hanging suet units on the little tree in front of the house, plus a couple times a day, I waded into the snowbank and put seed on the ground. And there were plenty of customers. We noted doves (22 at one point), juncos, cardinals, woodpeckers, chickadees, blue jays, titmouses, and even some crows. Fun to watch. *(01-10-94)*

A quotation: "The most serious charge which can be brought against New England is not Puritanism but February." We ain't alone, I know, but it was some week. The snow is piled up at least ten feet high where the plow has scraped it from the driveway. The problem now is that there is no place left to put it. And this morning, we had freezing rain. *(02-13-94)*

Nature note: I have a small bucket of bird seed on the porch, and the other day I dipped into to get a handful, and found a bunch of bees in the seed. *(03-18-94)*

A few minutes ago, Mom asked: "Do we say every year how green the grass looks?" I guess the answer is Yes. But the progress of the season, this season in particular, is slow, but beautiful. *(04-25-94)*

I watched some deer near the garden. They ran up the hill, and then slowly came back to about 100 feet away, and I began to wonder if they were going to charge me. They didn't. *(05-15-94)*

Lots of nature notes: I have sighted three different snakes-two in the gardens, and a large one disappeared down the outside stairs to the basement. I nervously checked out the basement today. On the subject of birds – the front porch is a mess. One of the hanging flowerpots is now vacant, but a second is chock full with little birds and the third now has a nest with two small eggs. *(07-04-94)*

The last few years we have had a couple 'hover' bees near the porch of the barn. They can hover in space, and then speed off, sometimes over your head. Well, they have multiplied, and it is now an experience to walk there. *(05-29-95)*

Bedford Pa. is a name we have passed oodles of times on the Penn. Turnpike. It is a neat old town that seems rather prosperous. Many antique dealers. And a Ford dealer. Who was very good to us. Our story starts in Pomfret Center, where I parked the camper in front of the greenhouse and under the maple. Well, the maple seedling pods came down on the hood. And a mouse/chipmunk took them into the engine area and built a nest. As we were leaving the campground, I turned on the heater, and smoke poured into the camper. The heater coil was in the middle of the nest. Happily, no flames, but it could have been a disaster. *(09-17-95)*

I think I may have saved a few birds. The bird book tells me that they are very resilient and can handle bad weather. But I have had to fill our five feeders each morning. And glad to do so. One morning, I found a hawk (one of my neighbors says he has seen a falcon near his feeder) on the evergreen bush in front of the house, and I suspect he was looking for a meal. Some debris near the front steps suggest that he was successful. *(01-14-96)*

Nature question: How is it possible for the finches (yellow and red) to have their feathers change so much as spring comes on? *(03-31-96)*

I think Spring has arrived! Because of the small buds appearing on the pear, apple and peach trees? Maybe. Because of the robins singing? Maybe. Because of the massive explosion of daffodils? Maybe. But really because of the motorbikes on a Sunday afternoon. Back and forth, back and forth. *(04-21-96)*

Nature news: Should we take a trip in the camper? If so, we will disturb a robin's nest on the front right tire, right on the tire. *(05-19-96)*

We are in a hurricane 'watch.' We have moved many items that could fly around, have filled the bathtub, and will have flashlights at the ready. Our real worry is loss of power and damage to the old trees. *(09-01-96)*

I think that the squirrels have won. First, I gave up on the hanging suet ball. Then I watched a squirrel turn the suet cage upside down and drop the suet to the ground. I decided to rely only on the two window units, but then the critters just climbed up the wall of the house and into the units. I noticed that Spag's carries a type of squirrel-proof seed, and I may try it. *(12-15-96)*

Nature notes: the snow cover has brought the deer back to the evergreens. I have covered them with pea netting. Too little – too late? Also, I was puzzled to watch a bunch of sparrows under the auto with necks poised upward. Do you know what they were doing? They were catching the drips from melting icicles. *(01-19-97)*

Next, the STORM. I think I am partly responsible. A few days before, I stored away the snow shovels and 'melt ice' container. We had snow from one noon till the next. It was a heavy wet snow, and we lost some branches and limbs from the evergreens. But we never lost power! With a bum wrist and a law that says heart guys like me shouldn't touch a shovel, we made a path, and the snowplow did the rest. It was fun to watch the birds at the feeders – a real feeding frenzy. *(04-06-97)*

Nature notes: a robin got into the greenhouse and for two days and nights banged himself against the glass. Finally got out. Also, we have a family of two or three snakes that watch us closely. And I watch them closely. *(06-08-97)*

Nature notes: we apparently have raccoons in the pipe under the driveway; the two snakes near the greenhouse have really grown; the woodchuck has a new entry into what was once a vegetable garden. My question is, how does he/she know to come up? First, there is a fence that goes down a foot, then about eight feet of grass, and then, the garden. And right at the edge, there is his hole. To add to the insult, he has entered the greenhouse to jump up on the bench and devour the remaining plants. *(07-06-97)*

Bird Watch. We watched a hawk sit on the front lawn, and then dash into the bushes to grab small birds. On [*many*] tries, he failed. I know this is part of the necessary food chain, but who should I root for? *(01-18-98)*

A Christmas gift here was a squirrel-proof bird feeder, and it seemed to be working. But the other morning, I saw an object on the field in front of the house. It was the bird feeder, dragged a hundred yards or so, torn open, and the bird food gone. *(03-08-98)*

Nature notes: we have a robin who built eight or nine nests in the overhang on the barn. And we have wild turkeys. And the other day Mom said to me "there is a bear in the field" And I said, "Good grief, no." But it was a bear. We looked through the field glasses, and, yes, it was a big black bear. One clincher was when a bear cub ambled by. *(05-17-98)*

We read much about the Census of 2000. Well, I started the game with one [*here.*] First, according to a plaque on the wall, there is an old gardener and his American beauty. And I have added 1 raccoon, 5 woodchucks, 2 rabbits, ? deer, 2 chipmunks and ? squirrels. *(07-05-98)*

Nature Notes: I have seen a solitary big heron flying over the fields in front of the house, and I hoped he/she had a partner somewhere. Well, I saw three the other day. *(08-09-98)*

Speaking of birds, we made a list of such visitors, and the total is 31. Last week two new ones were an Indigo Bunting and a Towhee. *(05-17-99)*

June is here! Okay, calendar, you can slow down now. We have had some beautiful days, although we could use some rain. Now I did it. *(06-06-99)*

How come August goes by so fast, and February goes by so slowly? *(08-15-99)*

Nature notes: I stood on the porch and watched a hummingbird about a foot away work away at the blossoms on the hanging plants. Also, we had two very young deer on the lawn, and I went out, and they spooked, but one was curious and kept coming closer. I was probably the first person it had come across. *(08-22-99)*

A mystery: A motorist stopped by here one evening to tell us that a deer was hurt down near the brook. Mom called the Audubon, and the next morning the Audubon ranger came and found the deer in the brook with both front legs broken. He called the DEP, and they came and searched the area, and we heard seven shots, and they left. But the Audubon man later came and found the deer (dead but not from gunshots). Question . . . what did the DEP guys do? *(11-07-99)*

It's fun to break away for a short visit. . . . It sort of refreshes and renews the body and the mind. Cape Cod is a good target, but even in this off-season it can be crowded. Lots of traffic. But I know why people like to be near the ocean . . . watching the surf is good for the soul. *(03-06-00)*

April! April! An Englishman once wrote that April was the 'cruelest' month. Presumably because of expectations. But I am full of expectations for what's ahead. Tomorrow, the next day, and each day thereafter. As Aunt Ruth once said: The Gift of a New Day! *(04-02-00)*

# The Working Life

**"I was asked to stay on longer, and so will be working until April 1, with some reluctance, I might add."**

*Pop wrote his own obituary. There was no mention of his thirty-year career in marketing, working his way up the corporate ladder at Procter & Gamble, Warner-Lambert, and RCA. By any account, he must have done well. He drove himself hard, with long days and frequent flights around the country. He was still working, commuting to New York when these letters started, and his weariness of the corporate life was plain to see. He wanted something else, and RCA helped him realize that dream by letting him go when he was just fifty-two years old. He couldn't shake the habits he accrued or his plain interest as he went to the business section of the Times first and pored over the Wall Street Journal and the annual reports. It's no surprise that what he most relished and wrote about were his business pals, as he regaled us with stories of the people he met along the way.*

Victrola by John Dickson

The Dunns are great people, and Mr. Dunn and I reminisced about the Crest toothpaste business of many years ago. Mr. Dunn has a big business in children's photography for advertising and they've also just finished their eighth book. We pulled chairs up to the roaring fireplace and sat up far too late. *(12-03-73)*

I must admit that I'd just as soon not go into the Big City today. It's been a busy and long weekend (I took Friday off) and I could use today to recuperate. I'm in the kitchen having coffee and apple pie, and not even too enthusiastic about tackling some projects in the basement. *(04-01-74)*

I'm sitting on a stalled train on the good old railroad. We have been here for forty minutes, and prospects are for a long wait. The train ahead of us had a fire, and things are really tied up. *(04-22-74)*

One of the participants in the service was Mr. George Depue, who Pop used to work with in the advertising business. Do you remember going to the Harlem church some years ago to hear him preach? *(09-17-74)*

Such a gorgeous morning – and brighter too because of the time change. But it'll be plenty dark tonight when the old train comes into Wilton. Last week was a bad week for the trains, with all kinds of switch, engine and track problems. It bodes ill for the winter. *(11-05-74)*

This is a special 'Weekly Letter.' The letter form is either the best way or the worst way to pass this news along, but it does have the advantage of telling the story the same way to each of you.
Poppa has realized his long-time wish to be a full time 'farmer.' I've been 'retired' by RCA, effective immediately. Tomorrow morning, I may go down to the railroad station and fulfill a long dream and wave to the train as it heads to the Big Apple.

This development may have been part of Pop's planning, but the timing was not. However, the initial reaction has been one of zigzagging between relief and joy vs. disappointment. It is one more piece of evidence of the difficulty or impossibility of precise planning of one's life. We can set a general course, and then only hope for the best.

The nature of Pop's separation from corporate life virtually demands a lengthy trial period of the much talked about idea of trying it on our own. This is *good,* for it will provide various times for all of us to talk about it.

I think we've got some exciting days ahead. It's great to think about them, and even greater when I think about how well each of you are currently situated. *(10-30-75)*

Among the items of last week was a very specific job offer to manage a London branch of a company. Some time ago that would have had high appeal, for now – no thanks. *(10-17-76)*

I spent an inordinate amount of time at work last week. [*Ralph Glendinning, an old friend from Princeton and Procter & Gamble, hired Pop as a part-time consultant for his company.*] I was in Westport the better part of three days, and in Greenwich one day. This meant two nights away from home, and a fair amount of driving. . . . I spent Monday night at Mr. Glendinning's new home in Southport, and it's some mansion. I think he's bought most of Europe's antiques. Pretty fancy. *(12-19-76)*

One of the reasons Pop went to Wilton was to get the final word on the tax situation due to the sale of the house and the land – and it was awful. Awful. And there shall be no more to say on that subject. *(01-02-77)*

Pop spent most of the week away – in Westport and Princeton. I was home for two nights, and on one of those, Mom and I went out for dinner to celebrate my first consultant's check. I was asked to stay on longer, and so will be working until April 1, with some reluctance, I might add. There's so much to do here, and the driving back and forth is getting to be a real pain. We've had the Toyota about 3 months, and I have 8,000 miles on it. *(01-31-77)*

Some sad news. Pop's old fishing partner from Canada, and former Warner-Lambert associate, Mr. McCaskill died last weekend. He was a magnificent guy, who had a chance to become President of W-L, but turned it down because he didn't want to leave Canada. He was also a good Princetonian, voted most likely to succeed at my graduation, a good fisherman, and a warm and decent guy. And only 50. *(04-04-77)*

The Vartabedians from Wilton dropped by yesterday, after leaving their daughter at the Pomfret School. Since he was one of my partners during the terrible days of commuting, I had my joys renewed as he talked about the train problems. *(09-10-79)*

This is the season for the corporate Annual Reports, and Pop has sent a couple notes to these giant institutions chiding them for commenting on record sales and profits in 1980 – but also making predictions about how much better things are going to be under the new administration. With some of these guys earning more than a million bucks a year and still deciding to use the Annual Report to take a swipe at my old friend Jimmy, it seems a little ungrateful. And so, they are hearing from Pumpkin Center. *(03-31-81)*

Some of the quarterly statements coming in from companies have had some interesting comments about the economy and its prospects. And so, to make life more interesting for them, I have written to a few of them reminding them of their claims for 1982 based upon the great new program of our great new president. Might as well rub it in. Certainly, no one inside these companies is telling the Chairman of the Board that he was wrong – dead wrong. Just old Pop in Pumpkin Center. *(11-22-82)*

I had gone to New London NH for a lunch with a guy from RCA who also had the experience of being thrown out by that fine company. But John Riewener had been a 27-year employee, and it was a tough blow. He did an unpredictable step by buying an inn in New London which he and his wife ran for two years and then gave up, in exhaustion. He now has an accounting business, a wonderful old cape house in the country, and is deliriously happy. So much for being fired by Big Biz. *(09-11-83)*

For some time, I have been looking at a small palm sander to help in the refinishing work – but the only model has been a Japanese brand. I waited until an American model showed up, made by Black & Decker. Well, you guessed it. When I unwrapped the package – it was made in France. *(03-12-84)*

The Marshalls were here for dinner on Friday – to celebrate Mrs. Marshall's birthday. The more interesting part of the event belonged to Mr. Marshall. He moved up here some years ago to basically retire and live a quieter life. He has slowly gotten back into some business ventures, and it was sad, for Pop anyhow, to watch his tensions, phone calls at dinner, and travel schedule talk. It reassured me to my way of life. *(11-12-84)*

I finally finished the New Yorker series on the Johns Manville asbestos story. The revelation about corporate activities went from dismaying to disgusting. What a bunch. *(08-05-85)*

We are now the owners of a VCR. There has been so much talk about a price increase in these items in '86 (stronger yen) that we made the plunge. It is an RCA, and you can suspect that last week's announcement by GE and RCA was a little disappointing. It means a big profit for our stock, but it seems a poor way to improve the lot of major corporations and their employees. *(12-16-85)*

One of the customers [*in the shop*] was a guy that I had worked with when I was at P&G. He was at an ad agency and then had gone to Richardson-Vicks, recently bought by P&G. To show how these mergers work, even by a good company, he and the marketing staff had just been fired. *(10-20-86)*

I 'won' in a game that rarely happens. If you look in the business section of the daily paper, there is a list of earning reports for corporations. Once in a blue moon, every letter in the alphabet is represented – and it happened last week, helped by reports from Quintel Corp., Xios Corp and Zeus Corp. *(02-23-87)*

Today's Times had a story about the ad agency business, and the feature guy was a fellow that Pop used to work with when at Warner Lambert. He engineered the sale of his agency to the dismay of many, but he now counts his bank account in the 100 million plus figure, and that's more than I count. A little more. I said it then and I'll say it now . . . he didn't impress me at all. *(11-08-87)*

There were two sad articles last week. One was about the Seamen's Bank (where Pop had his first job) which went belly up some time ago due to just plain poor management. Started in 1829, the bank had over the years built a collection of ship models, ship paintings, scrimshaw and mechanical banks, and now there is a great contest among museums and galleries to try and get their hands on the stuff. I can remember Mr. Thayer, who supervised the collection, adding banks and models. *(05-21-90)*

The Times had a big obituary last week for a guy named Tom McDermott. Tom was in the programming group at Benton & Bowles when I worked at P&G. He went to Hollywood and became a very successful TV producer. I was quite surprised to see him one day at RCA, and we ended up in adjacent offices working on SelectaVision. Tom was the ultimate entertainment-show biz type. He knew everybody, lived like an Arabian prince, had an unlimited expense account, and had an aversion to eating lunch alone. Thus, whenever his calendar was bare, he would take me to 21 or some other bistro – and these in the days when I was counting pennies (I still am). But Tom was good to me (and I believe I helped him) as we both struggled with that strange culture in RCA. He was fired shortly after I was. *(08-19-90)*

We read a bunch of books. Some serious – some escapist stuff. I read a great history of the oil business, a book about Stalin (horrifying), and we both read a very useful book about the Middle East. In the oil book, I learned that in the spring of '48, P&G interviewed me and George Bush. They did not offer him a job, and so he went south to start an oil company. *(01-29-91)*

Every town seems to have its Wal-Mart store. Sam Walton is the richest man in America. I wonder if he ever wanders through the downtowns of these small towns to see the havoc that his store has wrought on the small merchants. *(03-25-91)*

My old pal Ed Dooley has been nominated for the Advertising Hall of Fame, and I was asked to second the nomination. It is a giant step for a group that has concentrated on Chairmen of the Board to consider a practitioner of everyday effort – and I hope he gets it. *(10-06-91)*

There is a message or lesson here. When I joined P&G, I did my sales training in various eastern cities. The District Manager was Dick

Easley who I came to dislike (hate?) intensely. He pressed me on why no hat (I couldn't afford one), why only one suit and a seersucker at that (see above) and generally made life miserable for me. When we were both in Cincinnati, we had sort of a silent peace. But some time ago, I learned that he had a bad cancer, and so I wrote him a letter. He called the other night and in frail voice talked over 'old times.' *(05-01-94)*

Some time ago, I got into a discussion about plastic manufacturing with a pal here, Dave Parker (Pomfret's heart transplant veteran). He invited me to the plant where he works in marketing . . . and I was overwhelmed. It is in Clinton, Mass., northwest of Worcester, in a huge brick factory that started out as carpet factory for Bigelow, built in the 1870's. It is immaculate, beautiful paint everywhere, landscaping, and a modern facility. They work seven days a week, 24 hours a day. They make parts for Gillette razors, all of the contact lenses for J & J, and small parts for IBM etc. It is employee owned, with plants in Asia, Russia, England, Latin America and all over the US. I have never seen such clean and modern facilities – and in century old buildings. *(07-31-94)*

Still on the medical subject, I was outraged to read a story in the paper that IBM had proposed to its employees that they fight health care reform. To me, that is a case of "I've got mine – if you don't – too bad. Further, I will fight to keep you from getting what I've got." I wrote to the Chairman, who has a reputation of not caring what shareholders or employees think. But I am going to sell our IBM stock. I checked, and after 15 years of ownership, it is worth only 85% of what I paid for it. And, of course, meager dividends. *(08-21-94)*

I was saddened last week by an obit in the Times for King Herbert who worked for Pop at P&G. King was Princeton '54, a quiet and totally pleasant guy. He left P&G for Lever Bros., and some other marketing jobs. He had a heart attack in his office at Harvard Medical School where he was Director of Development. Too damned young. *(12-26-95)*

Some of you may remember Dever Gregg. We have sort of kept up with each other since the days at P&G and Warner-Lambert. He has bounced around a bit. We got a letter from him this week, and he is moving back to Phoenix. Someday I would like to tell you the wonderful story of the romance of Dever and Dawn. *(06-25-95)*

When I was at Warner-Lambert, early on, there was a bookkeeper by the name of Bob Dircks, who I tried to promote, and failed. But I finally prevailed, and Bob went on to become Chief Financial Officer and Director (after I left). His wife died a few years ago, and Bob set up a foundation to be administered by Warner-Lambert. And in January, he died. I made a gift to the foundation, and his son wrote this week to say that in his father's desk was the notice of his promotion . . . the only newsletter that he had saved. *(04-21-96)*

There was an obit in the Times for Saul Bass. Saul was a graphic artist that I worked with near the end of my career at RCA. He had won a whole series of Oscars for his design work. Besides RCA, he had worked for a bunch of companies, including AT&T and Exxon. He never wore a jacket and tie – always a sweater. *(04-28-96)*

Many years ago, when RCA was planning to move to New Canaan, it hired a local lawyer named Willard Overlock, and we became good pals. One evening, at his house, I overheard Willard reading the riot act to his son, who was about to be kicked out of prep school. The Wall Street Journal had a story about young Willard who announced his retirement from an investment firm at age 50. Incidentally, his income last year was 10 million. *(07-21-96)*

Headline of the week: Company stock jumps as chief says he will retire. *(08-11-96)*

Also, there was an obituary for Dr. Joe Muhler in today's Times. Joe was the inventor of Crest. Joe was an Indiana University scientist. I remember a trip to Los Angeles with Joe where I was commanded to stay with Joe, a wild man, and literally put him to bed. *(01-05-97)*

Speaking of RCA, today's paper carried this obit for Bob Sarnoff. He was a dillitant (sp?) and it proved his undoing, for a Board that tired of his personal spending. But at a low point in my career, he protected me. And when I was working on the project to move the company to New Canaan, I remember coming to the office one Monday morning, and being told to fold the project. Bob had been to New Canaan for the weekend, and at a cocktail party had been told by a citizen that New Canaan doesn't like Jews. *(02-23-97)*

And when I worked for P&G there was a guy named Paul Myers, who left to work in a local agency, handling his father-in-law's account. He had married into great wealth, and unhappily his wife died young. Paul inherited it all, and he has spent the years since travelling and partying. He built a house in Watch Hill that is so big, the natives call it Fort Myers. But he called – after about 45 years. *(01-05-98)*

Enclosed is a copy of an article about Mrs. Orswell [*who owned the bird sanctuary next to our house in Pomfret Center*]. It was the cover of a brochure from Audubon. Inside there was a list of contributors to a special fund, and one name was Paul van der Stricht. Paul is the guy who hired me at Warner-Lambert. He was a Belgian lawyer, urbane and fluent in five or six languages. He was very good to me. My mentor. As Executive VP, he essentially ran the company, since the president was an alcoholic. But the Board would not make him president and he was bypassed. It's nice to have a fond memory of a boss. *(02-28-99)*

Memory time: P & G announced last week that they were about to sell Prell Shampoo. A few days after my graduation, I showed up at a hotel in Plainfield and met Charlie Smith, a salesman of the old school. At breakfast, Charlie asked me, where is your suit, where is your hat? I had neither. Charlie, wherever you are, please don't ask me the question now. *(05-09-99)*

# Digging

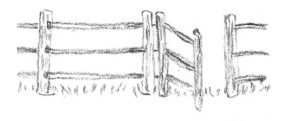

**"An old gardener lives here with his American beauty."**

*A friend of mine once shared her belief that putting your hands in dirt was beneficial to a long, healthy life. Well, Pop might be the best proof of that unscientific assumption, as his gardening helped him live far beyond expectations following his massive heart attack. He was hooked on vegetable gardening from the first harvest in the small bed near the patio in Wilton. From that start, he expanded quickly and set aside a large, fenced-in area for a grand garden when they moved to Pomfret. His letters were full of reports of the harvests, but also of the frustrations in competing with any number of animals that wanted to share his harvest. He spoke of giving it up, but he never did. He just loved putting his hands in the dirt.*

*Garden Gate* by John Dickson

Yesterday I planted the asparagus garden and began putting the raspberries in. I put in 4 of the 100 plants that Mom bought, so you see I have a long, long way to go. *(04-22-74)*

Before I ran for a plane to Indianapolis last Thursday noon, I put in 6 or 7 kinds of lettuce, carrots, beets, turnips, and radishes. The garden is slowly taking shape. Also, I started using the new tiller, and it works very well. Unfortunately, it doesn't work on sod, which I had counted on. But it will be a great timesaver after the crops start coming up. *(04-14-75)*

You wouldn't believe the apples we have. They are falling off the trees in such quantity that the Locke can't make it through. We've given them away and we've made applesauce by the bucket. The freezer is now beginning to bulge, for we had not counted on this particular crop. With Pop as the peeler, Mom cooked four huge tubs on Saturday. *(09-10-75)*

The garden is still delivering radishes, beets and carrots, but the crop is surely dwindling. Yesterday, David finished tilling the ground, and now I must find a weed killer to work over the winter to get rid of the monstrous weed that took over during the summer. *(10-31-77)*

On the garden front, I am puzzled. The peas, carrots and beets that I put in some weeks ago have not peaked through at all, and it worries me. I am wondering if the weed killer that I put down last fall may still be active. *(05-15-78)*

I've spent much time in the garden doing a lot of weeding. The replanting of the portion of the garden where I dumped all of the chemicals has not worked, and I guess I had better write off that hunk of land for some time. *(06-12-78)*

And the beans. And the beans. Mom estimates that there must be a hundred packages of beans in the freezer – and still they come. I have taken a couple big bags and boxes down to a "People's Store" in Danielson, which is sort of a Salvation Army place, and they are delighted with them. Yesterday, they said "Here comes the bean man." *(07-25-78)*

Thursday was garden day, and Peter helped me put up some stakes for some of the peas. I planted peas, onions, carrots and beets. The great process has begun! And none too soon, for Mom came home from the store the other day with some frozen peas. Horrors! I have not been a good provider. *(04-16-79)*

Another project – the garden – received a big setback last week. We had just about the most violent thunderstorm on Wednesday that I can remember, and a feature of it was a forty-minute hail barrage that ruined many home gardens. It flattened everything and tore off most of the blossoms on the peas, effectively finishing many of the plants for this season. I've re-planted some items, and yesterday's check showed some of the plants returning to vigor. The hail tore leaves off of plants like bullets. We had about a two-inch cover of hail on the driveway, and the temperature dropped so fast that it stayed around for a couple of hours before finally melting. *(06-04-79)*

The garden is beginning to pick up. We've had asparagus twice during the week, and I pick a few in the morning and a few in the evening. That had to be the fastest growing vegetable going. The beans are coming up (Mom has threatened to stomp them down), the corn is peaking through, and if you look hard enough, you can see a beet and a carrot or two. *(05-19-80)*

My regular pea crop has been devastated by a woodchuck, who has trimmed the new plants down to the ground level. He has a tunnel opening right beside the garden (handy) and I filled it with boulders, put an old door over it, and put rocks on top of the door. The next morning, the rock had been moved. Strong little cuss. *(06-02-80)*

Momma's Birthday! Hooray! Hooray! She got a bunch of cards and some items, including a "coupon book" of Promises and Things, one of which was a certificate entitling her to throw one bucket of beans on the compost pile. *(07-28-80)*

It's a chilly 18 degrees and I hope it warms up quickly for today. Bob and I tackle the job of putting the glass on the greenhouse. The framing is up, after a few days of joint effort of trying to read the instructions that were clearly written by a madman or a bureaucrat. Maybe both. *(11-03-80)*

The garden continues to look promising. One event in the garden was not too pleasant. I cornered a big woodchuck one evening and after some intellectual, moral and medical debate with myself, I killed him with a rake. Happily, my aim was good, and it was immediate and merciful. It has bothered me since. *(06-22-81)*

I told Mom yesterday that her wish for a garden of just peas, limas, asparagus and berries was going to be partially realized but that she might weary of the pea crop that looms. We froze (Mom did) a bunch of peas yesterday – Pop has the enjoyable job of sitting in the rocker and shelling them. It is a fine way to enjoy the sun and some music. *(06-29-81)*

I read one suggestion that creosote poured around the border of the garden would discourage some animals. And so, I poured a can of the stuff, including some on my trousers, and thus adding one more casualty to the war on the doggoned varmints. *(07-27-81)*

We also harvested a few tomatoes last week, but they were the ones hidden under the weeds. We have had some killing frosts and I bet there are close to a thousand tomatoes rotting away in the garden. *(10-13-81)*

The first tomato was harvested from the greenhouse! Everything is still thriving there, and I planted some seeds that are already peeking through. The colors of the flowers look mighty reassuring from the outside. *(12-06-81)*

I spent a fair amount of time in the greenhouse restarting flower seeds and starting a few vegetables. There are some encouraging signs. Yesterday was sunny and glorious here, and I sat in the warmth of the greenhouse reading and listening to good music. Actually, I even had a noontime martini in the greenhouse, but I'd appreciate it if you didn't broadcast the news. *(03-15-82)*

I have put the windmill in the garden as a scarecrow – for the crows have been pulling up the new corn plants. *(05-24-82)*

Peas have an extra ingredient for enjoyment. And that is the joy of just sitting and shelling. It's a job of doing something and actually doing very little. Mac and Sandy watch intently, as they like the pods that sometimes come their way. *(06-25-84)*

The greenhouse is filling up with little seedlings. The lettuce crop looks promising. And Mr. Rabbit, who lives under the building, is waiting for his share. *(02-25-85)*

I found the hole in the fence they had chewed and also bombed their hole – but the damage has been done. They also chewed to the ground about 200 bean plants. Some of this might have been avoided if my new fence was up. The posts and rails arrived about a month ago – but no carpenter. I moved them in the rain one day, 44 posts and 88 rails – one at a time, with the dogs following me back and forth. *(07-01-85)*

I had a happy time with the Rahrs. They are super friends. Dave gave me a bumper sticker which reads: Don't complain about farmers with your mouth full. It now is on the greenhouse. *(10-15-85)*

Once again, I peeked in on the greenhouse one morning to find that disaster had struck. The doggoned heater went out, and the repair man showed me 'points' that had rusted, a dead mouse that didn't help, and huge wasps' nest. Only a few things survived, and the question now is whether to just plain shut it down for couple months. *(12-09-85)*

The garden is really producing stuff. After a shaky start, it is beginning to be very productive. Gardens are unusual in their patterns. Last year, I couldn't grow a cucumber – this year they are coming in daily – and too many. *(07-29-86)*

I went out to the garden one day and saw a strange path around the inside of the fence. When I went to show it John, we saw the reason – a huge turtle. And when John tried to flip him out with a shovel, the turtle just about bit the shovel in half. He left the gate open, and the hope is now that he escaped. But I look closely each time I enter. *(07-01-90)*

Gardening was a big user of time. The house rule here is that whoever plows the ground, buys the seeds, plants the seeds, weeds the rows and picks the crops must play a major role in processing the crop. And so, each half bushel (daily) of beans has been 'happily' fixed (cut) so that Mom can do the freezing work. The freezer overflowed so that we took that portion destined for the soup kitchen up to the church freezer. *(08-05-90)*

I saw seven deer looking at my garden. I guess they are wondering when I am going to put the seed in. *(02-10-91)*

On the subject of gardens, a car drove in here today, saying that with all the flowers that they saw from the road, they thought it was a garden shop. Actually, the coreopsis, one of my favorite flowers, are in full bloom, and you can see them from a distance. *(06-09-91)*

I put the scare crow out this morning, and just a little while ago, I looked and found him [*the woodchuck*] chewing underneath the scare crow. Mom has suggested, and I have tried, putting cayenne pepper on the little plants. I may yet call one of my NRA friends with an assault rifle. *(06-16-91)*

On the garden front, the peas are coming in, although the varmint has chewed up some fifty feet of the stuff. He also ate 14 cucumber plants, all of the sprouts, all of the broccoli, all of the beets, and was working on the carrots. I put out a trap, and he managed to turn it upside down and escape. So, I borrowed Mr. Nelson's big trap, and caught him. The rest of the story is tough to tell, since I am not disposed to capital punishment. *(06-23-91)*

Garden Report: Perhaps I should find a new hobby such as betting on the horses or sky diving. When I went to check on the garden, I found that all of the bean plants (a few hundred) had been stripped of their leaves by the varmint or varmints. . . . I caught a small rabbit in the trap last night, and rather than go the unhappy dispatch of another animal, I let him (her?) loose a few miles away. Now I know what they mean by the phrase 'scared rabbit.' *(07-14-91)*

We have brown lawns, and the garden is suffering. I spend an hour or so each day carrying buckets of water to try and save some of the plants. We have harvested some beans, a second planting is now emerging, the raspberry crop has been better than expected, and the zucchini crop is in full swing. I also picked blueberries. *(07-21-91)*

Peaches, peaches. The two trees have provided at least a thousand peaches. The branches were so loaded that even the two by four props couldn't hold them up. We began picking them before they were ripe to relieve the pressure on the branches. Unhappily, it didn't work for one of the major limbs, and it has a large crack in it. *(08-17-91)*

The seed catalogs are on the table, and I have placed my first order! I checked the order first with the deer and woodchucks. *(01-05-92)*

I found a product at Spag's called Scent Fence, which they say will scare off some things like rabbits and woodchucks. Interestingly, the scent duplicates the odor of a red fox, and I saw a handsome specimen the other day. Usually, they are mangey creatures, but this guy looked good. *(06-22-92)*

About ten or twelve years ago, I started a compost pile – you have all seen it. Over the years, I have stuffed 'stuff' into it and have rarely taken anything out. But space compelled me to move, and I began digging out one section. Amazing. From garbage, from weeds, from plants from the garden, from grass cuttings have come a black soil that matches what one might buy in a bag of potting soil. It's a slow process of screening out pebbles and twigs, but the wheelbarrow load that is dumped on the garden looks beautiful. *(08-09-92)*

On balance, I would have to say that this year has been a gardening disaster or disappointment. The animals have eaten all the beets, the broccoli, the cabbage, and most of the sprouts. Sprouts are one of my favorites, and when I walk in the garden and see 18 sprout plants chewed to the ground, I could cry. But so far, the tomatoes and the lima beans (also a favorite) have been spared. Next year will be better.

And tomorrow, too. *(08-16-92)*

We have lots of tomatoes. And so does the varmint. But with 64 plants there is plenty for everybody. By the way, does anyone know how Green Giant gets the beans out of the pods? It is a long, tedious job for this gardener. *(09-06-92)*

The vegetable garden has been rototilled, and the peas are in. Five pounds of pea seeds. Now if the woodchucks will just give me a chance. *(04-25-93)*

As a testimonial to my green thumb, I planted a packet of about 25 sunflower seeds, and have one plant! *(07-17-93)*

This is the time of year when one looks at the garden and says, oh well. We are harvesting much stuff, and I am continuing the some-what stupid project of digging up the rows of weeds (to keep them from seeding), but the zeal is clearly diminished. The disappointments this year include the onions, carrots and sprouts. *(08-29-93)*

The varmints are back in the garden. This time they are working on, of all things, the asparagus. Big tooth marks. And also the beans. To counter this, I have put up the owl (it didn't work last year), a scarecrow, a windmill (for noise), have covered the beans with a fabric, and have spread crushed pepper on the plants. I am sure that buying Birds Eye would be cheaper. *(06-06-94)*

On the garden 'front,' much progress. Thanks to John's work, the area behind the red barn is now planted with a zillion marigolds and zinnias. I added some more this week. The problem with this garden, as in so many things in our lives, is that 'out of sight = out of love.' But last year, I figured if I crammed it with flowers, it would beat the weeds. And it did. In the vegetable garden, I have been hauling hundreds of buckets of leaves from the leaf mulch pile to help cover the endless parade of weeds. Hope it works. *(06-26-94)*

Much time in the vegetable garden. The peas are coming in nicely. Where are the pea pickers from Silver Spring? Also, radishes, rhubarb, lettuce (the best I have ever grown); and thanks to Mr. (Mrs.) Woodchuck I have planted my fourth re-do of beans. Most of the garden is now covered with some sort of netting or fabric. *(07-04-94)*

After all my groaning about the problems of varmints in the garden, the produce is really arriving. The peas are all finished – and it was a good crop; and now we have beans, beets, cucumbers, broccoli, zucchini (of course) and the best lettuce I have ever grown. *(07-24-94)*

The garden. Oh well. I returned a little while ago after disturbing three small rabbits – working hard to become big rabbits. The other day, I went out and found a deer standing in the garden, a woodchuck eating weeds, and a rabbit a few feet away. This is a garden? It's a zoo. *(08-07-94)*

Lots of time in the gardens. I was going to say work, but one shouldn't treat a hobby as work. But it is somewhat physical, keeps me out of doors, and has many rewards. Besides, it's all I think of (almost) all winter. *(06-04-95)*

What was life like before peas? Last week, I spent three or four hours each day picking and shelling peas. The crop is huge. We have frozen much, given away much, and eaten much.
Finally, I have a snake in the herb garden. About three feet long, and he stares me down. *(07-02-95)*

I picked and froze beans almost every day and picked raspberries and blueberries on alternate days. The freezer is really beginning to bulge. But as we work, we think ahead to the days of winter when we will enjoy the benefits of this labor. *(07-31-95)*

I did the dumb trick of giving away dozens of tomato plants from the greenhouse and left myself with mostly with cherry tomatoes. They are nice, but can *you* imagine that we bought tomatoes at the market the other day. (09-24-95)

There are lots of garden catalogs in the mail. What to do? The varmints did so much damage to crops and morale, should I do it again? *(01-14-96)*

The garden is a shambles. I think some of the peas may come back, but the second planting of the beans has been chewed up. On the good news side, the asparagus season is finished, and it was wonderful. And last year, I planted about 30 sunflower seeds, and only one came up. This year, they all have. *(06-16-96)*

As some of you know, or have learned, a Dickson can be stubborn. To prove the point, I planted beans for the third time and have tried all sorts of schemes to grow peas. Also, after watching broccoli and sprouts being devoured overnight, I decided to plant them in buckets near the greenhouse. Same result. *(06-30-96)*

The garden. Ah, yes the garden. It now seems to be a lima bean garden. The second planting of peas and the third planting of beans didn't work, and so I have put in more limas. For some strange reason, the varmints do not like limas. But I do. *(07-21-96)*

Greetings from Lima Bean Farm! Are lima beans beautiful? Yes, if it's your only crop. I pick a bucket each day, which is about as much as my fingernails can handle. For some reason, the woodchucks just don't like lima beans. Also, many children. *(09-01-96)*

I have tackled a lot of dumb jobs in *my* career, but I think I have now hit the best – or worst. The vegetable garden, destroyed by the animals, is knee high with weeds. For a variety of reasons, I am digging it up, shovel by shovel. Of course, I'll never do it all, but some of it will get done. It does get me outside, it is exercise, and I dig for ten minutes and sit for ten minutes. On the saner side, I picked a batch of blueberries. And Mom made some peach pies. And the pear trees are groaning with a big crop. *(09-06-97)*

Last week, I finally planted radishes, beets, carrots, and onions. I also lost a few tomatoes, but so far, the beasts have left the peas untouched. Are you tired of these tragic reports? *(06-07-98)*

For Father's Day, I got a plaque that reads: "An old gardener lives here with his American beauty." It now rests on the wall above the doorbell. But I am not sure what kind of a gardener I am. *(06-28-98)*

Crop report: we have loads of peaches and pears. And although I planted about 50 tomato plants, and only twelve have made it past the woodchucks, the remainder are plentiful suppliers. We have had three huge tomatoes, and there are more to come. The lima beans look promising, and we may even have some carrots. *(08-16-98)*

We have bulbs by the zillion peeking through. I don't remember planting that many new ones. We can look forward to plenty of color. *(03-23-99)*

The lima beans are all 'in.' But as I sit and try to get the darned beans out of the pods, I wonder how do they process these at Green Giant? Two nights of frost have basically ended the garden. It was a good year. *(10/03/00)*

# The Woodie, Ah the Woodie

**"The Woodie is running!"**

*Pop had a lifelong love affair with Ford Woodie station wagons. He bought a 1940 model for my brother David's high school graduation, but, unfortunately for David, it didn't run. It needed a lot of work. David started down the repair path, sanding down the wood trim, but engine repair was not part of the family talents. Still, Pop held on to the car, shipped it to Indianapolis, back to Wilton, and then up to Pomfret. It sat in the driveway like a decoration. There, he made the decision to turn it over to a restorer and get the thing running. His letters captured the journey and all the frustrations along the way. Still, the Woodie was the first thing we saw when we pulled in the driveway, and it became a backdrop for family photos. And it even ran . . . sometimes.*

*Uncle Don's Woodie* by Rell Dean

Andrew and I (mostly Andrew) put a new battery in the Woodie yesterday – and it runs. Now we are going to try and get the wiring system straightened out, and then on to some of the wood refinishing. It also needs a new roof. *(07-24-77)*

The Woodie was moved to a nearby garage to begin the long and costly job of restoration. I am very apprehensive (and Mom is more so) about the eventual price tag, and the restorer will not give even a ballpark figure estimate. It's to the poor house in style! *(08-24-81)*

I paid a visit to the Woodie last week and these visits are becoming rather unpleasant for both old Mr. Adams and me. My one-thousand-dollar door now doesn't fit. I don't think I will ever see this nightmare finished. *(02-21-83)*

The Woodie – ah, the Woodie. I paid it a visit last week and there is some progress. I know why they stopped making cars with wood. There's absolutely no end to the problems. The promise is that it will be finished in a month. Maybe. *(03-28-83)*

The Woodie is here, and it looks sensational. Unfortunately, I put it in the garage on Saturday night, and couldn't get it started yesterday morning. As an example of my frustration with this whole project, when it came time to pick it up on Friday, Mr. Adams asked me to delay the pickup until 'the rain stopped.' He never got the idea out of his mind that this was to be a museum restoration. And I paid for that mindset. *(05-23-83)*

The Woodie has been used daily, but the doggoned brakes locked on me while in Putnam. And so, it's back to the shop today. *(06-13-83)*

The Woodie, ah the Woodie. It's back again after a couple weeks at the shop. It has a new electric fuel pump backed up by a thousand reasons why it hasn't worked before and why it should work now. I got an inquiry from someone supposedly representing one of the Beach Boys – maybe I should just sell the doggoned machine. *(06-25-84)*

Forbes' list of the 400 richest families came this week and once again we didn't make it. I guess I put too much money into the Woodie. *(09-24-84)*

We had a couple here the other day looking at the Woodie. They haven't called back, so I assume they were stunned by the price tag. But they have just inherited a bundle – and I would hope that they would share it with me. *(11-10-91)*

The Woodie is running! Bob Hanley, who used to work at Putnam Ford, and is at loose ends, spent some hours fine turning the engine, and it has never sounded better. And it has been washed. Next comes a cleaning out of all the mouse litter (and dead mice), and a little work on the brakes. *(08-09-92)*

Some time was spent with the Woodie. My friend, formerly with Putnam Ford, has tried to get the doggoned machine going, and then to keep it going. We have stalled twice on back roads. He is now trying to rebuild the carburetor. A great adventure. *(08-22-93)*

The subject is autos. For you who have wondered about the dirty windows – I washed the inside and outside of every car! And the saga of the Woodie. Bob Hanley is the retired first mechanic at the local Ford dealership and has a few old cars of his own. He has been working on the Woodie at his garage, and drove here the other day to say that he had started the car 50 times. And it wouldn't start here. Back to the drawing board. *(08-29-93)*

I decided that it was time to get the Woodie organized. But before I called the mechanic, I decided to try and start it. And it started! Would you like the name of the battery maker? *(06-06-93)*

I got some material from the Transportation Museum in Boston. and it is quite a place. They are anxious to have the Woodie, and I am now checking with the lawyers about tax consequences – and then to get it appraised. *(12-12-94)*

The museum people from Boston came and took the Woodie, and I am now waiting for their appraisal. The deal was that if the appraisal was too low, they would bring it back. I was close to tears when it was taken out on the flat-bed. *(03-26-95)*

The odyssey of the Woodie, at least my part of it, is over. The guy from the museum showed here on Friday with three appraisals, and the needed paperwork. The highest figure was actually more than I expected but less than I hoped for. And far less than I had invested. But it was the right decision. *(06-04-95)*

Enclosed is a copy of a letter from the museum near Boston, where the Woodie now resides. On the wall next to me, in the big montage, is a snapshot of Mom and Pop about to leave on our honeymoon, with a Woodie as our vehicle. It was a gift for the week from the parents of Leighton Laughlin. And so, the affection for 1940 Woodies. *(06-25-95)*

I have just about finished a needlepoint belt. It has a bunch of old cars, but the real attraction is a blue Woodie. *(12-01-96)*

# On the Road

**"HOME! HOME! What a beautiful word! HOME!"**

*The only times Pop missed writing us a letter was when they picked up and hit the road. Or the air, but hardly ever the sea. Pop's seasickness was famous, even for a Coast Guard veteran whose nickname he told us was Breakwater Don, after his inability to withstand the sea outside of port. Upon returning home, we would get a longer travelogue, hitting the highlights, sharing an observation or two, never more than two pages, often written in bullet form. Their travel choices were near and far, by plane, train, automobile, and camper van. They visited family, friends, and the sites. They tried to get away for warmer climates in the winter and took more than one cross-country trip in each of the other seasons. Even though each letter following their return started out with a salute to the delights of home, they continued to enjoy their opportunities to see the country and the world.*

*Home Hearth* by John Dickson

Pop's big news concerns fishing. After seven years of trying to organize a fishing trip to Mr. McCaskill's camp up in Canada, it finally took place. And what a weekend! From Toronto, four of us flew in a small float plane to the lake, arriving in the dark, which made it a little nerve-wracking. There are obviously no lights and finding the right lake among literally thousands seemed impossible, but the pilot knew where he was.

Pop was a sensational fisherman, which totally changes my fortunes and experiences with a rod and reel. We caught speckled trout, pike, perch and pickerel. Pop caught the most fish (about 8) and the biggest fish (a 10-12 pound pickerel). The guide said that it was the biggest he'd seen in some years, and they are entering it in the North Bay contest. How's that for fishing luck? *(09-12-72)*

On Thursday, we got on an Interstate long enough to get us to old Route 20 and took it across that great farm country to Rochester, and I bet we stopped in 30 antique shops. By this time the car was really getting jammed. We had a great dinner with the Franks [*Paula's parents*], and Mr. Frank showed me his fantastic gun collection. They were busy harvesting and shipping cauliflowers for the last loads of the season. *(11-13-74)*

This Weekly Letter comes to you from Ripon Wisconsin! Mom and I arrived here this morning after a drive from Beloit through fog, rain and snow. Andrew, Mom and I are now sitting in a motel room enjoying Dr. Pepper, Dr. Martini and potato chips. *(01-24-76)*

We went fishing twice – once on Ralph's boat and once in small bone fishing boats. We caught strawberry groupers on the first trip – a very colorful fish. The bone fishing expedition was great. We were in a small boat with a guide, and we drifted over shallow water, and the guide stands and looks for the fish, which can be seen in the clear water over the white sand bottom. Mom and I hooked a fish at the same moment, and then the fun began. They are strong fighting fish, but we both managed to boat them. We saw many other fish, including sharks, which are plentiful in these waters. They and the barracudas, incidentally, make swimming a risky affair. *(01-13-78)*

We bought the tickets for our great trip to England! This week we get to work to get our passports renewed. And Pop has started to re-read Churchill's *History of the English-Speaking Peoples.* Also, Princeton has asked me if I would be willing to talk to an alumni group in London, and also the contingent at Oxford. Of course! *(03-12-78)*

We hit a rainy siege, and I guess about 12 of the 14 days were rain, foggy, drizzly or some other form of British wetness. Since our schedule was kind of loose, and since a prime purpose was to sit with Uncle Jim and Aunt Georgia, the rain was not that bothersome. Among the highlights of the trip, I remember:
—We saw the Canford School, Peter. Your teacher, Mr. Gay, was not on campus because of a hospital visit for knee surgery.
—We visited the Baldwin farm, David, where you spent a summer. We also saw Morris, the "pig man," as he led a huge hog into the barn.
—We went to Parliament and sat in the special Strangers Gallery and saw the Prime Minister answer questions from the opposition. *(05-11-78)*

At Lake Placid, the site of the '80 Winter Olympics, I saw the huge ski jump that has been constructed. I'd get the wobblies just being at the top of the thing, let alone thinking about going down the hill. *(09-24-79)*

Well, there's lots to talk about this morning. The first word is Nantucket! Nantucket! We were there for an all-too-short visit with David and Paula last week. They rented a house and went over on Sunday, and Mom and I and Matthew followed on Monday. It's a two-hour boat ride to an island that is steeped in history – and of course, very beautiful. We did a lot of sightseeing on the old streets and docks and visited the Whaling Museum. We spent time on the beautiful beaches which we practically had to ourselves. *(10-01-79)*

Mom and I took a trip last week to Shelburne VT, the site of a "museum" of Americana. It is actually 35 buildings on 45 acres, and each building has a specialty. One is toys, another is quilts, another cigar store Indians and carved items, etc. One building has 5,000 old tools. And there are wagons, sleds, railroad engines until the mind (and back and legs) can't absorb it anymore. The most spectacular item is a large steamboat that they hauled in from Lake Champlain and set up in a field. *(06-23-80)*

Flying across this country is a humbling experience. It is a vast and beautiful place. Even the deserts have a beauty. I look down and see a ranch or a farm or a town and wonder what the people are doing, what they are like, and whether they are really any different from the folks at Pomfret Center. *(09-21-80)*

The week started out with Mom and I going up or out to Cape Cod for a couple days. Monday was a super day although a little chilly and a little windy. But we enjoyed a day in a special place right on the beach at Orleans. Pop walked the beach as often as he could, and walked much further than his walks around here. Perhaps it was the atmosphere of the surf and the sand, but the walks were super and almost easy. *(04-19-81)*

The big news of last week was Mom's trip to Colorado. She left on Thursday morning and arrived home last night, full of news and chatter about all the great things that happened in between. Forty-one of her classmates and friends, from Carleton spent a long, exciting weekend at a lodge high in the Rockies (11,000 ft high).

She hasn't seen many of these gals in 30 plus years, and we can only imagine the good times. She brought back some photos, and they are all of smiling, happy gals. *(05-04-81)*

When we were sitting in the Prestwick Airport waiting for the homecoming plane, Mom asked "What are you most glad that you brought with you?" I said, of course, "YOU!" But next on our list was rain gear. Boy, did it rain. It rained every day – sometime all day, sometime just for a shower. The roads were flooded, the fields were flooded, the streams were flooded. *(10-06-81)*

Since we have been back from our trip, we have been checking the weather report for Aberdeen in the Times each day. After weeks of rain and clouds, Aberdeen finally got a sunny day last week! *(11-02-81)*

Where's your dear wife? Where's Georganna? Why did you come alone? These were the kinds of questions that greeted me everywhere during my little trip to Cincinnati and Milwaukee last week. Next time I had better not go alone. *(12-06-82)*

During our trip, we drove many miles in torrential rain and over bridges, through tunnels in and out of cities, and on high-speed turnpikes. Well, on Wednesday, while driving in Pomfret, the drive belt broke. I was angry until I thought of all the places the doggoned thing could have broken and caused real problems. *(05-02-83)*

One of the highlights of last week was our trip to the north country. Happily, we hardly saw a cloud during the whole trip. And we were very surprised to see that the foliage, even in the Adirondacks, was still in beautiful color. We drove along with oh's and ah's about the great views and colors. *(10-24-83)*

In looking back to last year, we record that we did touch base with you all in various places, but it's never enough. Our travels overall included New York City, Princeton, Boston, Washington, Denver, Taos, Santa Fe, Milwaukee, Block Island, Mannheim, Watch Hill, Gettysburg, Portsmouth, Lake Placid, Middlebury, The Point, Cincinnati, Kansas City, Palm Beach and Putnam, Woodstock, Dayville, Brooklyn and downtown Pomfret. The last named is best! *(01-02-84)*

What Did We Do [*on Petit St. Vincent*]? We spent many hours walking and sitting on the beach – with frequent plunges into the water. A large reef about a half mile out broke the waves, and so the water was relatively quiet. Good for swimming. A lot of reading – a book a day, needlepoint, gin rummy, crossword puzzles, opera cassettes, and radio (much gospel programs from the states – Falwell etc. – a rather strange intrusion). *(01-30-84)*

Well, we're home. Before we left, Mom estimated that we would drive 3,500 miles, and when we came into the driveway, the meter showed 3,500.5 miles.
Mom's college chum, Georgia, lives in a town near Orlando – right on a lake. She and her husband were our hosts for two nights. One of the events was to watch the launch of the Challenger – some miles away but clearly visible and it was clear that something had gone wrong when we watched. *(02-05-85)*

We fished in canoes in two rivers – one in Quebec and one in New Brunswick. In an attempt to revive the Atlantic Salmon, both provinces have taken stern measures. You can keep only one fish per day over four pounds in New Brunswick, and none in Quebec. Everything else must be released. But it is still quite an experience to hook and hold one as it jumps and runs up and down the river. It took me 25 minutes to bring one to the boat. *(07-22-85)*

On our way, we found a way to get through Providence (the marriage is saved!) but trying it in reverse on the way home we got lost (the marriage is in trouble again?). So, the eternal argument persists. *(09-23-85)*

In the nostalgia department – I finally threw away the big bags full of the old sleeping bags. We had used these in those great trips to Montana, Wyoming etc., and they were just plain worn and moldy from years in the basement. The passing of an era! *(10-21-85)*

It was a Great Trip. We arrived home last evening – pooped after the long drive home from Madison, but very happy that we had made the circuit. This is the kind of trip that is fun to plan, then nervousness sets in just as you are about to leave, and then your spirits soar as you get to places and people (it should be other way around), and finally on the way home you remember over and over again the good times. *(11-12-85)*

As we look at the Road Atlas to plan for a drive to the South in January, we wander to other pages in the Atlas. Last night, I looked at Wyoming and spotted a town called Lander. Do you remember Lander John? It's the place where your kidneys almost burst. We tried to get you to run off the road, but you were too bashful – and waited the interminable miles 'til we arrived at the motel. *(11-25-85)*

Thanks to some travelling, last week seemed to go by quickly. The first trip was to Princeton for the annual dinner of former Chairmen of the Alumni Council. . . . It also had its other moments: I ran out of money, I locked the car with the keys inside, I lost my hat, and I got a ticket for leaving the car overnight on the campus. As is my wont, I left early (5AM) and was amazed at the amount of traffic on the turnpike at that unreasonable hour. *(12-09-85)*

When I wrote last week of Ponte Vedra and called it 'gentile,' I really meant genteel – although the former word was clearly true. *(02-10-86)*

It was a good trip, but as always, it's good to be home. Further, I have had my fill of interstates for a while. They are essential for long trips, but they are hard on the fanny, and they seem to dull the mind. I don't know how the truckers do it.

Some observations – the national speed limit is 65. I (and everyone else) drove through countless speed traps at 65 or more. Trucks, trucks, trucks – they are endless. I even saw trucks carrying subway cars. It is deer hunting season, and the roads are littered with dead deer, possibly frightened or flushed out by hunters. Also, it is tough to find good music – but easy to find preachers. *(11-18-86)*

I went to Maine for an overnight and an antique auction plus some other errands. The auction was a disappointment. But I can tell you where all those people who decided not to travel to Europe are. They are on Route 95 in Maine. *(07-21-86)*

Well, the 4th Annual Marathon with Matthew is history. We arrived in Hartford on Sunday afternoon. I think it might be better described as an Eat-a-Thon, for that is how much of the time was spent. But all went well, helped along by a string of absolutely perfect weather days. *(08-26-86)*

Before moving some stuff into the new cupboards, I looked over some of the old scrapbooks of trips to the west. Besides all the great pictures, we saved menus, receipts, etc. Do you know that we all took a trip from July 28 to August 17, and spent a total of $467.32? Do you know that your rooms with three meals in one place cost $23.70; that a roast beef dinner in Sacajewa, Ore. cost $2.00; that a salmon dinner at the Seattle Space Needle cost $6.75 and a martini 67 cents; and a shore dinner at Ivar's cost $3.75!!!! *(10-20-86)*

In the evening, we went to one of the taverns in Williamsburg with three other couples. Pop had jambalaya – and he had it again at 2AM. *(11-11-86)*

Talk about contrasts! From bathing suits to snow shovels! We arrived at Logan about 3 AM on Saturday morning – almost six hours late. The reasons were various; snow in Boston, an airport closed twice due to snow removal and to a plane skidding on the runway, a detour to Kennedy to refuel and an unhappy discovery that an elderly woman behind us had died during the flight and that brought cops and doctors and much confusion. David had waited during this delay, and it was great to see him as we came down the corridor. We arrived home about five. *(02-02-87)*

And now for a few left-over thoughts from our trip . . . Bathing suits must be getting cheaper . . . they are certainly using less fabric. *(01-26-88)*

Also, did someone move all the Rolls Royces, Mercedes and Jaguars from around the country to Los Angeles for the week? Sitting on Wilshire Blvd, I counted at least one a minute in traffic. *(03-08-88)*

We traveled both ways in first class, thanks to the many milage points Mom had accumulated on American. It is a fine way to understand why rich people like to stay rich. And how it feels to be a snob. *(01-26-89)*

We're HOME! [*from Durban, South Africa*] There are so many things to remember, and in no particular order of importance, we will randomly report on our great Adventure . . .
The townships. Whatever you have heard or read about the Black Townships, they are worse than words can find. John took us on tours of some townships (one in Pietermaritzburg is called the Beirut

of Africa) and the conditions are appalling, if not frightening. Tin and wooden shacks, no power, no plumbing, constant violence and very crowded. We visited one home (much better than the others) of a teacher who worked an hour from his job. Others had to take 3–4-hour bus rides. *(03-12-89)*

Here's an item from the paper: Basically there are two classes of people – those who get up early and those who sleep late. Motels put them in adjoining rooms. *(03-26-89)*

The trip had a harrowing moment. On a busy spot on 495, with traffic zooming along, a teenager ran across in front of our car. I jammed on the brakes, and missed him by inches, and was thanked by an obscene gesture. I had fully expected to see him on top of the hood. *(05-21-89)*

Mom and I took a day to wander and visit various motor home dealerships, and we sort of settled on a particular model. What we want is something that is large on the inside and small on the outside. It was a used model at a pretty good price. But Pop vacillated, and when we decided to do something – it had been sold. *(07-24-89)*

Our first real trip in the Camper/Cottage had us clearly in the slow lane on Interstates, and the back roads of Nova Scotia are so bumpy that any type of speed would have us bouncing.
The camper worked beautifully. We had most of our meals in it, Mom used her [oxygen] machine in it, we spent five overnights in it, and it lived up to all our hopes. Mom is the camper – she pressed every day to find a campsite. And the provincial campsites are great, and often with spectacular views or in fine forests. At this time of the year, most of the tourists are old ginks like me. You wonder when you see them coming down a steep hill in their huge camper whether they are going to make it, and I suspect they thought the same about me. *(10-02-89)*

HOME! HOME! What a beautiful word! HOME! We did it! It was billed as a People Trip, and it sure was. We are very happy that we did it.

First, the inevitable statistics. We drove 8612 miles through 24 different states in 38 days. We stayed 16 nights with family and friends, 17 nights in motels and 5 in campgrounds. We tried to stay in more campgrounds, but they were either closed (despite what the guide book said), or just not our style . . .

We should make the obvious observation that this is an incredible country – the geography is fascinating. For those who have been to countries and continents far away, it is fascinating to drive and slowly see the changes in plains, deserts, mountains, etc. For example, we spent three days crossing Kansas, mostly on back roads.

If we met an unpleasant person somewhere, I've forgotten it. The friendliness everywhere seemed genuine. *(04-02-90)*

The usual way to park in a campsite is to back into the space. This is an event of some tension between husband and wife as the driver tries to maneuver a camper or trailer, often with shrill instructions from his partner. But not us, of course. *(09-30-90)*

This encouraged me to start cleaning out the file cabinets in the basement. First to be attacked were the travel folders. Plenty of nostalgia as I waded through the stuff from Scotland, Zurich, South Africa, New Zealand etc. The file on The Point included the copy of the songs that John sang. I have made copies for you to remember that fine evening. *(01-07-91)*

We're HOME! It's great to go, great to be there, and it is great to be home!

First, the low points of the trip – let's get them out of the way first. When I got on the scale this morning, I had gained four pounds. Another low point happened at the San Juan airport, when I was twiddling with my glasses, and they fell down a slot at the check-in counter. They had to take the counter apart to retrieve the glasses. Lastly, when you travel on a non-smoking flight, all the smokers puff endlessly in the terminal before flight time. There is nowhere to hide. One World . . . the towels were from Venezuela, the butter from New Zealand, the sugar from California, the bottled water from Scotland, all the cars from Japan, the soap from Cincinnati, the commuter plane from France, etc.

Also, why is it that on two successive days with the same wind, same temperature etc., one day would have a heavy surf and the nest day would be calm? Why do the bees march to the seas, and almost certain drowning? How did the lizard get in Mom's purse? *(01-29-91)*

We are having a great trip. Last week we stayed mostly in campgrounds in Tennessee and Mississippi. The national park service does an absolutely great job – clean, spacious, privacy, all sorts of facilities – and all for 5 or 7 bucks a night. We have our breakfasts and lunches in the camper, and sometimes dinner, too. *(03-25-91)*

The most popular sign on our route was "Work Area – one mile" followed closely by "Right Lane Closed Ahead." *(07-10-91)*

Florida – it ain't for me. On this trip we did a fair amount of driving back roads. When you leave the glamour of the cities, the small towns and farms are pretty bleak. Even in January, the humidity was high. Moops [*niece*] said there were about three decent months a year, and the heat was oppressive the rest of the time.

Campground 'society' – we spent some interesting time at a campground on the ocean in South Carolina. In this 'society,' nobody is under 60, everyone chats, some put up awnings and put down rugs, some guys spend endless hours shining up the campers and some of them are huge. I noted that one huge vehicle was owned by a guy with a Roadway jacket, so I guess he knew how to drive it.

People ride bikes, take long hikes, and the place is strangely quiet after lunch. Naps? *(02-09-92)*

Being THERE was fun – absolutely great fun – but getting there and back weren't no fun. The London to Durban and back flights were jam packed and very uncomfortable. And long – it was 30 hours of travel time coming back to Boston. And British Air food is awful.

We had some wonderful trips. We all went for a weekend to the mountains (Little Switzerland), we visited townships, schools, church centers, museums, health care centers (where we saw Jennifer Anderson, who is working on a year-long AIDS project in a Township), and Mom and I took a week-long tour of the Garden Route, from Port Elizabeth to Cape Town.

It was, of course, an exciting time to be there. The Referendum was the big news, and the results were quite remarkable. The turnout was heavy, and it was a resounding vote for change. The other issue was the World Cup Cricket Match in New Zealand-Australia. South Africa got to the semi-finals, in their first entry in 22 years because of sport sanctions. In this sports-crazy country, the isolation from international competition was a clear factor in the Referendum vote. *(03-29-92)*

The next event for the camper took place on the way home. After a night's stay in Utica, we left early full of plans for the afternoon in Pomfret. But, alas, something went awry on the Thruway, and a friendly trooper called for help. A tow truck arrived, and took us to Albany where the problem was diagnosed as a broken alternator. After a few hours, and a few more bucks, we headed home. Happily. Despite the mechanical problems, for us the trip was a great success. We hope it was for Joe and Jeffrey, too. We saw so much of Niagara Falls, and then went to Toronto for two nights and a long day at the zoo and the science museum. The Welland Canal is something to behold. We watched two huge ships go through, and it is an impressive sight. *(07-24-92)*

What did I do for four days? As an experiment in vacationing alone, I must admit to some loneliness. Everything is better with Mom. But I walked the wonderful beach endlessly, I read two books, did a lot of needlepoint, watched the passing parade, and kept a close eye on the surf and the horizon. On my last night, a fierce storm came through, and I woke up with water dripping on my face. The roof leaks. *(04-13-93)*

The trip was wonderful. We 'camped' in camp sites on Lakes Huron, Superior and Michigan. The weather was generally good, sometimes great, and the few rainy days we were scheduled for motels anyhow. Some thoughts:
—We have seen many strange sights in campgrounds, but never have we seen a *guy* cutting grass with a mower around his camper.
—We've seen campers towing cars, boats and various kinds of trailers, but never have we seen a camper towing a helicopter.
—In Canada, the foreign exchange game is just that. I had a long argument with a gas station operator (after the gas had been pumped – a lesson), in which I said that I wanted him to make a profit as a gas dealer, but not as a banker. I lost. *(10-03-93)*

We are packed – and are we ready! The cold and snow here have been intense. We have two vehicles with dead batteries, and with much sun, the thermometer on the porch now reads 8. And the icicles have broken two of the gutters. Ah Tortola, here we come. We hope. The forecast for tomorrow is for six inches of the white stuff. *(01-16-94)*

Now, we don't expect any sympathy from you folks who lived through some bad weather. But we did have some problems. Our departure date was postponed by one day because the Hartford airport was closed. We spent an 'exciting' day at the Ramada Inn at the airport. When we did leave the next morning, the plane skidded and got stuck in the ice. *(01-30-94)*

This is a problem you don't have. But I sunburn on the top of my head. Thinning (or no) hair, I tried to walk the beach five times a day. That is at least five miles. And the surf was spectacular. *(01-30-94)*

Travelling is hard on diets – no matter how hard you try. We had breakfasts in our room and made picnic lunches each day. That was the only way to keep some control. (03-29-94)

Then to a motel near Gettysburg. Andrew and Billy arrived at the Harrisburg airport, followed by David and Jeffrey. On Saturday morning, we met Peter and Sean and John and Joseph at the Battlefield Visitor Center and began a day of touring the many famous sites of this three-day battle. The favorite spots seemed to be the site of Pickett's charge, where the boys ran across the fields of the charge. Next came Little Round Top, made famous by the 20th Maine and Joshua Chamberlin.
The motel gave us breakfast, but other meals were a little problem. Everything within Gettysburg was jammed, and we tried two spots near the motel for Saturday night supper. My memory of supper includes a Buffalo Burger (not very good), huge ice creams for the boys, and long and happy laughter from the boys. *(05-23-94)*

The Grand Hotel – Mackinac Island: this place is hard to describe. It's beautiful, it's huge. The world's biggest porch, on a hillside on an island, with only horses for transportation . . . except for a fire truck and an ambulance. Now I know what America smelled like before the auto. But on Mackinac, there are crews with wheelbarrows that follow the horses and clean the streets.
My question was and is, how can it be economically feasible? And

how can they get the food and the tons of supplies from the docks in small horse drawn wagons? *(09-21-94)*

I believe there are two things that can threaten a marriage . . . picking the wrong Christmas tree, and backing a camper into a campsite. *(09-17-95)*

A driver took us to JFK early, very early on Wednesday. Living up here in the Quiet Corner, we tend to forget the nightmare of traffic in big cities. It was awful – but most of it going the other way. Bermuda was gorgeous. Flowers along the roads, narrow roads, and we arrived at the resort to find that we were the only guests of a possible 120. Our beach front cottage was comfortable, and the meals *were* sensational. We walked the beach, we read, listened to tapes, played gin rummy, did needlepoint and napped. Tough life. *(12-12-95)*

A fire in the fireplace, good music, a martini nearby, and tons of snow outside. It's good to be home. *(02-04-96)*

Reluctantly, we have made a decision to sell the Camper. It has served us so well, and we have so many great memories, including a photo album of the camper in different places. But when we made the decision not to use it on The Trip, that about sealed it. *(08-25-96)*

The camper is now for sale – on consignment at the place where we bought it. I hope it sells soon – the carpenters, roofers etc. are nice guys, but they do send bills. *(09-18-96)*

From Minneapolis, we went to Wagon Trail, the scene of some great get-togethers. We stayed in the same log cabin. They have added a new addition to the Lodge. Still a great place. On one of my walks, I wandered through a small cemetery, and noticed a headstone for a doctor that said he brought life to the world and love to his family.

Were there any sins? You bet. Pop had a steak at one dinner, and Mom had a chocolate milk shake for a lunch. *(09-29-96)*

By the way, when we embark on these kind of trips, I usually update our instructions in the event of a dual tragedy. The envelope sits in the small stand atop my dresser. *(11-16-97)*

Home Again! What glorious words. You who also travel know the feeling. It is so great to be in some places, especially with family, but it's true . . . there's no place like home. And for you who like numbers, the odometer on this new vehicle read 2,222 miles. *(12-01-97)*

How do you cover two weeks in a foreign land without sounding like travelogue or a diary? But, of course, we did spend it with family, and that makes it easy and different.
I do have some impressions, and in no order of importance, they are:
Lima: This is a very unattractive city. It is old, very old, and it has grown aplenty recently. But as you drive these congested roads and see the endless poverty as the newcomers moved further from the central city, it's like one long slum.
Language: Not knowing the local language is very limiting. I wish I had studied up a bit beforehand.
Misc: Mom saw more than I did, but I did a lot of reading and needlepoint. We did go to a private museum for a two-hour tour (in Spanish) of primitive gold, silver and ceramic items. Very impressive. I have a magazine page about it, and if it copies well, I will send it along. Bubba [*John and Mary's dog*] is still frightened of me. *(03-01-98)*

Travel plans: We are planning to go to Dundee on the 30th for a long weekend to meet Daniel [*grandson*] and members of his family. The ticket price is an interesting story. Some years ago, American invited seniors to join a special 'club' for $100 and receive special discounts. I wrote the Chairman to complain about the many restrictions. I got my money back, but kept the membership. Well, the average fare to and from Chicago is about $400, First Class is $1,500, and our special fare is $150 round trip. It finally paid off. *(04-19-98)*

But Pop is becoming a non-traveler. It was only a two-hour flight home from Chicago, but even with a good book, I looked at my watch every five minutes. While waiting for the plane at O'Hare, I thought I would try a martini. I knew it would be expensive, but I was unprepared for the tiny size.
There is a special joy in visiting a young family. And there is a special joy in being home. *(05-05-98)*

Have you been thinking about going to Ireland? Don't bother. The document that Peter sent us (and you, too?) is enough of a travelogue to let you stay home and enjoy the country. Thank you, Peter, and also for the fine picture of Sean. *(12-06-98)*

Weather has been a factor in our lives. There were a few days of bitter cold, and then the forecasts for Sunday were simply frightening. And therein lies an adventure for Joe. He arrived in Newark just as they were largely shutting down operations. After some phone calls, we learned that his Providence connection was cancelled, that there were no hotel rooms available, that he was worried about his money, and that the earliest flight he could book was Monday night. Mom's idea was for him to take a bus into NYC, go to Grand Central, and take the train. Which he did. *(01-04-99)*

On the way home on a four lane stretch of road in Morristown, I witnessed a high-speed police chase. The target was a Jeep that switched lanes and on and off the highway. I kept waiting for a major crash. But they turned off – and I hope they got him and then throw the book at him. Dangerous. *(08-23-98)*

Mom and I travelled to Nantucket on Monday to check out the site for her Carleton girl get-together in September. The place is great. The weather was fine, and the ferryboat ride smooth. The ferry had one of its large doors out of service, so that all the vehicles had to back in. It was fun to watch the big trailer trucks very skillfully do the job. The ferry leaves from Hyannis, and I don't know how the local citizens can stand the traffic. And this was March, not the height of the season. *(04-05-99)*

# Celebrate

**"Mom gave us one of those dinners designed to see
how much food can be put on one table."**

*Pop used to tell us that all he wanted for presents were a bag full of
laughter and a box full of kisses. Sounds like a Depression-era present.
And, in the first letter included here, he wrote, "Having you at home
will be the biggest gift." He had one rule—not to travel on the holidays.
He wanted to be home. And so, for years, we all descended on Pomfret
for the holidays, and when their grandchildren grew up, we celebrated
at our own homes but convened in Pomfret Center for the chaotic
"after-parties." Chaotic, yes, but fun.*

*Oh Christmas Tree* by John Dickson

We're also getting a little organized for Christmas and Mom did a fair amount of wrapping yesterday. Remember, we're planning a rather modest holiday – so all of you can keep the present purchases down. Having you at home will be the biggest gift. *(12-03-73)*

What a great Thanksgiving weekend it was for us! To have all of you here for so long a time was absolutely great. We remember –
The surprise at seeing David and Paula on Tuesday evening.
The good Samaritan at LaGuardia on the same evening.
The kitchen table – never vacant.
The gallons of Cokes, cocoa, coffee.
The ever-burning fire – compliments of Andrew.
The late-night arrival of Peter, Janet and John (not really – Pop was asleep). *(12-02-74)*

Andrew, you should be happy to hear that Pop and David (mostly David) planted the Christmas tree. We put it on the slope near the road. Hope it takes. *(01-05-75)*

Things are somewhat quiet here – now. Mom and Paula are doing a jig saw puzzle; David and Andrew are watching a Jerry Lewis movie (Jerry Lewis?!); Ann is zonked out (Pop was, until a little while ago) and Charlie is watching . . . carefully. Because Matthew is at work on his toys in the kitchen. All is well.
John, we have missed you for the second year at Christmastime, and hope that next year will see us all together again. We tried to start a tape last night to record our Christmas wishes, but the doggoned machine just wouldn't work. Perhaps we'll get it working by New Year's Eve, when most of us will be back together again. *(12-25-77)*

About 3PM, Mom gave us one of those dinners designed to see how much food can be put on one table. You can imagine what happened after that. *(12-26-78)*

Well, we've finished another eventful year – and are now ready to take on the youngster of '78. Pop, as usual, slept through the great moment, but the house was busy with Momma, David and Paula, Peter and Janet and Andrew chatting and drinking to the New Year. The other sleepyhead, Matthew, was also zonked out. It was grand to have some of you here – wait'll next year when we look forward to a couple others – namely Ann and John [*neither of us made it the next year*]. *(01-01-78)*

Wednesday was St. Valentine's Day – as I know all of you guys know – and I gave Mom a copper pot from the shop. The hint was very clear, since she had brought it in the day before for polishing. *(02-18-79)*

I had a piece of apple pie this morning – one of the leftovers from a wonderful Thanksgiving. Paula brought three pies, and there is just a little left, and it is being hoarded. It's also easy to guess who did the lion's share of eating – for the scale said that I had gained ten pounds during the past week. Good grief. *(11-26-79)*

We had a Christmas turkey dinner on Saturday evening with David and Paula, followed by a spirited discussion as to whether it was legal and proper to open Christmas presents before the magic hour. We decided not to, but by a close margin. Pop, you must remember, has 84 votes. We also listened to a Muppet's Christmas album. *(12-24-79)*

June 9, 1980. An Historic Day
Hey! Hey! Thanks for all the birthday wishes and things! We had quite a party here last night with John, David, Paula and Matthew helping us to celebrate. I was showered with gifts, including a book about Robert Kennedy and a tee shirt from Wisconsin that says MRF – Pop. I'll be the Beau Brummel of Pomfret. *(06-09-80)*

I'd like to report a happy note in this sometime gloomy world. I stopped the other day at the restaurant at the truck stop near the Mass. Pike and the road leading to New Lebanon, N.Y., and they had a big sign that said "Continuing our tradition – a free Thanksgiving dinner to every working truckdriver." Nice. *(11-17-80)*

I spent some time trying to create some order in the chaotic basement. Do you remember the long cloak that we found in the attic in Cunningham Road and which I think each of you wore at some Halloween? Well, it finally bit the dust (or mold) and is now at the dump. *(12-08-80)*

The "double table" in the kitchen on Thanksgiving groaning with so much food. And Uncle Bob's wonderful singing grace that seemed to set the tone for such a happy meal. We also remember the snoozing, the reading, the watching of TV that followed the dinner. *(11-30-81)*

Since then, Mom has been busy wrapping packages – some for mailing and some for hiding around here. She has also been hard at work on the annual Christmas note and letter project. She gets an A+ for the amount of personal effort she puts into personal letters to many people. *(12-06-81)*

Yesterday, Pop marched in the Pomfret Memorial Day Parade. Since the music was supplied by the grade school band, it was more of a walk. But, a great event. Some National Guardsman, three fire trucks, three antique cars, Boy Scouts, Girl Scouts, Brownies, oodles of Little Leaguers, a gymnast class, two horses, and of course the Lions. All in the pouring rain.

It was interesting to note that this town of some 2500 people sent 79 men to the Korean war and 52 to Vietnam. *(06-01-82)*

On my birthday, our carpenter friend here asked me what my goals were 'after 60,' and I replied, 'June 10, June 11, June 12 . . .' *(06-13-83)*

We sure wish you were here, and we remember some July 4ths together. We wish you were here, but . . .
The but has to do with the refrigerator, which went on the blink during the night. Therefore, how would we keep the beer cold, the ice for the martinis, the salads cool and the ton of food ready for cooking? *(07-04-83)*

And yesterday was Father's Day. . . . The card from Mom showed Snoopy on top of his dog house saying "In your honor on Father's Day, a nap has been taken in your name!" Very appropriate. *(06-18-84)*

We got some happy Valentines from around the circuit. In olden days, there would be gifts here of such great things as nightgowns. But this year, I got a bar of soap and Mom got a printed banner that said "Georganna, I Love You." *(02-18-85)*

The trains are also up, on a train board in the old dining room. The tracks have all been nailed down, so that you don't spend endless minutes putting the track back after each run of the engine. It all worked just fine for Matthew yesterday who was the chief engineer for a good part of the afternoon. *(12-23-85)*

And the birthday last Monday! I have heard that you can tell much about a man just by reading his check stubs. Well, how about his birthday presents, too? Do you know who received a camera for picture taking at reunions, a package of pasta, a bottle of gin, a bow tie, a book about Yorkshire, 3 blueberry bushes, and a survival kit for a trip to Wisconsin? Thank you for all these gifts and for the phone calls on Monday evening. *(06-16-86)*

Saturday was TREE day. On a bitter cold and windy day, David and

I roamed the tree farm, finally settled on a tree and then lugged it to the van and began the process of trying to install it in the living room. It's about 15 feet tall, weighs a ton, now has 700 lights on it – and is probably one of the more stupid things that I do. There were quite a few times on Saturday that I vowed Never Again. But it does look super. *(12-15-86)*

Another wonderful holiday has come and gone. Peter and Janet left yesterday morning, taking along two fine little characters. And this place is quiet. And after stepping on the scale this morning, it is apparent that one person had too many brownies, too many martinis, too much pasta, too much turkey etc. It's back to the straight and narrow.

Thanksgiving Day found the folks from Marlborough joining us around the busy table. They also came out Saturday, and Paula, Janet, Johanna and Mom went up to a church fair for lunch. We all went to Hank's for supper. Amidst all these activities, we played backgammon, there was plenty of chasing, there were long walks, there were many times to answer the question "Where is Mac?" There were calls to Kensington (where Andrew visited), to Uncle Gil, and calls from Uncle All and Uncle Jim. Peter fixed the movie projector, and some old movies were reviewed. *(11-30-87)*

I had a rehearsal of the town Christmas pageant in which I suspect I am a rather stiff shepherd. And such a costume. *(12-08-87)*

It has been a good Memorial Day. The Parade (Pop wore his red, white and blue tie), a Post-Parade party, a Historical Association reception, and lunch here (and a groaning board) with the McCobbs. And a nap. *(05-30-88)*

We had a fairly busy Halloween. Part of the game on Halloween is to make sure the trick or treaters take all the candy, so that there is none left to tempt us. *(11-07-88)*

Saturday afternoon, I went to pick out and cut down a tree. This year, without David. And so I was resolved that the tree had to be smaller. Further, I had given away some of the tree lights, so it really had to be smaller. But. But, it ain't much smaller. *(12-18-88)*

We went to the annual Pomfret School Christmas carol sing . . . to me it is the 'official' start of the season. *(12-18-89)*

We have a tree! We just came back from the annual Christmas party at the Aicher's, at which each person gets to pick out a tree. If all goes well, we'll put it up tomorrow. *(12-16-90)*

This old farmhouse has seen many holidays and many family get-togethers. But this one was special. Thank you all for coming. We know the effort it takes to travel up to this place, and we appreciate all you do in getting here, and making it all happen here. *(12-30-90)*

We had a note from John along with some 'lists' from Joseph and Margaret, in response to Mom's request about their Christmas desires. One of Joe's items was a stretch Lincoln limo, which I suspect came from John's creative mind. *(11-03-91)*

When we first started putting outdoor lights on the evergreen, it was of a size that with a small ladder, I could reach the top. Last year, Paul Nelson brought his tractor with front loader over and put his nephew in it to get the lights to the top. This year, I said 'no more,' and the lights are now strung along the bushes. *(12-16-91)*

The tree is up, and most of the lights are on. I 'rented' a carpenter with a pickup to go up at the Aicher's and cut the tree and to put it up in the living room. It is about 10-11 feet high and quite handsome. *(12-20-92)*

We normally open our presents on Christmas Eve, and it was our plan to do it again. But we came home from a party, and I decided to light a fire in the fireplace. Unfortunately, I forgot to open the dampers. The smoke had about cleared out by the next morning. *(12-27-93)*

One of my New Year's Day projects has been to clean out the Weekly Letter file, before putting them in the notebook. A year ago, I wrote that the tree was too big, and I would not do it again. Well, I did, and once again I vow not to do it again. It does look spectacular with all the lights and ornaments, but the disposal is a major problem. So, come early December in 1995, please remind me to get a smaller tree. *(01-01-95)*

We spent much time during the week catching up on mail and papers, and writing notes in Christmas cards. Some of the Christmas mail includes 'letters.' One this year was entitled Dear Everyone – and that started me off wrong, and it followed with a description of lunch with the Queen Mum, and ended with plans for trips to London, Wisconsin, Montana, and Australia. Who cares, says I. *(12-17-95)*

We got a long e-mail from Paula that included some items about Jeffrey. He has a job working in a bakery, he became a senior patrol leader in the Scouts, and was working on a haunted house project for you-know-what. Speaking of that, we had a bunch visit here. I think part of the attraction is the Polaroid print that I take of each visitor. *(11-02-97)*

Today was the Memorial Day parade, and Pop had marched in at least the last 23 parades. But today, I stayed home. As we Brooklyn fans have said for so many years – Next Year! *(05-31-99)*

A Christmas thought: I don't have a list of gifts from you all to us. But the range of the gifts is startling. There is a real sense of real thought in the range. And we take that as a wonderful compliment.

An example. I got some books. One on pro football and its history, another a biography of General Bradley, a Bird book, a travel book on Mexico, a Lincoln book, a review of a battle in Africa and a story about the Boston Tea Party. How's that for range? *(12-27-99)*

Well, here we are! Quite a milestone. It arrived very quietly here. I haven't made any resolutions per se, but I am determined this year to really clean up the basement. Those of you who have braved the stairs to get there can vouch for the mess. *(01-03-00)*

Halloween was a busy night here, partially because we think the word is out that we take a Polaroid shot of visitors. *(11-05-00)*

# The Left Side of the Brain

**"The time each day also saw me in that comfy chair with a book."**

*The* New York Times *asks authors what's their favorite place to read a book. For Pop, it was in his chair, in front of the bay window, and tackling, for the most part, nonfiction—history, current affairs, biography, with anything related to the Civil War at the top of the list. His appreciation for the arts ranged beyond the written word, from opera to choral and big band, performances in the big city or up the road at the school or church. The letters regaled us with the occasional film, either out at the cinema or, even rarer, at home on the small screen. The* New Yorker *cartoon on the fridge was apt—"Don is kind of an intellectual and a regular guy."*

*The Heavy Tome* by John Dickson

I'm just about to finish two books. And I'm in the middle of a few others. I heartily recommend *The Bridge*, which Peter gave to me for Christmas. It's about the building of the Brooklyn Bridge, and it is hard to believe how exciting a story can be about a subject you might consider to be potentially very dull. *(01-07-73)*

I am now reading *The Legend of John Brown*, and it is a huge volume that will probably take quite some time. (Particularly when I slump in the chair and snooze). *(01-14-73)*

Mom and Ann and Pop sort of held the fort here, with the prime entertainment being a TV viewing of "It's a Mad, Mad World." Very intellectual evening. *(01-02-77)*

Pop has just returned from a church concert of sacred music, as part of the 150th birthday of the little church up the road. It was good, but a little heavy on the fiddling of some squeaky Bach stuff. How's that for an appreciative music lover.
I've also been working on Churchill's *History of the English-Speaking Peoples* – but it mainly helps to put me to sleep, rather than to educate me. *(04-02-78)*

Mom and I have been doing some "heavy" reading. At least, the books weigh a lot. She is reading *Trinity* and Pop is working on a Civil War book of some thousand pages. *(09-18-78)*

I also finished a spy book this week and am frankly not too sure who won what. These spy stories, with their subplots and code names, are hard for my simple mind to follow. *(12-10-78)*

Mom finished *Chesapeake* and Pop finished *Six Men*, and am now working on a book about the Irish and English struggles in the late 1500's. Those people could really fight. *(01-21-79)*

Another great feature was the Muppet movie, which we all saw on Monday evening. We went to Marlborough for supper, and then to the Muppets! It was a birthday present for Poppa, and it was Matthew's first movie. And it was good fun. *(08-13-79)*

On Friday, we went up to Annhurst to see the New England Opera's version of Madame Butterfly. After all these years of listening almost daily to records and tapes of Butterfly, Pop saw it! And it was absolutely beautiful. It was enhanced by the fact that Butterfly was a Korean singer, and so the oriental feeling came through clearly. It was a wonderful evening. Even after all these "listenings," the story still brings tears. *(10-29-79)*

Last evening, we went to an organ recital at the Pomfret School, and that building shook with some sensational music. And then we watched "The Sting" on TV. I remember Ann trying to coax me to go see it, and I finally did and thoroughly enjoyed it. And did again last night. *(04-21-80)*

I'm also into the third volume of *Lee's Lieutenants* and have just finished the very detailed chapters on the Battle of Gettysburg – a long sad story for the South and for Lee. *(11-24-80)*

As you all know, Pop listens to a most unusual classical music program each morning from Boston. Yesterday, when the host signed off, he said it was not time for the Hallelujah chorus, but rather time for the famous prayer from Hansel and Gretel. But this morning at 7 AM, he came on and said, "it is time" and he played some great music, including Great Day in the Morning. Thanks be to God. *(01-19-81)*

When Uncle Bob gave me a book on the Yorkshire vet of TV fame, he didn't realize that I would get out the maps and try to retrace some of the towns and places shown in such beautiful color. Nor did he suspect that I would come to the fine conclusion that Mom and I ought to try a trip to that fine land this fall. Probably just dreaming, but that can be fun, too. *(05-04-81)*

I also finished a book on the siege of Vicksburg – pretty grim reading. The largest military cemetery in the US is at Vicksburg, which says something about the losses suffered there. *(11-09-81)*

On Saturday evening, we were in the Pomfret chapel again, this time for the Christmas chorale of the Northeastern Choir group. The music was sensational, but two hours on those oak benches was hard on a few things, including attention. (12-14-82)

I spent some time re-reading Sandburg's *Lincoln.* It's amazing to realize that only a hundred years ago or so, the President's office was open for any citizen to walk into and to chat with The Man. *(01-25-82)*

Mom and I went up to Shrewsbury for an Italian dinner and then to our annual movie – this time "On Golden Pond." We enjoyed it immensely, particularly since we had both read *Fonda.* *(02-01-82)*

Oh yes, last Wednesday was Mozart's birthday! *(02-01-82)*

I spent considerable time reading the series about the potential for nuclear holocaust in the New Yorker. It is heavy reading, but the message is very grim. *(02-22-82)*

Friday, I took off for Otega N.Y. for an antique auction on Saturday morning. I drove through snow, and it was bitter cold there. I spent Friday night in a motel room – never a happy experience, but this time I was buoyed by the television set which had the greatest of all films – "Shane." *(03-29-82)*

Among my acquisitions last week were albums of "The Music Man" and "Fiddler on the Roof." They were two of my favorite shows, and the music has been ringing through the back room since. *(11-08-82)*

I finished Russell Baker's book *Growing Up*, which is about his childhood during the depression. The environments are quite different from Brooklyn and my own experiences, but there were similarities, particularly in the attitudes of adults. Since few people had any money to do anything, he recalls that it was a time of endless talking. People sat around the kitchen table and talked and talked. *(01-10-83)*

Then, after a visit to Barnes & Noble, we refreshed at the Princeton Club and headed downtown to a restaurant called Asti's, that neither one of us had visited in many years – and then under the auspices of expense accounts. This is the place where there is much opera singing by various bartenders, waiters, etc. Lots of fun, and Pop was even recruited for a hooded procession for the Anvil Chorus. *(01-17-83)*

On Friday, we went to the Imperial Cinema in Putnam to see "The Verdict." First, I must report on the walls and there seems to be new carpet on the floor. What a change! The movie was great, but it had an unintended result. It had been my plan to get up early on Saturday and go to an auction in Albany. But I relived the movie all night and when dawn came, I realized how little sleep I had had and dumb it would be to take off for a day of driving and sitting. *(03-14-83)*

The day ended with "The Sting" – one of Pop's favorite movies. The last time I saw it was when we were in Scotland. And I remember being late for dinner so that I could see the card game on the train. *(04-04-83)*

Pop went to the Library of Congress to check out the Playbill from Ford's Theater (Lincoln's assassination). The expert said he thought it might be authentic, which was good news. Further, he took me back to the vault to show me the Library's collection of Lincoln material. Quite an experience. *(04-27-83)*

On another evening, we went to see "Gandhi." It is a long picture – but it was longer for us because the film broke down in the middle and we had a half hour wait. *(05-09-83)*

My favorite morning radio program of classical music had a departure the other morning and had Tom Lehrer as a guest. He is an old singer of ditties that take on the establishment and various political and social dogmas. I only remember one song that had to do with the nuclear movement – entitled "Down by the Old Maelstrom." *(10-11-83)*

And now I am deep into a book *The Nightmare Years 1930-1940* by William Shirer. I remember his radio reports from Europe during those days when the world was staggering to the start of World War II. It makes uncomfortable reading to be reminded of the many times Hitler could have been stopped. *(08-27-84)*

Mom finished her normal two mystery books last week. She is one the library's best customers. I finished a biography of Wendell Wilkie, one of my boyhood heroes. Wilkie started his career as a lawyer in Akron in the '20s. It is hard today to realize that at that time Akron was controlled by the Klan, and there were 400,000 members of the Klan in Ohio. *(09-24-84)*

We went to a movie on Wednesday night – our second this year – and enjoyed it thoroughly. It was "Places in the Heart," and I can't remember when I have been so engrossed in a movie. Just plain great. *(11-13-84)*

A great opera idea! The Met is having a Gala in January that features great singers doing portions of four operas. AND the portions all happen to be the Third Acts – and Mom shouted that she could finally see the end of an opera. Since it starts at 6:30, I might even make it to the end. Our request for tickets is in the mail. *(11-30-86)*

Pop is trying to read a spy story – which means I fall asleep in the evening with the book in my lap. And then I can't remember who did what to whom, and must re-read the next night. And so it goes. *(04-13-87)*

Among other events of the week was the Monday Luncheon Lecture– and this was about Greek and Roman art. It was a slide lecture, (imagine slides after a lunch) and I worked hard to stay awake. *(10-19-87)*

My neighbor Frank Lamb, who was quite a hero with the Marines on Guadalcanal, gave me some books to read on the subject. I had just finished a book on the Civil War, and I was struck by the similarities in the number and tragic scope of poor military leadership. *(11-30-87)*

I am reading Jimmy Carter's book on fishing and hunting. He relates with incredible detail his fishing plans and equipment. Perhaps this attention to detail is a character trait that hurt him at the White House. Incidentally, one of the subs he was on in the Navy was the USS Pomfret! *(07-31-88)*

On the 'presidential front,' I am reading a series in the New Yorker about LBJ, and it is absolutely disgusting to read about this guy. And the Times today had book reviews about two new books about Nixon. Where do we find these guys? *(11-12-89)*

Since I could not stay awake to watch the "Tale of Two Cities," I did the next best (or best) thing, and read the book. I enjoyed it more than most of my recent reading. It was also interesting to read that the first and last sentences of the book were familiar lines: 'It was the best of times, it was the worst of times" . . . and "It is a far, far better thing that I do, than I have ever done." *(12-04-89)*

When you are here, I will probably bore you with my playing of a Tennessee Ernie album of gospel hymns. I can remember my mother playing some of these on the piano in Sunday School. *(12-18-89)*

I forgot to mention in last week's letter that we had gone to see "Driving Miss Daisy" when in Rochester with David and Paula. Did you know that it is a true story of the grandmother of one of Mom's Carleton pals? *(04-09-90)*

And last night we went to see "La Boheme," at least the first act. I think the first act is the best in opera – and that's enough for me. Besides, it's about 9PM, and you know what happens then. *(05-06-90)*

Also, we went to a movie! We saw and enjoyed "Dances With Wolves." And we went to the Lion's Valentine Party. Back to the movie . . . if you see it, perhaps you can tell me how they got the wolf to perform so well. *(02-18-91)*

Actually, a bad storm came by in the evening, and the power went off, so we went out to the camper for some reading. *(06-10-90)*

My reading last week concerned the RJR/Nabisco event (Barbarians at the Gate), and it made for some moments when I could no longer stomach some of the players and their greed. Disgusting. *(09-16-90)*

I have just finished a book called Mother [*Mother; May You Never See The Sights I've Seen*]; I hope you never see what I have seen. It is the story of a regiment from Fitchburg, Mass., that started out with

950 men, and after one year had 100. The details of each man's death, illness, desertion, captivity are full, as are the descriptions of battles and death. Slaughter. *(08-11-91)*

When we visited the Rahr's some weeks ago, David had decorated the guest room with pictures of Nancy Reagan. And he insisted that I take the book. Well, I am about finished with it, and it is very discouraging reading. If 10% – or even 1% is accurate and true, she (and he) are very troubling people – for different reasons. *(10-27-91)*

It pays to read. The Wall St. Journal had an article recently that suggested that one should fight the town tax assessor. And so, I stopped by, (we have recently had a reassessment of all town property), and found that they had us down for 39 acres. Would that it were. But they are going to change the books. *(11-10-91)*

Mom had her Book Club group here for an evening's discussion of *You Just Don't Understand*. No men allowed. At Mom's urging, I have read part of it – and I think I personally am a target of the author. Incidentally, the author is a visiting professor at Princeton. *(11-24-91)*

Mom had her book club here one evening, and the book to be reviewed was Anne Lindberg's *Gift From the Sea*. That has been around a long time, but is still relevant in today's world. *(12-22-91)*

I have been reading *Den of Thieves*, about the Boesky-Milken affair. I felt so sorry when one of the players was cast aside and his salary was reduced from 23 million to a scant 5 million. *(01-05-92)*

We are both doing our classroom reading for the Civil War College in Harper's Ferry. Some of it pretty grisly. One day at Antietam was the worst day in American history for casualties. A slaughter. *(05-03-92)*

I've read so much on the Civil War, and yet we keep learning. Antietam was/still is the bloodiest day in American military history. For the total war, 25% of white Southerners were casualties, and the ratio to population for both sides would mean 5 million casualties today. *(05-13-92)*

Mom gave me a book by Molly Ivins, the columnist for a Dallas paper. It makes great reading as she delivers irreverent jabs at her fellow Texans. She states that the problem with Texas Baptists is "that they don't hold them under water long enough." She describes one legislator "if his IQ slips anymore, they will have to water him twice a day." *(06-22-92)*

I finished the huge book about Truman. It reviews many of his campaigns, particularly the great one in 1948. They were all tough, with lots of charges, but nowhere does it mention charges against wives or families. What the heck is wrong with us now? *(08-24-92)*

Family Values time. In a respite from the sometimes heavy history books that I cherish, I picked up one of Mom's novels. All went fine for a while, but then I entered a series of steamy sex interludes. Good grief. *(09-13-92)*

Mom had a Book Club meeting, I went to Spags, and we both finished some books. My book was about George Bush. . . . Why do I do it to myself? *(10-04-92)*

Mom and I are going to an Alumni College in October on the environment. The textbook has to do with the diversity of life, and it is a real struggle. *(09-24-93)*

It was a revival of "Jesus Christ Superstar," and I'm afraid I didn't realize it was a rock musical. From the first blast of music, I realized

I was in trouble. The amplifiers in the pit were huge, and each performer had his/her own microphone. The noise was deadening. We left at the intermission. *(11-16-93)*

Last evening, we went to see "Schindler's List." To me, a fine movie (I only try one a year), too long, but utterly gripping. There were parts that I was tempted to leave the theater. If I can't stand it, how can the Germans? *(04-10-94)*

One of my Sunday hobbies is to check the wedding notices to find unusual name combinations. Today's candidate was the marriage of Amy Udo to Howard Fine, and from henceforth she will be known as Amy Udo Fine. *(09-25-94)*

Back to the Old Values? I'm reading a book about Paul Revere, and I learn that in colonial New England one-third of all children were born out of wedlock. Good Grief! *(10-09-94)*

I have finished a biography of Justice Hugo Black of the Supreme Court. I can remember my father being very angry about his appointment. But Hugo became a strong defender of the Bill of Rights – and read and re-read all of the proceedings of the group that wrote them. I was going to quote one of his opinions in a case that had to do with Loyalty Oaths – but I will just repeat the last sentence . . . loyalty comes from a love of good government, not fear of a bad one. *(01-22-95)*

Among the books read here last week was a book lent to me from Peter about a regiment that had personally killed 38,000 Jews. These 500 men were older, family men. Why? *(01-29-95)*

We have just come back from a concert by the Northeast Concert Choir group, in a program billed as 'Psalms, Hymns, and Inspirational

Music.' Well, the last, and major piece was a bone rattling thing by Leonard Bernstein with organ, drums, harp, and a great choir. But hard on the ear (and stomach). *(04-30-95)*

Surprise! Mom finally got me to watch "Sleepless in Seattle." I had been enjoying the music background on a gift CD. I did enjoy the film, so much so that I watched it a second time. *(07-31-95)*

Mom had a library board meeting. And she must have read a dozen books. Because of the weather, it was a book week. Quote of the week, from a baseball book: Yogi Berra, who said, "Yeah, we may lose again tomorrow. But not with the same guys." *(08-1-95)*

These are obviously days for reading. One of the books is entitled *Reporting World War II*, and it is discouraging to read the bulletins by reporters in 1938 and onward about what the Germans were doing to the Jews, and what they said they were going to do. It was common knowledge, and we did nothing. *(01-07-96)*

Since I use the treadmill these days (boring), I listen to books on audio tapes. One book has been *500 Nations*, a review of Indian tribes in North America. The Serbs didn't invent ethnic cleansing. The horror stories of the missionaries in Mexico and California and the endless pressures of Messrs. Grant, Sherman and Sheridan after the Civil War are not one of our finest hours. *(01-07-96)*

I am reading a new book about Lincoln. After all the books that I have read about Abe, you might think there was nothing new to report. There is a long section about the Lincoln-Douglas debates, and I recall my visit to the Library of Congress some years ago. . . . I also remember the thrill when the curator took me back into the vaults and showed me the original notes of Lincoln and Douglas for those debates. *(03-17-96)*

Pop was reading a newspaper story about the early advent of Lyme ticks when he looked down at his hand and saw . . . a Lyme tick. *(04-21-96)*

Friday night we went to Opera New England's presentation of the musical "Can Can" – a rather strange subject. I attribute many of my gripes to my age (I think), but I really am bothered by the assault on the ears of microphones and amplifiers in theaters. We sat in the back row, and the noise was deafening. *(11-17-96)*

Also, on books. Mom got a little book about Grandmas. One page said: My Grandmother started walking five miles a day when she was 60. She's 97 now, and we don't know where the hell she is. *(01-05-97)*

Another book was on the tobacco business. 763 pages of mind-boggling detail. Two items: the chairman of RJR belonged to 26 golf clubs and built a ten-plane air force with 36 pilots. And a lawyer in New Jersey, with a secretary and a paralegal fought the companies for four years, against 100 lawyers and staff. He lost. He spent 3 million; they spent 100 million. Tough reading. *(01-19-97)*

The time each day also saw me in that comfy chair with a book. I finished a great book about the Civil War, a novel about an airplane, and am back to learning more about the Islam nation. A few weeks ago, the Times had a story about the "hated Presidency of Bill Clinton." If anybody would read the papers and editorials about Abe Lincoln, they would know about hatred. *(02-15-97)*

Early on Sunday mornings for these many years, I have listened to an hour-long program from Boston of a classical music lecture by a Prof. Du Nord (sp?) from Northeastern University, who has sat at the piano, along with recordings, and has enthralled me with his chatter. Today's program ended with a statement that it had been recorded and was in his memory. Sad. *(11-09-97)*

I finished a Christmas book. A biography by Bishop Paul Moore about his career in Jersey City, Indianapolis, Washington and New York. If you thought Mom is a liberal, Paul Moore was much further to the Left. I can't imagine that the folks in Indiana called him to be dean of the cathedral. Of interest was his comment that during his first year there, he and his wife were not invited out by a parishioner once. And this is a guy with enormous wealth. He also remembers Eli Lilly coming to see him and saying, "You can paint this building pink with yellow polka dots . . . and I will still support you." *(01-05-98)*

I also read many pages from a Christmas book about Jim Herriot, the Yorkshire Vet. Ann gave me my first book about Jim Herriot many years ago, and at first I was puzzled by the choice. But I have come to love his stories. Because of this, Mom and I spent a week in Yorkshire some years ago and it is such beautiful country. We stayed at a country-inn, where we met a couple from northern Scotland. I remember our departure where Olive, an artist, came across the cobblestone courtyard, kissed me, and gave me a watercolor of a flower. Treasured. *(01-11-98)*

And this afternoon, we watched "Fried Green Tomatoes." I read the book, we both saw the film, and last night Mom watched the tape, and we both had a question about a character. I still do. *(01-18-98)*

Also, for the zillionth time, I've re-read Andrew's booklet for our 50th. I know, I know, I am just re-reading parts of my own Weekly Letters, but it is still joyous. *(02-01-98)*

It's reading time. I am working (poor word) on a wonderful biography of Teddy Roosevelt (800 pages!), a baseball story, and a history of the Jews. How's that for diversity? *(06-28-98)*

I am reading a remarkable book entitled *Letters of a Nation*. There are about 400 letters to and from presidents, from soldiers in various wars, from Indians, from farmers etc. Fascinating reading. Also, Mom bought a book of health care hints entitled *Age Protectors*. I could have used it when I was in my 40's or 50's. *(08-09-98)*

I also signed up at the Community College for a short course on Shakespeare's Henry IV. With all the books in our library, including one on his plays, there is nothing on Henry. *(09-21-98)*

Lots of reading. I pulled a big book from the library titled *The Two Ocean War*. Written by a naval historian, it describes the events of World War II. A reader becomes very aware how close we came to losing both the Atlantic and Pacific struggles. During the low points there are many stories of heroism. *(11/28/99)*

I too am a regular reader of the obits. Some of them make good reading. But one last week really surprised me. It led off with the woman's name and age, and then said, "died while brushing her teeth." Good Grief. *(10/15/00)*

You know that I read the Times closely. A recent issue had a small ad as follows: Anniversaries. Mr. and Mrs. Gregory were married November 17, 1990. They have a daughter Hayley and a dog Marley. They now reside in Charlotte N. C. He is a stud entrepreneur, and she is a hot babe. *(12/03/00)*

# Friends, along the way

**"My advice? Look out for friends. . . . They may be hiding close by."**

*Interesting tidbit. As Pop aged, the amount of space dedicated to friends and neighbors in these letters grew. Part of it was that my mother and he kept in touch with people from the many places they lived. Much of the typewriter ink detailed their illnesses and then obituaries. Another part was that the longer they stayed and the more involved they were in Pomfret, the more friends they had—neighbors, doctors, school faculty, church parishioners, and members of Pop's luncheon groups that were affectionately called The Old Goats and the Intellect Club. And, as often as possible, he filled us in on every visit with Mrs. Casendino, a woman who worked in our house in Chester, New Jersey, and became a fixture in our lives from that point on.*

*Maple Syrup* by Jim Nealon

Sad news. Mr. Hugger was killed in an auto accident in Cincinnati. He was just weeks away from retirement and a new marriage. As you may know, he was one of the very first employees of American Airlines. It seems hard to believe that both Mr. and Mrs. Hugger are gone. When Mom and I moved to Cincinnati, and began our life on the wonderful Fleischmann farm, our closest friends (and helpers!) were the Huggers. Such friends really have great meaning in life. Watch out for these friendships as they arrive and sustain them. *(01-07-73)*

Billie Smith (nee Rowland) and her husband were with us from Tuesday to Friday. Wednesday (Pop took the day off) evening we went to Silvermine Inn for dinner and Thursday we went to a Chinese restaurant in Ridgefield. Since they had both lived·in China (Mr. Smith for 45 years), they are experts on the food. Mr. Smith cleared the table of utensils, ordered the food, and Pop struggled through about ten courses with shaky chopsticks. *(06-24-74)*

Our social life was marked by a spectacular dinner that Mom put together for the White's on Friday night. It was a most pleasant evening, and Mr. White has the heartiest laugh around, but he's also a night person. And so-o-o, when Pop climbed the stairs early Saturday morning, he had a big pumpkin stem growing where his hair used to be. *(02-23-76)*

We went to [*our*] first social event in Pomfret. The postmistress of Pomfret Center had us to their annual Christmas "bags," and it was a delightful and colorful collection of townspeople. I had good discussions with a member of the sanding crew, a man who ran against Abe Ribicoff and the owner of the local liquor store. Nice people. And, as you might suspect, we will be known forever as the people who live in the old golf course house. *(12-12-76)*

Speaking of neighbors, when Pop asked the Dean at Princeton for permission to marry this fantastic girl, he suggested that I talk also with the Asst. Chaplain – Burton MacLean. Well, he is now the new headmaster of Pomfret School. I stopped by to see him the other day, and while he didn't remember me, it was still fun to talk about great old days. I told him I still loved the girl – even more so. *(02-07-77)*

Mr. Nelson came by yesterday with his tractor and cut the high weeds near the garden and between the blacktop and the shed. He got stuck a few times in the deep holes, and I feared that he was going to break either his neck or the tractor – but he finished the job. *(08-28-77)*

On Monday, Mom went down to Wilton for a surprise party by her sewing group for Mrs. Anderson – designed to replenish some of the clothes and stuff that the Andersons lost in their fire. *(03-26-78)*

Life is unpredictable, yesterday afternoon, when Pop drove in here after a long, long Reunion, there was a strange auto, and in the house were three visitors – Mr. and Mrs. Wright and CIII! [*neighbors in Cincinnati*] What a surprise. The Wright's original one night stay has been extended at our demand so we could "visit" longer. Such great friends! *(06-05-78)*

Last Sunday we had a visit from the French's, who lived here and who ran the golf course. He came over to point out some of the outside water connections. We had been warned that he was a crusty old Yankee, but it turned out otherwise, and we had a pleasant visit and they exclaimed over and over again about the changes we have made to this old place. *(05-07-79)*

This is the weekend of the Woodstock Fair, and the road has been mighty busy. This morning there have been lots of horse trailers going up the road, so I guess there must be some special horse events today.

On Saturday, Mom, David, Paula, and Matthew went up for a tour and they said it was jammed. Well, it was a great day for a fair. *(09-03-79)*

One sad note of the week was that Mr. Blodgett had a heart attack on Thanksgiving morning. He is out of the intensive care unit, and Pop visited him yesterday and he seemed in good shape and good spirits. This will change his lifestyle drastically, since he is the handyman for a couple homes around here. *(12-01-80)*

Thursday night we went to a Lion's testimonial dinner for one George Boss of this fine town. George is 73 and the ultimate do-gooder. He dresses in Indian clothes for all sorts of Boy Scout functions, is Santa Claus at all the schools, cuts the grass for the Congregational Church and various town properties, sells raffle tickets endlessly to the unwary, runs the Lions Club birdseed operation, and along the way he and his wife have raised and adopted about a dozen retarded children. It's a good thing the world has such saints. We need them. *(02-16-81)*

Paul Nelson gave us a small jar of maple syrup that he and his boys had made from sap collected on their trees. We had some yesterday morning – the elixir of the gods! *(03-23-81)*

Friday night, we went to the Follies for the Community School, with a variety of amateur acts, such as a recitation, a guy playing a saw (great), a grand dame singing (awful) and a dozen Lions in drag as a chorus line (awful – but fun). *(03-28-83)*

There was a hearing one night on a proposal to put in a used car lot up the road. It was poorly advertised (by design?) and only eight people showed up. Pop was the only negative vote, and for this I was mentioned on the local radio broadcast. *(11-05-84)*

Mr. Thayer lives on! We have a fine young man in the area who has just started at Yale under tough financial circumstances. And so, Mom and I have made an anonymous contribution to his education. *(09-02-85)*

The Storm had been less than anticipated but still did plenty of damage here – mostly to trees and power lines. . . . We have good neighbors. Paul Nelson came with a chain and his truck opened the driveway, and John Rauh came with a chain saw and cut the tree into manageable pieces. And Paul returned with his generator to help with our freezer, but we suspect we lost some stuff. *(09-30-85)*

We went to a party on New Year's Eve. We really did. Actually, I had my pajamas on at 9PM but Mom was intent, and so I happily changed, and we went up the road to a party. I broke some sort of record by staying up till 11:30 – and was in the bunk when the new year rolled in. *(01-06-86)*

Did you know that all of the sails for all of the boats in the Cup races in Australia were made in Putnam? Unbeknownst to us, there is a small outfit in Putnam that specializes in sail finishing. *(10-26-86)*

We went to some parties last week. One was given by Dr. Elmen of the church, and it was marked by his falling from a chair, and his wooden leg scooting across the floor. *(01-05-87)*

Pop went to his first meeting of the new Agricultural Land Use Committee (how's that for a Brooklyn boy?), and it was marked by a blast and resignation from one of the members, using an obscenity. I returned the word plus a few thoughts. *(01-13-87)*

We went to the annual faculty play at Pomfret School on Friday night. They are always good fun. This year it was "Bye Bye Birdie." *(01-19-87)*

We joined in a potluck supper at the church on Thursday evening, prior to a service. These suppers are my downfall. No resistance. *(04-20-87)*

We may be getting something new in Pomfret. A prison. This frightening news came because a farmer has offered his land to the State that has the usual problem of locating a new prison. If you think the average guy is distressed, how about the developer across the road from the farm who is currently putting up seventy homes for sale? *(09-14-87)*

Pomfret has a museum! Saturday afternoon was the dedication ceremonies for the Grist Mill and Blacksmith Shop in the red building at the entrance to Mashmoquet Park. A remarkable job has been done. The program listed Pop as a 'woodworker,' but the work was really done by David, who built two large display cases. They look great. *(09-21-87)*

The Putnam fire was something to behold. It occurred just as I was reaching town for some errands and involved a huge old mill complex. Various small companies had located there, including a welding operation and some with chemical stores. It was a chemical explosion that started it, and explosions continued all day. Twelve fire companies responded, and the buildings were a total loss. Happily, no one was hurt. But poor Putnam has suffered another reverse. *(12-08-87)*

One evening we went to a meeting of citizens who want to have Route 169 designated as a scenic route. Mom and I are the finance co-chairmen, and I guess that means more fund-raising. *(06-27-88)*

The Pan Am tragedy hit this town. A family, who lives in Plainfield but go to our church, lost a daughter. As did another family that we know from their great work in the Democratic Party. *(12-26-88)*

A tragedy was played out here last week. A local judge was up for re-appointment, but he had a record of alcoholism. His expected re-appointment was challenged by Mothers Against Drink Driving, including some of his neighbors. He withdrew and then committed suicide. The memorial service was held at the Data General auditorium, with about 1,000 people present, including the governor, all of the judges from the state, oodles of lawyers, and those of us who never knew him. A sad tale. *(02-13-89)*

Renewed-faith-in-mankind story. On Monday evening, during some snow, a little car skidded down the hill and plunged over our wall. I went out and the young man said he would come back and repair the wall. Well, he came the next morning, surveyed the damage, and the following day, he showed up with a partner and they put the wall back together. *(03-26-89)*

Wednesday evening was a town meeting to vote on an additional appropriation for the new school building. It included an exchange between Pop and the architect who I charged with double-talk and with 'lecturing' us as if we were bumpkins. A real smart ass. *(04-17-89)*

The Alumni Weekly this week carried the notice that Dick Deupree from Indian Hill (moved to Scottsdale) had died. Dick took me under his wing when we moved to Indian Hill, and one of his suggestions one time was that he sponsor us for membership in the Camargo Club. Little did he know that we were having a tough time paying the grocer's bills. *(05-08-89)*

I am a member of a local committee to plan the retirement party for our school principal – and we had our first meeting. It will be an emotional affair, since Bob has multiple sclerosis, and is going downhill rather fast. *(07-10-89)*

The week ended with a burst last night (at least my letter writing week) with a retirement dinner for our School Principal. Pop worked on the affair, and it was a resounding success. Because of Bob Glenn's poor health, (multiple sclerosis), we worried about the mood, but we shouldn't have. Over the years, Bob Glenn was one of the absolutely worst story tellers imaginable, and all the terrible jokes came back to haunt him last night. It therefore turned out to be quite a hilarious evening. *(10-16-89)*

Mom went to a town meeting to discuss the Roadway company's plan to build a tandem trailer facility across from the school. You can imagine the passions released by such a subject. Interestingly, the opponents do not have a single bit of legal support. To thicken the plot, the guy who owns the land is a wealthy character who moved to Florida to save on taxes, and he complains about the newcomers denying him his birthright to do what he wants to do with his land. *(10-22-89)*

Yesterday, Paul Nelson came by in his ancient truck (49 Ford) and we went to a nearby farm and loaded it with three-foot-long logs for the fireplace. I have had good neighbors here and there, but Paul is some guy. *(11-20-89)*

On Wednesday, I drove down to White Plains to pick up my buddy, Bob Glenn, from a rehab center connected with NY Hospital. He is in bad shape, and three hours in a car with a guy who wants to talk but is so hard to understand can be frustrating, mostly for him. They have changed his diagnosis from MS to some form of nerve disease. The prognosis was bad for MS. . . . It's even worse for this new syndrome. *(11-27-89)*

We sat here last night talking about past New Year's Eves, and I remarked about one we had shared with the Wright's . . . and then the phone rang, and it was Mrs. Wright. *(01-01-90)*

Before we left for Tortola, I had planned to write to Phoebe Dunn, widow of my old pal Tristram, and who had sent us a nice, long Christmas note. But I didn't get to it. And we read in the paper that Phoebe and her daughter were on a Costa Rican airliner that crashed . . . no survivors. *(02-05-90)*

We also went to a church supper and service on Thursday, and of course to the big Easter service yesterday. And yesterday was the party that almost wasn't. To join the Rectory boys who we have each year for Easter dinner, we had asked some others to join us. But one couple had to back out due to a family problem, Cousin Rell called to say she had to change her plans, and then there were no Rectory boys. So, Mom and I and Phyllis Smith sat down to a huge feed. It was an unusual but pleasant afternoon. *(04-16-90)*

Saturday was graduation day at both Pomfret and Rectory schools. We took the overflow from the McCobbs up the hill. This place was packed on Friday night. Every bed was occupied, as well as two bunks in the camper, plus one sleeping bag in the field. I don't know how people handle the bed and breakfast business on a full-time basis. It's a real chore, and of course, most of the work belongs to Mom. But the guests are mighty nice people, and that makes it a little easier. A little. *(06-03-90)*

We learned the details of the fire at the Nelsons last week. It seems that Matthew (16) and a pal were in the room above the garage/barn with sparklers, when one fell into a box of fireworks. I suspect the real fireworks came when Paul Nelson arrived home that night. *(08-19-90)*

Friday was the dedication of the new school addition named for Bob Glenn. Also, an announcement was made of the gift by an anonymous donor (?) of the Bob Glenn scholarship for students from the Community School to attend the Pomfret School. It was a very moving event, with quite a few tears, as Bob continues his slide in health. *(11-04-90)*

The mails have brought many cards and letters from old friends. It also brought a book from Billie Rowland whom I hope you remember from Indian Hill. It is basically an autobiography, with emphasis on her years in China, Japan, India and Europe. We were close to Billie, but I have learned many things about journeys. *(12-24-90)*

On a happier note, Paul Nelson had twin calves born last week. It is an unusual event. *(02-18-91)*

Sign of the times . . . one of the best volunteers in past Cancer drives cannot do it this year because her husband has lost his job and she has taken on two jobs. *(03-11-91)*

The big news locally is The Robbery. A house at Four Corners, (near the Vanilla Bean Cafe), and the elderly sister of Mrs. Blodgett, was 'cleaned out' one night. The police estimate that four people did the job, which included moving an antique highboy down the stairs, and removing jewelry from her bedroom while she slept. *(08-11-91)*

We went down to Essex for a visit and lunch with the Tuckers. They are both in their 80's, and Luther's eyesight ain't so good, but they are a remarkable pair. Luther has this great laugh, and he had folks turning around during our lunch at the yacht club. And despite his great wealth, he drives a secondhand station wagon, and a 25-year-old VW. They were both angry with Mr. Bush on a variety of subjects. We made plans to stay with them in Indian Hill during our western trip. *(08-17-91)*

There is an interesting question or thought here. There are such good friends, e.g., the Rahrs, the Eanes, the Tuckers, that mean so much to us now. But there must be others that we have met along the way, and what have we missed by not trying to be as close? *(09-29-91)*

We have a good friend in this town who has a few bucks and is putting them to good use. One of his projects is a project called Study Circle Resources Center, which attempts to duplicate the old neighborhood discussion groups. We went to a trial session of a group meeting on the subject of "Are there moral justifications for the use of military force?" This week's subject is on Homelessness, which may be a tough one for him, since his daughter in London was working on that subject when she started to come home on Pan Am 103. *(11-17-91)*

Last night we went to a 'celebration' party for the Selectman who won, and whose finances I sort of managed. It was a small group, made smaller by the fact that the main guest forgot to put it on his calendar. And so, they arrived late after a reminder phone call. *(11-24-91)*

We went to the Lions Christmas party last night. It is such a great cross section of life, and we always remember the small (but nice) circles that we enjoyed in other homes – but the wide variety here seems very special. *(12-16-91)*

And we took part in another Study Circle Group. This time the subject was Welfare, and we reviewed four options ranging from having the government do more to killing all welfare programs. This, of course, meant that we had to consider the idea of 'my brother's keeper' and what our obligations as citizens were. A lively discussion. We went back to the Aicher's yesterday noon for a brunch and then into the fields to pick and cut a Christmas tree. *(12-16-91)*

We went to Hank's for supper via a gift certificate and splurged on a once-per-month piece of beef. It is so good – and so big. And then to the annual faculty stage show at the Pomfret School. I don't know who has more fun – the faculty in their outrageous roles or the students who scream at the antics on stage. *(01-12-92)*

I got a call from our friend and my old pal in Scouting – Will Ludwig. When they pass out halos, I am sure he should get one. He has taken care of his multiple sclerosis wife for about twenty years. Some time ago, she fell from her little cart, broke a leg and was in the hospital for six weeks. And now, Will along with three nurses are trying to cope with her at home. To top it off, and it reveals much about the guy . . . I have never heard him complain. *(04-19-92)*

For the last few years, we have had a local debate about a thing called KELP – a wood burning plant in Killingly sponsored by a Pomfret citizen who is a close pal of Jesse Helms (that is an unauthorized editorial comment). Many of us have fought it, because it meant trucking in 200 loads of wood each day and pouring junk into the atmosphere. In a bizarre piece of government, they have folded their tent, and the state has agreed to pay the towns their legal fees ($800,000) that they spent to fight the project, but also to reimburse, with profit, the developers. To find the money, each consumer of the local utility will pay 36 cents each month for a year. Ralph Nader, where are you? *(05-31-92)*

Memorial Day was a busy time here. Pop spent part of the morning helping with the Soup Kitchen preparations, then marched in the parade with the Lions. It is a given that such ceremonies must have the loudspeaker system go flooey – and it did. *(05-31-92)*

First, some sad news. Bob Glenn, retired school principal and good friend, died on Saturday. His last five years were spent almost totally helpless and speechless from a terrible disease. Pop will be a pallbearer. I cannot conceive how they are going to get all the people into the church. *(06-08-92)*

Bob Glenn's funeral was on Wednesday. The town virtually shut down. As a pall bearer, I went to the wake, and to the very emotional time at the funeral home before the church service. There were so many people outside the church, and it was a long, long service. The pall bearers included a couple guys with by-passes, and a few others with operations here and there. And the casket was heavy-very heavy. Bob was buried in the cemetery across the road, and afterwards there was a buffet lunch at the school prepared by the teachers and the PTO that had enough food for the Fifth Army. *(06-14-92)*

With the whole nation cutting back on gas stations, Pomfret is about to have a new one! Citgo is about to open a fancy new station along with a general store. *(09-20-92)*

And on Friday, I drove to Wilton to see Herb Salter, who is slowly and painfully succumbing to pancreatic cancer. We always thought the cigarettes would be his undoing, and he has a dozen years of endless operations on eyes, heart, etc. He is still smoking, but now it doesn't make any difference. He is down to about 70 pounds, in a wheelchair, but his humor hasn't changed. *(09-27-92)*

We went down to Philadelphia for Ruth Ludwig's funeral. It was a little puzzling, in that there was very little emotion – perhaps everybody was wrung out after 30 years of coping with the multiple sclerosis, and my own judgment is that there was even some relief that the suffering was over. And here's a poor soul whose body and face has been terribly distorted, and the casket is open. The casket was the biggest thing I have ever seen, and the heaviest, since I was a pallbearer. Finally, the white stretch Cadillac limousines seemed kind of gross, I have written instructions as to how I want to depart, and if you don't follow them, I promise you I will come back to haunt you. *(10-04-92)*

I have just come back from an organ/choir concert at the Pomfret

School. It was spectacular. It was long. Just when I thought it had ended, I found that there was a page two to the program. And those oak benches are hard. *(02-21-93)*

On the local scene, the big news was the break-in at the Nelsons. Amazing. Here is a house on the road with four family members with varied and unpredictable schedules, and yet sometime after 10 AM on Wednesday someone broke in, ransacked the downstairs, and made off with a bundle of cash. *(04-18-93)*

While reviewing medical news, I should comment about George Faunce. George preceded me as chairman of the Alumni Council. Those of us who worked with George wondered which part of his body would go first because of his heavy smoking, drinking, eating etc. Well, it was the kidneys – plus diabetes. He is now (I talked to him and to his wife last week) on dialysis with nurses, and with a leg amputation. A sad story, but he was chipper in our talk. *(04-25-93)*

And last night we went to the Lion's Man of the Year dinner, with Newell Hale as the most deserved recipient. Pop had the honor of reading the proclamation from the State Assembly. This morning, we went to a youth group breakfast at the church. The menu had all the wrong things. And strong coffee. *(05-09-93)*

We had a town referendum in which the town budget passed – an important item was the purchase of a town truck, but the school budget was defeated. The school budgets in most of the towns near here have all been defeated. This says something about our priorities. *(06-06-93)*

Mom is at church for the ordination service of the Rectory School's Headmaster's wife as a priest. It has not been without controversy among some of the more conservative folks, and Mom has gone to the service to add her support. Naturally. *(06-13-93)*

Also, they had a motorcycle rally at the Fair, and almost every motorcycle in the eastern US went by here today. *(08-29-93)*

I went to an Old Goats Conference, a group of about a dozen mostly retired businessmen. I was shocked by the level of feelings, even hatred, against Bill Clinton. But then, I looked at their resumes, and they were heavily in the insurance business. *(10-03-93)*

This week brings Election Day, and Mom has been busy on the phone in get-out-the vote calls. Paul Nelson and John Rauh just stopped by. . . . They are running on the Republican ticket for the Board of Finance and Board of Education. Our big hope is that our man, Tom Pahl, wins in the race for Selectman. *(10-31-93)*

That evening I had dinner with my pal from the agency days – Ed Dooley, better known as the last angry Irishman. It was sad. Ed is about to move to Malibu to be near a daughter – and he will need her. Just a few years ago, Ed was a vigorous tennis buff, and now he is a hunched old man. He has arthritis in the back, has just finished a prostate operation . . . but he still is the last Irish angry man. A wonderful friend. *(11-07-93)*

Elections? Tom Pahl, our candidate, won. It was a busy day here at Democratic headquarters. Our good Republican friends, Paul Nelson and John Rauh both won terms on the Boards of Finance and Education. *(11-07-93)*

My pal, Dave Rahr was there, and we had some wonderful time together, including a three-hour breakfast. Dave had a back operation last summer that had the unhappy result of cutting a nerve to his leg, so that he drags his foot. Dave stunned me with the news that he had set aside a fund in his will for a perpetual gift to Annual Giving honoring four of his Tiger buddies – including Pop. Talk about immortality! I then had lunch with Leighton Laughlin. As the days go by, these old friendships seem so much more important. *(12-05-93)*

There is a group in this area that believes (and probably is) the cream of society. Of all things, it is a boat club . . . with no boats. We got a nice letter advising us that we were invited to be members. I have just written a letter thanking them profusely for the honor, but that I had an age-old quirk that says that I don't belong to any club etc. that has a peer review. So, when you or your kin wonder where you got a stubborn streak: remind them of Pop. *(12-12-93)*

Mom went to a Christmas tea at the McCobbs one afternoon (no men invited), and we went to party at the lawyer's offices. While there, I saw Jeff Davis talking to a few people, including one woman who seemed to be his wife, Nini. So, I came up, hugged her and learned that it was not Nini. I told her that there were plenty of lawyers around if she wanted to start a harassment proceeding. *(12-19-93)*

The piles of snow along the road have moved my daily walk inside . . . on the treadmill. It does the job, but it can be boring. And no cars to wave at. *(01-10-94)*

My plan on Thursday was to drive in the camper to Hanover and take Gil Ferguson to Boston for her back operation. But, on Monday, she had a massive stroke. We talked to Doug Ferguson today, and she is to be transferred to a rehab center near Boston this week. She is paralyzed on her right side and can't talk but the doctors are encouraged by her progress. *(01-16-94)*

We went to the annual meeting of the church today. Not very encouraging. The Sunday School is a disaster, volunteers are scarce for the altar guild, the youth group, etc., and pledges are down. My suggestion that a church with a 3/4 million dollar endowment that spent 90% of its funds on itself was part of the problem was met with a polite silence. I am always amazed by the response that a church is 'like a business that needs to be prepared for rainy days.' For my part, the rainy days are here. Just read the daily paper. *(01-30-94)*

It takes all kinds dep't. One morning about 3AM I awoke to an idling engine on the road. When I got up later, I saw about twenty large cartons of rubbish dumped on the road and grass. *(02-08-94)*

Sad news. Ellery Baker, who owned the nursery at the top of the hill, died last week. He had been plowing in his truck, came in for a rest, and had a heart attack. He was the classic Yankee – a quiet, good man. He will be missed. *(02-13-94)*

Rich and Cindi were here. Do you know who they are? Well, I had forgotten, too. Their car broke down some months ago, and we helped them with phone calls etc. And yesterday, they stopped by with a plant, and many thank yous. *(2-20-94)*

We made a trip to see Mrs. Ferguson. The therapists believe she is making real progress. And we watched a session where they were working to get her to move her arm. The great concern is that the muscles will atrophy. And I learned that in these stroke cases that the last part to return is the speech. But Gil said Gosh and Damn at two points. It was a poignant moment when we left and I asked her, in her wheelchair, where she would like to go, and she said 'home.' So, there is some progress. *(04-10-94)*

Paul Nelson came by with his tractor and dragged the big limbs to the back '40.' Paul just doesn't work on a problem, he attacks it. He tore off with his tractor dragging these big limbs, got stuck in the mud, but finally finished the job. A great neighbor. *(04-17-94)*

She [*Mom*] also went to a Board of Education meeting, filled with rancor (not Mom – the meeting). As in many towns, a very vocal right-wing group has taken over the Republican Town Committee and filled some of the Board slots with zealots. It is very divisive. John Rauh is Chairman of the Board and has infinite patience. *(05-01-94)*

I picked many raspberries and blueberries. I delivered one of the baskets to the home of a retired minister, whose wife has had an absolutely awful case of cancer. I remember this handsome, tall woman at the 8 o'clock service, head wrapped in a turban. Dick told me, it was a matter of hours. And it was. Courage, courage. *(07-24-94)*

We spent an overnight with the Gibsons in New Hartford. We had a great time. And once again proved the ancient maxim that Pop doesn't want to go . . . but enjoys himself once there. *(08-14-94)*

We got a long letter from Billie Rowland (Smith), in which she described a long trip to Israel. Billie is 85 – a remarkable person. Speaking of Israel, I was impressed by one of Mr. Rabin's comments, to wit, "One does not make peace with friends, one makes peace with enemies." *(09-12-94)*

I went to Boston and took Mrs. Ferguson out to lunch. I think she is doing better physically, for she can shuffle along better with her right foot. But the communication problem persists. Most of the chatter involves a yes or no. The words just don't come. *(10-02-94)*

We went to 4:30 Christmas Eve service at the church – jammed with children. It is one of the few services that I sit at the rear of the church. For it is a candlelight service, and I want to be near an exit with all the children and their candles. *(12-26-94)*

We have talked to each of your households during the past few days. That's always a good event, but too much of the talk this time was about an unhappy event . . . Mom's fall on the ice. You now know all the details. After all the pain killers from the hospital, she is now slowly 'coming out of it.' But she still hurts. Thank goodness nothing was broken. A minor but interesting sidelight came from Ann Navarro, who brought a jug of chicken soup. Ann, a nurse at the Pomfret School, said that half of the EMT group (there were a dozen here) were special ed. students. And here they were, in the middle of the night, performing a great civic function. *(01-08-95)*

Mrs. Casendino called today. We have known the Casendinos for some thirty plus years, and she now calls us Don and Georganna. It takes time. *(01-29-95)*

Today was the Lion's pancake breakfast. It is billed as a mid-winter social event, and it surely is. Pop's job this year was as cashier and ticket-taker – usually reserved for the elderly and infirm. Do I fit? I suspect so. *(02-05-95)*

I had a fascinating day visiting in Rhode Island with a couple from the church. The Paquettes both taught in Turkey before the war, got married, and decided to take the long way home. They landed in Manila in December of '41, were interned, and spent four years in a prison camp. Last Tuesday was Rosemary's birthday, and also the 50th anniversary of their release from prison camp. She has Parkinson's disease and Bill has Alzheimer's. She has a small apartment at one end of the complex, and he is 'locked in' at the other. Last fall, he wandered off and broke his ankle. They see each other for meals, and the affection was good for the heart. Here is a couple that has truly showed us what values are, and they are in trouble. *(02-26-95)*

Mom had a busy week of meetings. She attended a Board of Education meeting one night, where the Board wrestled with the problem of cutbacks, primarily due to a vocal and also vote-carrying group that has refused to submit to any tax increases. Among the messages of that night is that Pomfret is 99th of 169 towns in the state in terms of some measure of wealth, and 169th in terms of spending per student. *(03-12-95)*

It is almost 60 years since four guys named Dickson, Lemaire, Ludwig and Norton joined Boy Scout Troop 87 and were assigned to the Blazing Arrow Patrol. We have sort of kept in touch. This morning, a phone call told me that Al Lemaire had suddenly died. A classic case of a guy who had really never been sick – and boom! *(05-21-95)*

May 29, 1995 Memorial Day – Observed
Except that we did not observe Memorial Day. And in Pomfret, it's a bigger day than any other. Half the town marches, and the other half watches. There are Lions (the sponsors), Girl Scouts, Brownies, Boys Scouts, Little Leaguers, Fire Engines, Ambulances, Horses, Sheep, National Guard, an Air Guard fly-over, etc. And the inevitable recitation of the Gettysburg Address by Howard Baker, now in his '90's, and afterwards, many people will say, this may be Howard's last year . . . and we have been hearing that since we moved here. *(05-29-95)*

Mom spent many hours at the Muir's house helping to sort out and price furniture and stuff. They move to Naples next month. Last night, we had a party for eighteen of their friends. A happy evening, for an unhappy move, at least for us. Dr. Muir has been a super doctor and friend. *(06-18-95)*

This is the week of the Special Olympics, and Connecticut has gone all out. I hope the national coverage has been good. Each town has a banner proclaiming their hospitality. Putnam has a banner for their hosting the athletes from St. Kitts-Nevis. The Pomfret School is the host for a group from Spain. There are 4,000 athletes from 140 countries – the largest sports event in the world this year. *(07-02-95)*

This town is still debating the subject of the education budget. At a meeting the other night, Mom complained to the radio interviewer that he talked only to the opposers, and not to those who supported the budget. And so, she was on the radio the next morning. Good for Mom. *(07-02-95)*

The Lemaire internment at Arlington. It was hard to believe, and harder to describe. Al was an enlisted man for four years in the Navy, but apparently stayed on and became an officer in the Naval Reserve. In indescribable heat, a Navy band, a 30-man (and woman) drill team, a rifle squad, and a caisson with six horses, a Navy chaplain, and the Arlington 'Lady' to watch over the widow. And everything in slow motion. It took the sailor honor guard 10 minutes to fold the flag. *(07-17-95)*

The next time you are here, we must show you a thank-you card from a Girl Scout troop in Woodstock. Carolyn, who is our designated house sitter and weekly helper is the Scoutmaster of the troop. We have given for many years to the regional group, and this time we decided to help Carolyn's troop. The thank you from the girls was worth it. *(09-24-95)*

Newell Hale and I made our regular trip to visit the Parquettes in Rhode Island. (Parkinsons and Alzheimers) Rosemary insisted that we have lunch on the premises. We did, and never again. It was delightful, but the sandwich was tiny. The reason? These older folks do not eat big portions. *(10-08-95)*

Mom spent the afternoon on the phone at the 'headquarters' for the campaign. She also spent some time on Friday evening as a checker as they installed the voting machines. The enclosed flyer includes a photo and a message from Mom about the Library. Since she is unopposed, I think she will squeak in. *(11-05-95)*

Mom had a Library Board dinner meeting, and she attended the annual meeting (and pot luck supper) of the local Historical Society. And last night she attended the 25th Anniversary Meeting of Common Cause in Conn. (and USA) at which our friend Paul Aicher and his Study Resource Center won an award. Typically, Paul did not accept the award, but let his staff take the honor. Also, typically, Pop did not attend for it promised to be a midnight affair, and it was. *(11-19-95)*

You-never-know-department: Our UPS man is a happy guy called Bill. UPS rules are very strict in that there should never be any time for small talk between driver and customer. But last week, Bill told us that his wife had had a liver transplant and was doing well. We seldom know of the drama in the lives of people we see each day. *(12-17-95)*

I went to the quarterly meeting of the Old Goats Conference, this time in Worcester. I commented to this group of about ten guys, mostly still at work in banks, brokerage houses, insurance companies, etc that while the discussions always began with issues of interest rates, the price of gold and other commodities, the status of the Japanese and German economies, the long-term bonds etc., we always seemed to veer into very deep talk about the safety net, health care, education, teen age pregnancies and other moral issues. I find it very healthy and also encouraging that a group of very wealthy (at least some) and very conservative (at least most) men would realize the moral effect of economic policies and decisions. *(01-28-96)*

Today was the Annual Meeting of Christ Church, and for the first time, I didn't go. It's not good for my health. Each year, I have commented about the increase in the Endowment, the decline in pledges and the decline in average pledge. I see a connection. The endowment is now over a million bucks – and to me, that's obscene. Maybe the new rector will see it also. *(01-28-96)*

Today was the Lions Pancake Breakfast. I worked for a while before church, but left to hear the sermon by our assistant, Virginia Army. She does a magnificent job of preaching, and I just wish she could do it more often. *(02-11-96)*

I had an interview with a young man from Pomfret School. Blue blazer, chinos, button-down shirt, and a large Bugs Bunny tie. I expected an exciting interview, but he was so quiet. The School Bulletin came yesterday, and it had a story on the many awards he has received – none of which he revealed to me. *(02-18-96)*

Also enclosed is an ad and letter to the Editor of the Pomfret Times – a monthly paper. It needed contributions to get it started and so we have run a monthly ad – and it has provoked some comments. Good. *(03-03-96)*

When Mom came home from church last Sunday, she said: "After all the sneezing, sniffling and coughing by the Rectory School boys, be surprised if I escape unscathed." She didn't. She has a case of pneumonia, amid much coughing. *(04-21-96)*

We went to the annual Lions Man of the Year Award dinner. Last night it was a 'she,' the town Librarian who has been involved in a zillion do-gooder projects. *(05-12-96)*

The Olympic Torch went through Pomfret this morning. Not quite what we expected. To the biggest crowd I have seen here, a parade of state police, Coca-Cola trucks, and a motorcycle bearing the torch sped by. We waited an hour for something that took about 15 seconds. *(06-16-96)*

I worked for the Community Kitchen, I picked strawberries, and Mom worked at the church and had a Democratic Town Meeting. And we spent many hours at Positively Pomfret Day (a town fair) where Pop served fried chicken for the Lions, and last night we went to a fund raiser Gala for the Bowen 1846 House in Woodstock. A great band . . . and Pop was on the dance floor, but absolutely impossible to chat with your dinner partner. *(06-30-96)*

A newspaper clipping from Cincinnati brought the news of the death of Dr. Mike Upson – Pop's doctor for many years. But I remember Mike for something else. After Grammy's death (Mike had taken care of her), Mike told Gramps "I have no bill. . . . Pay me what and when you can." *(08-05-96)*

Do-it-now! For the past year or so, Sally Faunce, the widow of my old pal from Princeton days, and I have promised each other that we would get together. It never happened. Friday's Times carried an obit for Sally. Do-it-now! *(09-01-96)*

I went to Boston for a meeting of the Old Goats. It was held in a brewery, run by a son of one Old Goat. I guess you call it a micro-brewery. But it was an eye-opener into the operations of a small business. It is called Harpoon Beer. On the weekend they had a gala in their parking lot with 13,000 fans. *(10-20-96)*

We had a visit from Lillian Lemaire, the widow of my Boy Scout pal, Al. And you may remember my description of his burial at Arlington. Lil decided to move back to Connecticut to be near family. I give her grades for spunkiness in handling widowhood, but it was actually a teary time, with many pictures, and with too much detail on how Al died. All of us face these events, and I guess there are few guidebooks, but there should be some guidance as to how to handle chats with such good old friends as Lil. It was tough. *(10-20-96)*

We went to a Historical Society potluck supper and presentation, and it was marked by Pop dumping a bunch of chili on my jacket and trousers. I left early. *(11-24-96)*

I stopped to see Mrs. Casendino on the way home. There are many changes in life . . . but Mrs. Casendino is unchanging. She sends her love to all of you. *(12-08-96)*

The Christmas tree is up – and that's another Christmas story. In recent years, I have relied on local guys to go up to Paul Aicher's Christmas party to cut a tree from his farm, and to put it up here. But this year, the current guy demurred. In desperation, I called Paul Braaten, who has worked for us as carpenter for many years. I met him at the farm, he cut down the tree, and put it up here. I then asked him "how much" – and he responded with "I don't work for pay on Sunday," and further, "this is my Christmas gift for you." And he added a Christmas present for us. Things don't get much better in life. *(12-15-96)*

Good deed department: I lugged a bunch of food items from the church to the local food bank. And I drove our neighbor, Frank Lamb, to the first of his seven weeks of radiation treatments for lung cancer. The same day, his wife Trudy was in Boston for work on her jaw cancer. Tough days for one family. *(01-19-97)*

Paul Nelson just dropped in for a visit. He brought a package of hamburger meat and said that I might recognize it from one of the fine animals that roam across the road. Good neighbor. No, Great. *(02-15-97)*

We went to a Lenten Soup/Study group on Monday evening, which had one unexpected ingredient . . . the couple that was to bring the food never showed. After some scrambling, we sort of had a meal. *(03-16-97)*

But another emotion. One of the prayers was for Carin Laughlin. We learned, in church, that she is undergoing treatment for cancer of the esophagus. Once again, Mom made a quick and right decision. We visited them for a few minutes. Lots of tears. But the prognosis is good. Leighton is about my oldest Princeton pal. We all know that these events face all of us. But it doesn't make it any easier. *(4-20-97)*

We keep learning – and there are surprises. At a meeting some time ago, I took issue with the School principal's comment that half of Pomfret's citizens were college educated. She sent me the figures, and it sure seems to be true. But hard to believe. (04-27-97)

Finally, to add to the great benefits of Mom's machine (computer), she has been corresponding with Lynn Anderson, her old pal and partner in the antiques business from Wilton, who is now in Hanover NH. Lynn's comment was "imagine two old broads keeping in touch via this machine!" *(05-26-97)*

The other was Frank Lamb, our neighbor at the top of the hill. Frank was a highly decorated Marine from Guadalcanal. He spent two years in hospitals after a grenade blew most of his middle apart. He had prostate cancer, lung cancer, an aneurism (sp?), and finally, a brain tumor. I am sure he wrote his obituary, for it ended with a great bit of humor: "he was a founding member of the Pomfret Intellect Club," which he called our Thursday luncheon group. *(09-01-97)*

On the brighter side, we think we have a new neighbor. Mrs. Orswell has turned the golf course land over to the Audubon Society. So, we will not have a development in front of our home. But, we do have a great crop of goldenrod – the field is totally yellow. However, we are really happy to see this new neighbor. *(09-14-97)*

We had a lunch with the Wrights from Santa Barbara. Life is funny.

My introduction to Clifford Wright was so negative as I realized his wealth and his control of my hopes to buy 9655 Cunningham Road. And here *we* are, friends of so many years. My advice? Look out for friends. . . . They may be hiding close by. *(10-05-97)*

Indian Hill. I have some thoughts about such reunions – at our age. It often seems to be a tale of health problems. And that's after you realize who you are talking to. Here were friends that we knew and worked with for years. And I didn't know them. Heaven only knows what kind of trouble they had in recognizing me. The evening was a major event of the church's 50th anniversary. The biggest potluck supper on record, many old friends (Chuck Fullgraf). And biggest of all, I was asked to stand and be recognized. *(12-01-97)*

On my way to Princeton, I stopped to see Mrs. Casendino. How do you describe her? To me, she is exactly the same as when she tore through Far Hills. An incredible woman. And she loves each of you. And talks about you. I hope you remember to send her a card. *(12-07-97)*

And today, we went to a town 'burning of the trees,' monitored by the fire department. It was an idea of Mom's, on a committee to think of town events. We used to have it in Indian Hill. The fire was mostly smoke, and the chief said, "We know how to put them out, we are not too good at starting them." But a good event. *(01-11-98)*

The forecasts on radio and television were frightening. I have been taking Paul Aicher to Worcester for his radiation treatments, and on Wednesday, he asked me to come the next day because he was about to find a generator and take it to Maine where his son had been without power for days and with a sick child. I said, "Take ours." And he did. But then our forecasts turned awful, and Paul was worried about our lack of a generator. And so, he rented one locally, and left it here. But the Thursday forecast of eight inches, and the Friday of ten inches turned out to be zero. *(01-18-98)*

Our neighboring town of Putnam has signed a lucrative contract with a trash hauler, who will be bringing ash from Bridgeport, New Haven, and other places. Fifty to one hundred truckloads a day right past our house. Pomfret is trying to fight, but I suspect it's a lost cause. *(02-08-98)*

This morning's church bulletin had an announcement: "The flowers are given to the glory of God and in grateful thanksgiving for the birth of Daniel Andrew Dixon by Don and Georganna Dickson." Good grief. *(03-08-98)*

Also, we both got haircuts! But, when I entered the barbershop, he greeted me with "My, you have put on weight." Unhappily, true, but there must be a better Hello! *(03-29-98)*

Mom had a meeting of the Civic Pride Committee and I met with the Old Goats group. There were two main items on the agenda . . . the Japanese economic crisis, and the pending computer crisis when we reach the year 2,000. I can contribute little to either subject, but I learned enough to be concerned. *(04-13-98)*

Attention all girls! TJ Maxx has come to Putnam! *(05-24-98)*

Interesting, but the bride-to-be's name is Linnard, and her parents were here. I asked her father if he had a relative named Irving, and he said, "He was my Dad." Irv Linnard was an old hand at Warner-Lambert, in charge of manufacturing, and he was a wise counsellor to this guy fresh from P & G. He helped me out of some scrapes. *(06-07-98)*

My Thursday lunch group gave me a party at The Harvest with cards, cake and a package of Miracle-gro – as a substitute for Viagra. I also had calls from all over, including one from my cousin in Carolina. Overwhelming. *(06-14-98)*

We also went to Watch Hill one day for a lunch with the Wright's from California, plus Kathy and her two daughters. When Kathy was born, I put up a big homemade sign welcoming her . . . and Sis Wright said that she still had the sign. *(06-23-98)*

Mom went to a town meeting about a very controversial subject. A non-profit group with enormous financing from the state wants to buy a local estate to house about 15 teen-age boys with sexual abuse background, and who are presumed to have poor futures in that department. You can imagine the heat generated on that subject. Mom also had a Library Board meeting. *(08-09-98)*

Ed Dooley. Perhaps some of you remember his name. Ed and I worked together for 12 years at Warner-Lambert and RCA . . . Pop as the Client and Ed at the Agency. A late-night call on Friday (anyhow, late for me) awakened me. It was Ed's daughter Lynn calling from LA to tell me of Ed's death. Ed knew every fine eatery from coast to coast and we sampled quite a few. He was also the host to Mom and me at many great evenings in the Big Apple. Ed and I were walking in Denver one evening and I spotted a pool hall and I invited Ed to a game. I never had a chance. He had put every ball in a pocket before I had a turn. I then learned that he was a Midwest champ when in college.
Once at Rex Ranch in Arizona, he and I rode to a roadside tavern for a beer. There were three rough looking guys at the pool table, and Ed innocently asked them if he could join. They looked at Ed, the city slicker dude, and suggested some bets. Ed cleaned them out.
Ed, long a widower, was as honest a man as I will ever meet. I loved Ed. I will surely miss him, but the memory bank is full. *(09-13-98)*

Mom went to a Democratic Town Committee meeting. And we both went to a 'wake' for Uncle Mike, Paul Nelson's uncle who died in his 93rd year. Some years ago, during a snowstorm, Mike was up on a roof shoveling down snow, when his sister screamed at him "Get down – you're not 75 anymore." *(11-30-98)*

Mom and I drove to Princeton on Monday, with a lunch stop at Mrs. Casendino's. Do you know what this fine Italian lady served us? Matzoh ball soup! She hasn't changed at all, and she sends her very best to you all. A grand person. And Patty was there, and she looked just great. *(12-13-98)*

Last night, we went to a Christmas party at the Nelsons. It was like a town meeting. Such wonderful people. Of the many towns we could have picked, this place of Pomfret has proved to be a gem! *(12-20-98)*

Our small men's Saturday morning group had a tour of the Frito-Lay plant in Killingly. The plant manager belongs to our group. The figures were incredible. They get 24 trailer loads of potatoes a day, and they empty one each hour. In an hour, those potatoes are finished packages of chips being loaded onto other trailers. Some parts of the process with huge machines were handled by only a few people, and they merely watched computer consoles. *(01-18-99)*

Last night, Mom and I went to the Pomfret School for an evening talk by a visiting lecturer. He was Bob Ballard, and he is the guy who found the Titanic and other sunken vessels. But the high point, to me, was his description of what's ahead in mapping the ocean floors and the mountains that are under water. *(01-18-99)*

There was an obit in the Alumni Weekly for Buddy Mack, who lived near us in Indian Hill. When a member of the Country Day School group approached Buddy about a contribution toward the annual

Athletic Banquet, Buddy asked when the English Banquet was scheduled. Buddy's family figured in a famous Civil War incident when Grant expelled them from Kentucky for dealing with Southern cotton farmers. *(02-15-99)*

We had some drama here last night. A snowplow hit a car on the hill, with minor damage, and the plow driver took full responsibility. But the woman from the car used our phone to call her husband, who said he "would beat her to a pulp." She tearfully described the beatings. I told the truck driver to alert the trooper when he arrived. We don't know the final episode, but I don't feel good about it. *(03-07-99)*

My meeting schedule was limited to the Men's Gathering on Saturday morning. Our speaker was the guy who invested so heavily in the antique business in Putnam, which eventually became a great success for him and for the town of Putnam. There are now 400 dealers in Putnam and the antique traffic has rescued the town from oblivion. *(03-29-99)*

Do you remember Shelley Longmuir? She rented a stall [*for her horse*] in Wilton. She is now the chief Legal Officer with United Airlines, an Executive Officer, and has moved to Chicago. She sent us pictures of her newborn, and her huge new home. All of this raises an interesting question . . . of all the people we meet en route, why do some stay on as pen pals? *(05-09-99)*

Starting at the end, we had a shower for Matthew Nelson and his bride-to-be here yesterday. It was a catered sit-down luncheon for about 30 and it seemed to go off quite well. It was good to do something for the Nelsons, who have been so good to us since we arrived here. *(05-17-99)*

There is a new sign on the house, and it reads Benjamin Sabin – 1719.

The old sign was refurbished by Andrew, and it looks just great. *(07-05-99)*

We also attended the Hospice tree lighting ceremony at the Village corner, and then joined many in the annual Pomfret School candlelight carol and reading service. It is a wonderful event with music and student reading. Very emotional and very Christmasy. Mom and I fervently agree that this Service is the real beginning to the Season. *(12/13/99)*

One day we drove up to Andover, Mass. to visit Jessie Flouton. Long overdue. Jessie and Bob (Bob is sequestered in an Alzheimers section) are in an enormous Assisted Living complex. Jessie and Bob were good friends in Wilton. . . . She and Mom were in a sewing group together. Jessie has had a stroke, uses a walker, and her speech is a little awkward. But what a gal! Jessie was a speed skater in the Olympics for Canada. She has a great laugh and is a charming lunch partner. Jessie and Bob have daughters in the area who seem to be very supportive.

Now this is a long story. But all stories have lessons. To Mom and me, it reinforces our appreciation with our current lives. More importantly, it strengthens our resolve to reach and touch base with those fine folks who are going through bumps in the road. *(02-28-00)*

Social notes: we went to a surprise birthday gala for Betty Hale, wife of Newell at the Harvest replete with Band and 100 friends. Importantly, Mom and I 'danced' when they played 'our song.' Newell sold his inherited mill company for 8 million shares of Monsanto and is the least unlikely rich man who you will encounter. *(04-02-00)*

When we got home, I learned that my frugal ways had resulted in an out of stock of beer. And the stores were all closed. But I called Newell Hale and he 'loaned' me a six pack. Newell also came by on Friday with his pick-up and his handyman, and they loaded up the truck with stuff too big for the normal rubbish pickup. Good friend. *(07-16-00)*

The Rector has two beagles. And they escaped last week. After five days he caught one in the hills above our house. In bad shape after days of running. And last night Mom came home from a church project and found the other asleep on our porch. Mom had worked at the Habitat auction. *(10-03-00)*

# Spag's and Other Material Stuff

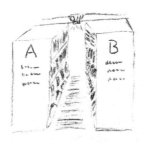

**"What is Spag's like on a Saturday afternoon?
Well pretty good, <u>after</u> you find a place to park."**

*Is it Spag's or Spags? Or even Spagg's. It doesn't matter because Pop spelled the iconic store in Shrewsbury, Massachusetts, different ways in his letters. And he mentioned his trips to the store so often, and in such humorous, loving ways, it deserves its own separate chapter in this book. For Pop, it was all about the prices. Or mostly, anyway. He would drive the forty miles with a list (of course!) of the odds and ends he needed—and sometimes didn't need. Everything from toothpaste to snow shovels and work boots was there. He would save a few dollars, and fill up with gas, and save a few dollars here and there. But it could have also been about the donuts on the way or the other restaurants that he would combine for an outing. He wasn't alone, as Spag's was famous for miles around. Sadly, it closed a few years ago.*

*Crowded Aisles* by John Dickson

We also made a trip one evening to Worcester to a very unusual hardware store that discounts prices very sharply. We went up with a long list of needs. Pretty exciting life. *(05-09-77)*

Pop went to Spagg's this week and loaded up on a lot of things, including vegetable seeds. Many of them were only 7¢ a pack, so I came home and crossed off a bunch of items from my Burpee order (at 55 and 75¢). *(02-18-79)*

Mom and I went to Spag's one evening and really loaded up with stuff. We were looking at snow shovels, and I said to Mom, "Well, you're the one that's going to use it – so you pick out the one." A man standing nearby said, "I overhead that statement and I can't believe it. How do you do it?" *(12-10-79)*

On Thursday night Mom and I went to Spag's – and I lost my wife in Spag's. We got separated and I thought I would never see her again. *(11-09-81)*

Speaking of letters, a few weeks ago I found a letter from Poland in the Spag's parking lot – addressed to a woman named Kosciusco (what else?) in Worcester. I mailed it to her, and last week we got the nicest letter from her telling us of her efforts to find the lost letter which was from her niece in Poland. *(09-20-82)*

There was an article in the Wall Street Journal about Spag's. I went there last week for my usual haul of items. I've been looking for a small band saw, and a catalog came recently that had one from Shopsmith for $250 plus shipping; then a catalog came from Shopsmith itself with the same item priced at $199 plus shipping; Spag's has it for $152 and a $15 dollar rebate certificate. *(01-31-83)*

I went to Spag's last week and met Mr. Spag – a celebrity. *(05-31-83)*

Last week was the week of the rain. Boy did we have we weather. At least we didn't have to shovel it. But the first day the rain froze when it hit the roads and there were many fender benders. I defied the rules and made a planned trip to Spag's anyway, and had the pleasure of shopping in a store with clear aisles. And that's because not many nuts were out shopping – like me. I bought a new pair of workshoes, and I have been hobbling around trying to break them in. The old boots look pretty good now. *(12-19-83)*

Mom and I went to Spag's one day and then decided to have lunch at Legal Sea Foods. But first we decided to check out some stores in the mall. While there, we were approached by a lady with a clipboard asking us to participate in some research – for five bucks apiece. The research was taste-testing of instant oatmeal – six variations – and by the time the test was over, I had lost my appetite. Hence no sea food. *(01-14-85)*

A couple of months ago, Paula noted a discrepancy in a checkout slip and wrote to Spag's. They sent her a refund. And then, a week ago, she got a case of fruit from Ollie Spag. How's that for consumer relations? *(02-06-84)*

The big event of last week was the celebration of The Big 38! After many days of discussion as to how we should honor this great day, including various ideas for trips here or there, we did the Ultimate. We went to Spags. *(06-24-85)*

We talked to John yesterday and they are getting excited about their planned trip home. They have changed their destination from Boston to NYC, in order to avoid coming through London (and the concerns at that airport.) He said that Joseph was wearing a shirt that said, "This is my first Spag's t-shirt." *(05-06-86)*

I also braved Spag's on Saturday morning. It opened at 8am, and I had my stuff by 8:30 – and as I left I saw cars trying to find parking places. *(12-21-87)*

I went to Spag's – they said they had missed me – as did the people at the dump. Pretty exciting stuff. *(01-30-89)*

I tried to think of a reason to get to Spag's, because it would have meant a triple sweep (dump plus haircut), but the list was just too small. *(04-17-89)*

I went to Spags and got a haircut . . . but no more triple plays since I don't go to the dump. Only double plays. *(08-13-89)*

I went to Spags on Saturday morning, and modernization has arrived. But it is still an amazing place . . . where else can you find a section devoted to bowling, to bird seed, to maple syrup etc? *(09-29-91)*

I went to Spags on Saturday morning, and in one of their buildings is a collection of awards and newspaper features. One shows Mrs. Spag in front of her $2 million jet which she piloted. Unhappily, she is now in that great Spags in the sky. But it shows that the business not only helps Pop, but the owners, too.

I went to Spag's one morning, and discovered that Spag's opens its doors an hour early on Wednesday for the handicapped. The place was filled with wheelchairs, people with crutches, canes, etc. Incidentally, we now have a handicapped license plate to make it easier for long walks in parking lots. *(02-21-93)*

No week would be complete without a visit to Spag's. *(12-19-93)*

Pop went to Spag's. It is a great visit, but no longer a challenge. The new addition makes a visit so 'lonely.' There are now 38 checkouts. *(12-04-94)*

I went to Spag's. Surprise, they now have automated checkout machines. *(12-07-97)*

I went up to Spag's on Saturday morning, and there were six trucks (two trailers) unloading plants and flowers. The girl at the checkout told me there would be a total of 20 trucks that day. *(06-08-97)*

Bonehead play of the week. I went to Spag's on Monday, and I learned that it was Patriot's Day in Mass. The population that didn't run or watch the Marathon were all at Spag's. *(04-26-98)*

# Medical Notes

**"Something's wrong. I have to go to the hospital."**

*Health issues plague all of us past the age of fifty, and, so understandably, they take up a sizeable chunk of the weekly letters. Rarely were there complaints, though. Pop used the letters to keep us apprised of medical incidents and status reports. That way, no surprises. Still, they were often laced with advice for those who carry the same genes. Looking back, following the deaths of both our parents, you can see the references to issues that had a hand in ending their lives.*

*Intensive Care* by John Dickson

Good grief. I got all organized to write this week's letter, went into the bar room to get a you-know-what, grabbed a potato chip – and a big hunk of tooth fell out. Mr. Dentist, here I come. So far, no hurt. *(09-28-75)*

By the time you get this, Poppa should be out of N.Y. Hospital – well on the road to full repair from a heart attack. Right now, I'm in the Intensive Care Unit – all wired up with hoses and tubes, and I've been told that I'll move out on Monday to a regular room for 2-3 weeks rest. And then home.

You should not have any worry or concern. This isn't the worst thing to happen to a guy, but I have had such excellent care that the confidence alone makes you feel better.

I drove down to the City on Thursday for a 10 AM meeting with Mr. Rahr of the [*Princeton*] Alumni Council. About 10:30 I began to feel weak and have chest pains, and by 11:00 AM, after a wild ambulance ride from the Princeton Club, I was in a room with nurses and doctors swarming all over me. And the head doctor was Princeton '60 – and you can't beat that can you? *(06-17-77)* [*Handwritten note to John in Gabon, which read on the back "This is the letter we sent you in June! It was just returned."*]

As I was saying before the interruption . . . Gosh it's good to be home. Mom came down to the city on Thursday afternoon, spent a few nice hours with me, and then picked me up on Friday morning, for the wonderful drive home. And here I am, where I belong. . . . There are times in each day when I feel a little wobbly, but there is a clear feeling of getting stronger. The good doctor gave me a five-page letter describing what happened, what's ahead, and how to take care of myself. The sergeant in this place has seen it, memorized it, and is in total control. *(07-04-77)*

Poppa is mending – but slowly. The old body really sends out signals when it is pooped, and I have felt just a little rotten at times. . . . One day last week, during some warm weather, Mom said that my problem was the heat and humidity. I called the doctor in New York, and he said it was the heat and humidity – and did Mom want a job there? *(07-11-77)*

We decided to wait a day before putting together this week's letter, for today I had my first check-up, and we thought you might like to have the results. Mom and I went to Hartford to see a cardiologist, and the results were quite interesting. First of all, he said that my cardiogram was very good for a guy who had had such a major heart attack. It seems every time some doctor talks about the event, it was worse than the time before. *(07-18-77)*

Pop is feeling pretty good. I seem to poop out rather easily, or else I try to do too much, and very quickly am reminded that I must take it easy. After losing 12 pounds, I am having mucho trouble losing more. Anybody got any ideas? *(07-31-77)*

I have been bothered with a very noticeable skipping to the heart beat. He [*the doctor*] heard it, and it registered on the machine, but he claimed it is not of serious concern. But sometimes it bothers the heck out of me. Incidentally, I have now lost 18 pounds, which is all to the good, and I am sticking to the diet. But it ain't easy. *(08-15-77)*

Poppa went to NYC on Tuesday for a visit with Dr. Scheidt. It turned out very well, and he continues to be very positive about my situation. My tests apparently went very well. I am now on some medicine which should relieve some of my frequent discomfort. But anyway, I left there feeling pretty doggoned good. I needed to, for I faced a nightmare ride through the deluge of rain that hit the city. I drove uptown with the water at hubcap level and managed to get around some places where the water was over the hoods of cars. *(11-13-77)*

Part of Pop's problem is that his morning and prescribed hike of three miles really eats into the work time. But I've managed to do it (and like it) each day, despite some bad weather now and then. *(12-04-77)*

Pop also had a visit to his new cardiologist in Worcester on Friday, with most of the conversation centering around the possibility of surgery. This seems a little fast for me, particularly since the New York doctor appears to be lukewarm on the subject and has a more positive view about my condition. At any rate, since my medical insurance is so poor, and since it won't improve till next year, I am stalling on the subject. But this means that I must be extra cautious, which I certainly intend to be. *(05-30-78)*

I received a very sobering two-page letter from my cardiologist, and there is no question now that I must change my lifestyle, as quiet as I now think it is. *(06-05-78)*

By now, I think you are all aware of the results of Pop's test. There seems to be total agreement that the by-pass operation should take place, for there are three blockages of main arteries that need attention. Dr. Scheidt, until now, was reluctant to advise surgery, since he claims to be very conservative on the issue of by-pass operations, but he says the evidence from the catheter tests is quite conclusive. *(07-17-78)*

Pop went to the internist in Southbridge, and he confirmed the judgment that an operation is in order. Only he would prefer it earlier than November. *(08-13-78)*

Pop left here on Tuesday morning for a date with Dr. Scheidt at New York Hospital. We picked the date of Nov. 1 for admission and Nov. 3 for the operation, but he called later in the week and asked to change it to Nov. 5 and Nov. 7. So that's where it now stands. *(09-18-78)*

Home – home – home – home! What a lovely word! And how great it feels to be back here again. It seems hard to believe that it was just two weeks ago that Peter and Janet dropped me off at the hospital for the "adventure" . . .

I celebrated the arrival with a you-know-what – very dry. The previous evening, Dr. Gay had told me that shortly after I got home, I would feel like I had been hit by a ton of bricks. Well, I decided that was so much hogwash. And so, I read the paper, had a good lunch, had a nap, and when I wasn't looking – then came the bricks. Things are somewhat better now, but I really was faked out . . .

I learned a few things this past week or so. Or had some things re-impressed on me. The love and support of family and friends has a meaning all to itself when you're staring up at a hospital ceiling. Also, I am astounded, and this is a new lesson for me, at the bounce-back or resiliency of the body. The mending process is amazing. *(11-19-78)*

Pop's first week of "home care" has been pretty good. I have a lot of aches and pains, and it has been affecting my sleep. The leg, in particular, constantly hurts, and I guess this is part of the healing process. The appearance of the scars is very good, and they seem to be clearing up nicely. Yesterday was my best day, but I seem to have slipped back a little today. *(11-26-78)*

I'm feeling pretty good, but expected to feel better four weeks after leaving the hospital. I have had some pains on my walks to the post office and am not sure whether it is the cold air or what. About once per day I manage to sneeze, which is about the most painful thing that you can imagine. It feels like my chest is about to explode. Maybe I'm trying to rush things. Slow down, Pop. *(12-17-78)*

I think Pop was asleep, for I have a humdinger of a cold, which started out with the usual sniffles and then turned into a cough-cough deal, and it hasn't been much fun. Thank goodness I didn't have this about four weeks ago. I think it's a little better today. *(01-01-79)*

The purpose of the trip was to re-visit the good doctor, because I have suspected lately that "things" haven't been going just right, and he agreed. The reason at this point is not clear, but I am back on some medicine, and he has suggested that we watch and track my progress closely for another couple months. It's a little discouraging, but he indicated that this kind of problem is not too unusual. *(01-07-79)*

I had a date with the good doctor, and his news wasn't exactly good. There are apparently three explanations for my current problems, and two of them would require going back in with surgery. The third option is even worse, in that they could not do anything. So the "good news" is that I may require another operation – but that would be some time off. For now, they are boosting the pills, and maybe in a couple months, I'll go in for another cath test. *(03-12-79)*

Wednesday, I had a meeting with the good surgeon (Thumbs Gay) who did the job on me, and he is as puzzled as anyone why I am as I am. But in mid-June I go back into the hospital for a few days of tests. *(05-13-79)*

Also, I sometimes wonder if some of my health problems are in my head, for here I stand on the ladder swinging away with a paint brush and with no chest pains, and then I walk up to the post office and feel punk. *(06-04-79)*

Pop had a poor time in the hospital. Everything seemed to go wrong. I checked in on Sunday, June 10, after Mom and I had left a Princeton garden lunch at Pres. Bowen's, and after a moving church service in the Chapel. I was scheduled for two tests – one on Monday and one on Tuesday – designed to clue us all in on why I have been having pains. The Tuesday test was snafued, and I had to wait until

Wednesday, and then it became a very difficult one, and they then put me in Intensive Care for two days. This is the doggoned test where they send the tubes and needles into your heart to probe around, and a year ago it took a half hour, and this time it took two hours. The unhappy result of both tests is that I have major blockages again, and another operation is on the schedule. My plan, if I can make it stick, is to stall until early 1980. *(06-18-79)*

Pop went up (to Boston) on Thursday to see the doctor at Mass. General Hospital for a second opinion on 'what's next.' It was kind of sobering, for he described his judgment on the serious nature of my clogging, and he also tentatively suggested that I stall any operation, for the reason that he was doubtful how much good might be done, compared to the risks. He's an impressive guy, a friend of a fellow that Pop worked with at Princeton. *(07-30-79)*

The arrangements have started for Pop to start using a new experimental medicine, which means a parade of visits to hospitals for weekly checks. It also means that I must slowly stop using my current medicines, which will make for an interesting ten days since the medicine has a stabilizing effect on heart beats. *(12-31-79)*

Pop went to New York Hospital for an early morning start to a series of tests. I found out that the first pill I had been using for the past two weeks in this experiment was a placebo – or sugar pill. No wonder I have had so much trouble working around here recently. But now I'm on the new drug, and I just finished carrying wood and starting fires – and no pain. The tests yesterday were the usual, plus a new one. It's called a nuclear scan, and you lay down with your feet in the air on a bicycle apparatus, and you pump away until you are basically exhausted. And I was. *(01-29-80)*

A day late this week, because Pop graduated yesterday from the test for the new drug. I was in NYC for a morning of those terrible tests, and now that it is over, I am back on medicine. And that's good news. I still have to check in with the doctors once a month for a year, but only for modest checkups. *(05-06-80)*

My walks are continuing, and I've been doing fairly well with a longer version. On a scale of 10 (like Bo Derek), I'd rate them a 6 or 7. *(04-13-81)*

This is from the "there's always hope" department. In reading the obituaries in the Princeton Alumni Weekly, I ran across an item about an old Tiger who had retired in 1923 because of <u>ill health</u>. (05-26-81)

Pop has a candidate for the dullest food. In my search for diet crackers, I have found dietetic matzah – a new low in the taste sweepstakes. *(06-15-81)*

Three years ago today I was in NY Hospital getting prepared for an operation tomorrow. I sort of prefer what my plans for today are. *(11-02-81)*

I learned last week that my old friend (and best man) John Sawyer who has never smoked, never drank, jogged five miles a day, and was in fine condition, had a bypass operation. This is an unpredictable disease. I hope to see him in Cincinnati. *(11-16-81)*

I got a letter from Dr. Scheidt at New York Hospital today thanking me for my participation in the new drug study and to advise me that it is all over. That is good news, but it also means that I will be paying for doctor's bills and medicine for the first time in two years. *(04-05-82)*

The BIG news here last week was that Mom stopped smoking – and she is upset that I am writing about it. She is fearful, and who wouldn't be, that she might not be able to keep her daily record going. Now, if only Pop would give up those martinis . . . *(05-03-82)*

This is the week Mom takes off on her great trip – and she will be seeing some of you. Remember to congratulate her on her continued discipline and resolve vs. the tobacco industry. It ain't been easy. *(05-17-82)*

Mom is happy to report that she has lost all of the ten pounds that she added after the end of smoking. She deserves a great round of applause. It's easy to stick to a diet when the pounds drop away quickly – but it has been a very, very slow process for her, and she has been very diligent. *(12-20-82)*

I have been limping around with a sore left foot and with no apparent reason for the problem. It was compounded one morning when I bumped it into a door. Did you hear me? At any rate, the morning walks have been temporarily stopped. *(04-11-83)*

The week also marked the first anniversary of Mom giving up you-know-what [*cigarettes*]. Congratulations. *(04-27-83)*

And, I am proud to report that except for two lapses, last week was a no-martini week. I am going to try and break this awful habit. *(12-05-83)*

And Saturday was the seventh anniversary of Pop's 'event.' The average life span after a heart attack is seven years and so I am now ahead of the odds. *(06-18-84)*

Mom is now minus ten pounds! Every morning, she spends about an hour on the bike and these mornings are not exactly the best for heavy work. And work it is. *(07-16-84)*

Also enclosed is a copy of a page from a newsletter called Cardiac Alert. Since the unhappy genetic 'thing' that created my heart problem may be passed onto other generations, I thought you all might be interested in the advice of the Letter. Nothing new, just reminders. *(11-25-85)*

A party week it was – just like Wilton. We went to a few and then last night Mom put together an extravaganza for about 90 friends. . . . I became ill and our friend, Dr. Muir, quietly whisked me to the hospital for a bunch of tests in the emergency room. They all came out OK – and I returned to the party with nobody the wiser. But for a few moments there was some quiet fright here. Weird. *(01-06-86)*

Among the many words, phrases and sentences of last week, I remember one vividly. It was Mom at 1:32 AM on Sunday morning saying: "Something's wrong. I have to go to the hospital." And something was wrong as we found after a quick dash to Day Kimball. It was a reaction to a drug she has been taking to help her breathing and it was having the opposite effect. A quick shot at the hospital helped, and she recovered happily and there were two less scared people in the world. *(06-23-86)*

Mom saw a few doctors last week and this morning she hopes to see another – a dentist – for last night she broke a tooth. No fun. The many tests seem to indicate an 'adult asthma' that has been interfering with her breathing. *(06-30-86)*

Dr. Steve called with the results of last week's blood tests. It seems that I have lost 50 points in the cholesterol count in one year. I find the change hard to believe, but welcome it. The real honors go to the menu planner here. *(08-04-86)*

Finally, I went to the dentist to have a broken tooth fixed, a tooth that I broke while drinking a martini. I guess I have been making the martinis too strong. *(08-31-87)*

Just as I was to start the letter a few minutes ago, I heard some strange noises – and it was Mom with an asthma attack. Now I know. Good grief, it scared both of us. Her trip to Denver was a success – not in terms of cures or promises of cures, but in terms of confirmation of the problem plus some ideas on how to cope and some new medication. She was absolutely impressed with the whole operation. *(11-14-87)*

Mom also discovered that the pharmacy made a mistake in a prescription, and she has been taking one medicine at ten times the prescribed rate. She is lucky, for even the druggist states that it was a very dangerous mistake. *(06-06-88)*

While waiting to see Steve (cardiologist), I watched a poignant scene from the window of the waiting room. First, two vans rolled up with a couple dozen wheelchairs. Then a bus came, and soon, children were being carried from the bus by what were obviously a camp staff. None of the children could stand or walk. The signs of affection among everyone were noticeable from four floors up. There were teary 'farewells,' as some re-entered the hospital and others seem to go home with parents. *(08-28-88)*

The mystery. We felt fine after our arrival home but in a few days began to drag (postponed jet lag?). As it worsened, I even went to the hospital for an EKG (OK). Then chills, fevers and splitting headaches (side effect from the malaria pill? No, said the doctor). And then we began to get very unattractive red sores. On Saturday, we decided to call John, but he called us first – Mary, Annie and Margaret all had the same thing. The verdict – African tick fever, a souvenir of the game preserve. And so, we are on antibiotics, with a quiet life planned for the next couple of years. *(03-20-89)*

In cleaning out some files, I ran across a letter from the fine doctor in Boston that I went to see for a second opinion about a re-do of the bypass surgery. It was exactly ten years ago – and his letter describes in detail what a mess I am in. And here I am. *(08-27-89)*

There is a new game at 233 Pomfret Street. The idea is to see who can cough the most during the night. Mom is ahead at this time. We cannot seem to shake the colds that have bothered us for a couple weeks. *(09-19-90)*

On the medical front – or perhaps I should say medical rear because that's where the action was – I had one of those uncomfortable exams that older or old men must handle. The results were fine. *(11-24-91)*

Medical news – good grief. Mom had a check-up, an x-ray, an eye exam, and new glasses. Pop had a flu shot, and miracle of miracles a wart that has been on one of my fingers for many years, suddenly disappeared. Overnight. *(12-08-91)*

Also in the medical news, I sensed during my morning walk that I had an 'irritation' on my left side. Mom looked at it, and it was a tick that had buried itself. I went to the emergency room at the hospital (since we could not get it out), and they cut the critter out. It was a deer tick, and I am now on medication for ten days. *(02-23-92)*

My week started fine by a session of picking blueberries, some garden work, and some painting. But then it fell apart. A visit to John Muir and to an orthopedic MD confirmed what I really already knew – arthritis in my right hand. The day before the blood test to identify the type of arthritis, I called John to tell him I was sure that I had another Lyme tick bite. He added that to the test, and put me on a pill. The Lyme test turned out negative, and when I went to show him my side, he said 'Shingles!' He also told me to get off the pill, but it was too late. . . . I have lost six pounds in the last two days and nights, and you can guess why. *(08-16-92)*

One big winner last week was the phone company. Thank you for the many calls.

By now, I think everybody is now a medical expert on the subject of heart tests. While I was disappointed in the decision not to do the angioplasty (although I really didn't want to have it done), and I am disappointed that the future may hold another by-pass operation, still there are good reasons to be optimistic. Steve said that the heart itself is in great shape, that the "pictures" from 14 years ago vs. now show very little change, and that if surgery is required that I am in good shape for the routine. (Routine?)

I checked in at 6:45 AM, and went in for the procedure at 1PM. It takes about 90 minutes. From then, I had to lay on my back immobilized with a sandbag on my leg, for eight hours. A very long eight hours. New York Hospital's idea of a semi-private room is four beds. My companions included a man with weeping women visitors and his only reaction was a periodic scream of "Cremation," a Redd Foxx type who mumbled a lot and snored even more, and a Greek who spoke no English and who called every Greek in the phone book. But he really didn't need the phone – he could have been heard just by opening the window. *(11-15-92)*

Let's get the medical report over quickly. I got the second opinion from the fine doctor in Boston. And he clearly told me to go ahead with another bypass operation. This is the guy who counseled against one some 13 years ago. But he was very firm this time. Do it. But Steve is still hesitant. I talked to him and he again suggests a waiting period. *(12-06-92)*

As for me, Steve called it a 'fielder's choice.' The dilemma is what to decide between one of the nation's foremost cardiologists (Do it) and a doctor who has taken care of me for 15 years, and who says 'let's wait.' Steve rattles off statistics about the odds of those who do and those who don't. So, we will 'wait.' *(12-20-92)*

I spent some time getting the material together for the tax man. It was discouraging to add up the medical bills and realize that the expenses were over five figures. There is a health care crisis. *(01-17-93)*

We will soon be off to Boston. Mom is not eager for the surgery [*to unblock sinus passages*], but she is eager for a solution. And John Muir said this morning that the procedure may even help the asthma. Let's hope so. *(01-24-93)*

It has been a long (and painful) week for Mom. The positive changes are subtle, but they are there. Importantly, we thank you for the many calls, flowers, cards, gifts and letters. And we had David and Paula asking and asking if they should come east. And we had John leave Silver Spring at 4AM on Saturday, and drive up to be with us for the weekend. We have had great support from our friends, including full course meals delivered to the door. *(01-31-93)*

We had a trip last week. Separately, I went down to see Dr. Steve on Monday, and got a very fine report. It's hard to believe, and I am not sure that I do, but apparently some of my problems have 'reversed,' and he concludes that I am in better shape than last year. *(07-25-93)*

We get a nutrition newsletter, and the last one was about Pasta. Very dismaying. The pasta is good, but restaurants put so much stuff on it that the message was very clear . . . do not eat pasta in restaurants. What's left? *(02-13-94)*

Also, on the medical front, Mom arose from the couch in the back room in an awkward manner, and apparently broke a rib. In much pain, she talked to Dr. Muir, who hustled here, confirmed the problem, and said there was not much to do except pain killers. Surprisingly, the pain has dulled, and she is doing nicely. *(06-13-94)*

Such good news! Great news! We went to Boston on Friday fully expecting some doctor to suggest surgery . . . and they did not. So, we have had a sinus guy, a gastro . . . (sp?), and a pulmonary guy all say, 'do nothing.' The expected villain, an obstruction in the esophagus, is there, but is still small and hasn't changed in two years. The real villain is the pneumonia that Mom caught last August in the hospital and has remained dormant for some time and has flared at other times. She has it now, but is under control. One happy thought for us has been that the specialist at Mass. General agreed with everything that John Muir has been doing. That is called confidence. One other thought: the doctors at this famed place were patient, thorough, with a sense of humor, and no rush. *(01-29-95)*

Speaking of doctors, we have reported that John Muir makes house calls. But he also sends flowers! *(02-12-95)*

First, some great news. We went to Boston on Friday, and Mom was poked and probed by two sinus specialists (an unpleasant process), but they both pronounced Mom to be "in fine shape." Mom's habit of asking questions prompted Dr. Salman (a wonderful guy) to finally say, "No matter what you ask, I won't answer." *(02-26-95)*

One of these Letters I am going to skip the medical report – but it seems to go on and on. It was an overdue suggestion, but John Muir (a pulmonary guy) said that I should have a local cardiologist, and he knew just the guy. Well, I had a session with him, and among many things, he said (1), it is remarkable from my reading of your files that you are even here, and (2), there are very few people in the nation that can point to two giants in the cardiology business on their 'resume,' Dr. Scheidt in NY and Dr. DeSanctus in Boston (for second opinions.) He also said that I should cut back on the evil martinis, which I have. I had one test last week, and the second to come. Will keep you posted. *(03-26-95)*

Are you tired of medical reports? I am tired of the subject, too. But the test results are in. There are two parts . . . the "fuel lines," and the "pump." My problem all along has been blocked fuel lines, and the expectation was that the lines were further blocked – but I did even better on the test that measures them. But the pump which has been my salvation has had a problem surface in the form of a valve leak. Is it minor or more? Only more tests will show. I see Steve next week to hear his judgment on these developments. *(04-09-95)*

Good news! No medical report. Oh, but I forget that I tore the nail on my thumb. Do you know how many times you use your right thumb? *(04-16-95)*

I had a date with Steve in NYC on Thursday, and it lasted 2 plus hours, including a fine lunch at the Faculty Club. Steve had all the material from Dr. Bradbury, and his basic reaction was . . . "Good, you have a competent and eager young cardiologist in your backyard. I'm impressed and I look forward to working with him. But, as with many young doctors, he has rules and levels that are right and desirable, but that he will have to yield a little bit as time goes by. His cholesterol, liver etc., levels are goals, but you are a 71 year old guy who has survived nicely these 18 years with a good life style. Let us fiddle a bit with the medications . . . go back to your long walks, and stop worrying."
I really don't feel any better, but I feel better about not feeling better. *(04-23-95)*

Hi! This is Lefty. As I think you have heard, I fell one evening, from a post-dinner snooze and hurt my wrist. A visit to the hospital emergency room the next morning confirmed that I had broken a small bone.

I have a new respect for people with disabilities. Such ordinary things as tying shoelaces, shaving, brushing teeth, buttoning shirts, signing checks, and of course, eating were real challenges. *(03-16-97)*

Last things first. We just left the doctor at the hospital and his firm instructions were – NO KISSING! Pop has been dragging for a few days plus coping with a bunch of sores in his month. It seems it's a kind of viral infection that he hopes to control by the end of the week. If not, he says, change the trip. You have just met the ideal patient. *(06-08-97)*

The big word here last week was Tick. After one bad night, I seem to have recovered quickly from Lyme Disease, but for Mom it was a much different story. Mom had a rash on her thigh, but the doctor's office said she would have to wait two days for an appointment. So, we went ahead to Wilton, and during the night, the rash had spread and painfully, too. We cancelled the New York trip and came home directly to the Emergency Room, where the doctor noted that he had never seen such a big tick rash. By that time Mom was in real trouble. So much so, that we tried to get the attention of her doctor, and failed. I went to the office and ended up in a shouting match with a doctor. We then went to my doctor, who treated her forthwith. He also gave us some literature which proved my side of the shouting match. The records are now being transferred.

She is recovering, but slowly. *(08-03-97)*

This week's Letter includes a few pages of the Harvard Heart Letter. Since my sons have, I believe, some of my genes, these items about the heart may be useful. *(10-19-97)*

Uncle Bob, at 78, is an old man. Therefore, when hospitalization occurs, it is a shock to see the patient. At our first visit, he was really out of it, and heavily sedated, and he looked it.

The stroke happened in church, during the sermon. Luckily, the church is only blocks away from the hospital, for in a stroke/heart attack, time is of the essence.

The stroke damaged the part of the brain that controls speech and swallowing. To make sure that he gets nourishment, they put some sort of an entry device to his stomach.

Aunt Ruth is remarkable. After the trauma of the auto accident, her vision problems, and now this, she is still in there fighting.

A very sobering experience. It is repeated endlessly each day. And we are so unaware of it until it hits near home. We will keep you posted. *(03-24-97)*

Medical Report: More. Pop had a regular checkup except that just as the doctor was getting serious, the speaker called for Doctor Cooper to come to Birthing Now. He ran out. Later, he called to tell me that I had arthritis in my right knee and that there were some swallowing problems. More tests and x-rays are to come. *(01-24-99)*

I have lost 14 pounds. Mom says it is the absence of martinis. Perhaps. But a diet based upon applesauce, Jell-O and Popsicles ain't much. Popsicles? Yes, Popsicles. One of the new medicines leaves a metallic taste in the mouth, and a Popsicle alleviates that, temporarily, but nicely. *(06-20-99)*

I get a monthly newsletter from the Harvard Medical School. This newsletter was about arthritis, which I surely have. It suggested 15-minute hot tub baths. I just got out of the tub, and I fear that 15 minutes of a hot bath would have me asleep. *(08-22-99)*

My original plan for the week was to go to see Aunt Ruth after

Princeton, but this lingering cold caused me to cancel. This is no time to pass a cold around. She is planning to go to Houston for Christmas. Good idea. *(12-03-00)*

[*A week later, he died from a fall that broke ribs and his collarbone and pneumonia.*]

# A Good Citizen

**"Mom went to a church meeting on Wednesday and advanced the great Dickson theory that church and volunteer groups should not have large reserve or bank accounts. Put the money to work is my theory."**

*Pop was a joiner. So was Mom. They had no ties to their new hometown when they moved to Pomfret, and this was their way of becoming part of a community. Church, library, historical society, Democratic Party, cancer drives, the schools, and friends in need all filled the letters each week, often nothing more than a list of all the meetings and work. Pop reserved his highest praise for people he called "good citizens." They both were.*

*Civil War* by Andrew Dickson

Thursday, Mom went to a church lunch, which featured an opera singer; in the evening Pop went [*to the*] Lion's Club, which mostly featured a bar. *(02-26-78)*

We've been accepted into membership in the Grange. Since Pop will be out of town next week, our induction has been postponed until April, and it will be held in Brooklyn [*CT*], which appeals to me in a strangely sentimental way. Full circle. *(03-19-78)*

And we went to Grange on Wednesday night. It's hard to describe Grange, for I am not sure most people would believe that such an organization and its rituals is part of this day and age. But there we were, singing old hymns and participating in a ceremony that clearly was designed for the last century. *(10-01-78)*

Mom went to a church meeting on Wednesday and advanced the great Dickson theory that church and volunteer groups should not have large reserve or bank accounts. Put the money to work is my theory. *(01-07-79)*

The big news of the week is that Mom was elected to a three-year term on the Vestry of Christ Church! I wonder if the good old conservative status quo Vestry really knows what they have wrought. Yesterday's annual meeting was just like the meeting of the ABC Corp., with most of the emphasis on how well their investments have grown during the past year. *(02-01-82)*

Yesterday morning was the annual Lions Pancake Breakfast at the Community School, and it was a huge success. Pop's responsibility was orange juice – in keeping with his intellectual and physical talents. *(02-08-82)*

There is a controversy boiling at our church. It seems that the minister and warden gave permission for a mental health group to use part of the church for a school for about a dozen retarded teen-agers. To Mom and me, it seems like a logical use for a largely unused room. But there will be difficulties for an occasional church dinner, and therein lies the rub. It is a small price in our judgment. *(09-07-82)*

We went to a Vestry dinner on Wednesday night, and I was an observer to the business session – and you would have been proud of Mom. This church has a record of zilch giving to others, and Mom said that if the church taught us to tithe – why didn't the church itself? And she prevailed – and promised that it was only the beginning. Three cheers for Mom. *(01-17-83)*

I had the fun to teach another class at the school about the Civil War. This time, I brought along the record of old Confederate songs, and it helped a lot. I sure spent some hours of preparation for a short class, and I'll bet John is shaking his head in agreement about preparation time. *(12-19-83)*

On Monday, Mom and I were guests of the Community School, for a tour of the classrooms and a visit to the library to see where our 'booster' contributions are going. We are the only members of the library 'booster club,' begun after the athletic booster club was started some time ago. It was great fun to see youngsters in action. *(10-29-84)*

The Lions have a raffle each week, normally a bottle of booze. Two weeks ago, for the first time in all these years, I won. But the prize was a coffee liqueur that I didn't want and so I put it up again last Thursday. Do you know who won? *(05-13-85)*

Thursday was Daffodil Day. Another guy and I spent the day with the flower cart from the shop, big signs, and 100 bunches of daffodils for sale for the Cancer Crusade. We did our business from the front of the Variety Store, and it was a long, cold day, but we managed to get rid of most of them. *(03-23-87)*

I taught my Civil War "class" at Rectory School one morning. Actually, it was four classes in succession. And I was really pooped at the end. *(04-27-87)*

Among the down points of the week, I realized I had made a mistake in the big needlepoint project (church kneelers) and had to rip out a fair amount of the stitches. *(06-15-87)*

I finished the big needlepoint, and immediately started on another one for the school chapel. The theme of this one is science and math, and it will be fun to do. *(07-27-87)*

I am slowly getting organized as Campaign Treasurer for a friend running for Selectman. Also went to Lion's, where I picked up a 10-year plaque. Doesn't seem that long. *(09-14-87)*

Mom sure had a busy week. She had a Hospice meeting one afternoon and she spent another afternoon working as a volunteer at the Hospital for a cancer screening clinic. And she made batches of pepper jelly and chili sauce. This involved long hours of stirring. But the results are sensational. *(09-21-87)*

It was a busy week. It was the week of Mom's soup kitchen work, and that takes a good part of two days. It is also a tiring job, and so we went out to supper the second night. Pop had his lunch-and-lecture series on Monday (Judean-Christian heritage) and a meeting of the Agricultural Land Use Committee. We are finally about to recommend something, and I am enthusiastic about it, and I also have the chore to write the recommendation. Mom had a

Democratic Town meeting and a meeting of the Arts Festival group and I went to Lions. How the heck did this meeting stuff get out of control? *(09-28-87)*

Mom and I have signed on as co-chairmen of the special gifts group for the Church building project. I am somewhat lukewarm about the project, but we will do our best. In fund raising drives of this kind, you always find out things about some people that you would rather just as soon not know. Such as their priorities. *(10-12-87)*

Mom was busy with the Community kitchen and with a library meeting. I went to another rehearsal of the town's Christmas pageant, in which I am a slow-moving shepherd. This is in sharp contrast to a Christmas card we received showing three wild-eyed shepherds running up a hill shouting 'We found him, We found him! Just like the angel said!' Great card. *(12-14-87)*

Yesterday, at the annual meeting of the church, Mom was elected a Warden. She is going to have a busy year, because this is the year the addition to the building is started. *(02-01-88)*

I continue to spend some hours each day painting in the new church area. There are six new Sunday School rooms, and the assignment is to stay ahead of the carpenters and plumbers and get walls and windows painted before heating fixtures, etc. go in. We're making it, but it's close. *(12-11-88)*

Yesterday was the dedication of the new church building – and it was a great event. Mom had a part as the Warden, and I did too, as a "Fund raiser." Communion was in the new big hall, packed with choirs, children, a music ensemble, and loads of people. The procession from the church was led by a bagpiper in kilts. A grand and happy affair. *(01-30-89)*

I did my Civil War talks at Rectory school on Tuesday, and on Wednesday we went to a Kitchen 'Shower' at the church in the evening, which was followed by a brief talk about South Africa by the Dicksons. *(04-25-89)*

Our First Selectman has decided to run for the State Representative's job, and I have signed up to be the campaign treasurer. The Cancer Crusade is going slowly, and we are behind last year. And I spent a quiet afternoon at the Grist Mill, as a guide to only two visitors. *(05-28-90)*

Today Mom was a hostess at the Prudence Crandall house in Canterbury. Prudence started a school for black girls in the 1850's and had quite a bit trouble but stuck to it. It is now a Historical place, and they have a fine new exhibit detailing the history of Route 169. *(10-21-90)*

I did my weekly trip to Mass. General in Worcester with the old girl undergoing chemo treatments. This trip was a little tense, since she was also battling diarrhea, and we both worried about whether she would make it each way. She did. *(11-11-90)*

And yesterday, at the Lion's pancake breakfast, they had a glaucoma screening test – and I did poorly. So, I have just made a date with the eye doctor. Incidentally, my job at the pancake breakfast was the coffee, a new job for me, and I suspect that those who drank my first batch may not have calmed down yet. It was STRONG. *(02-24-91)*

I also learned that though we think of this generation's famous children's book of Curious George, the early settler's best book was Generous George. We thus established the unique idea in the world of giving time and money. Did you know that 45% of our citizens claim to spend five hours or more each week at helpful work? *(10-06-91)*

John and I attended a celebration ceremony at Inanda Seminary [*in South Africa*]. It was started in 1868 by a 41-year-old missionary named Mary Edwards, who was principal for 57 years! Once a year a celebration is held, and John and I were guests (Christ Church makes an annual gift.)

In the chapel were 500 girls, grades 7-12, in white blouses and black skirts. The hymn singing was forceful, some in English and some in Zulu. It is surrounded by high fences and barbed wire because of the crime problems in the surrounding area of grinding poverty.

The address was by an alumna, a large woman in a huge hat, and flowered dress. Her theme was "when you train a boy, you build a man; when you train a girl, you build a nation."

She listed 40 or so of the graduates of the Seminary, and when she mentioned their achievements, each was greeted by an approving murmur. But when a graduate was listed in an American job, there was loud approval. The American presence was mentioned again and again. In the chapel was a large plaque listing six memorials, three of them Congregational Churches in Connecticut. *(03-29-92)*

I did my annual Civil War routine at the Community School for two classes. They are a remarkable bunch of kids, and I leave feeling that I must be the best educator ever. But I ain't. *(04-05-92)*

The Pomfret Cancer Crusade has started, and I have made a couple dozen calls. I guess I have said this before, but requests for money bring out the best and the worst in people. But, happily, we remember the best longer. *(05-03-92)*

When we were in Fairport, Matthew told us about his trip to Virginia to work for Habitat for Humanity, and his plan to be a counsellor at a camp for terminally ill children. Both he and Jeffrey are at Boy Scout camp this week. *(07-24-92)*

This is the weekend of the Woodstock Fair. The Lions Club have the 'franchise' for soft drink cans. This means emptying our cartons (too often with rubbish) and clearing out the rubbish cans for cans. Intellectual work. I worked this morning. The Fair attracts about 100,000 each day, most of whom seem to arrive via Rte. 169. *(09-06-93)*

Mom . . . officiated at her first wedding! As a justice of the peace, she married a couple at the McCobb's B & B. Her uniform was John's graduation robe – which she found in the attic. *(06-26-94)*

Mom's Carleton Alumni magazine had a story about eight Carleton students who went to Mississippi during the summer of '64. They stayed for the summer; Pop stayed only a week. It seems they were as scared as I was. To me, it was interesting that the idealism that took them there also guided their careers. All in challenging jobs. *(07-31-94)*

I 'worked' at the church's community kitchen. I really don't cook, but rather run errands. But it is good fun. But I did work at the Lion's Chili Booth at the Woodstock Fair – and it is work. A bowl of chili, a cup of chili, a chili dog . . . what'll you have! *(09-01-96)*

I had two interviews at Pomfret School. It is a humbling and joyous experience. Both youngsters from broken families. The girl (young woman) is a sensational long-distance runner, a great student, and I must add . . . a beauty. The boy (young man) started in Ghana, and has overcome, with his Mother's help, a truck load of obstacles. *(11-17-96)*

Yesterday was the Annual Meeting of the church. Things are looking up. But there are still money problems, despite the fact that the endowment is close to a million bucks. I made my usual speech about how we needed to do more in outreach giving, and I was stunned to hear that our percentage was about the best in the diocese, and better than any in Fairfield County. Further, the Bishop had congratulated our church on its percentage. No wonder the Episcopal Church is in trouble. *(01-26-97)*

This morning was the Lions Annual Pancake Breakfast. It really is the social event of the year. For the first time in almost 20 years, Pop didn't work. Nobody noticed any difference. *(02-15-97)*

Our tax lawyer has pleaded with us to reduce our contributions, and I think we made some 'progress' in 1996. But what can you do with parents who have been tithers for so many years? *(02-13-97)*

Election Day. No surprises here. Our dining room table was the scene of a group working to get out the vote. Pomfret had a 52% vote, which was good considering the real absence of issues. *(11-09-97)*

I was a chauffeur for Ted K. as he had his 20th radiation treatment at the U Mass Hospital in Worcester. It is a very sobering experience to sit in the waiting room and look around the room and realize that most people there are there for the same reason . . . to treat a cancer. All ages, all types, all very quiet. *(01-05-98)*

Pop was asked to talk to the Library Committee as to why anyone would or should help the library start an endowment fund. My credentials were based on the various funds Mom and I have helped at Carleton, Pomfret and Princeton. *(01-25-98)*

Today was the annual meeting of the church. One of the highlights, to us anyhow, was the budget item that showed a dramatic increase in outside giving. *(01-25-98)*

And I foolishly volunteered to add some personal words to a Class Planned Giving letter. It was a good idea, but I forgot about my arthritic fingers. But I did it – all 750 of them. *(10-12-98)*

Mom had a Library meeting, and also was the Librarian on Saturday afternoon. I went to a Lions meeting, marked by the aftermath of the admission of a woman member. I was not there when the Club did it, and they really had no choice. But some guys got really upset. *(10-12-98)*

Pop worked for the Community Kitchen, and this time they put me to work on slicing onions. Ugh! *(11-30-98)*

Mom and I witnessed four living wills at the hospital. And I was the 'presenter' at the Men's Gathering. My subject was the Civil War. *(04-19-99)*

# Much Ado About Nothing

**"Another failed experiment: I bought unsalted pretzels. Not good."**

*How do you fill up a letter each week? There's only so much family news, trips to the dump, or medical updates. So, Pop added tidbits about nothing at all really—the stuff that could have very well appeared on the Seinfeld television show, which I should hasten to add he never watched. Fun, funny, touching, nonsense.*

*Mailbox Calamity* by John Dickson

Of course, last week had one tremendous advantage, and that is that I took a day off. Yes, an absolutely honest-to-goodness vacation day. *(03-15-71)*

Mom came into New York on Friday to do some shopping and to visit the Passport office. I took her to lunch at the Princeton Club where an amazing thing happened. Mom announced in a loud clear voice that she wanted a Bloody Mary! Not root beer, not a weak sherry – but a real live Bloody Mary. Now you know how your parents are carrying on while away from the discipline of you kids. *(01-14-73)*

Pop just came back from the pond, where I tried to catch a nice big fish that I could see – but time and time again the little ones went for the lure. I guess that's why he's big. *(09-17-73)*

Mom is working on the NY Times puzzle. She has finally relaxed after a long weekend of work and errands. And when she relaxes with the puzzle, she really disappears! (That's Pop's envy showing through). *(09-23-73)*

The last piece of exciting news is that Mom has changed her hairdo. I don't know how to describe it – but it looks nice. *(02-18-74)*

There is no getting away from WABC [*A NYC pop music station that his children listened to, but he couldn't stand*]! Am at my desk and there's a scaffold outside the window, with WABC radio blaring away. Just like home. *(06-10-74)*

First, the big news. Mr. Big Fish is still in the pond. I hadn't seen him lately, but last night at dusk I wandered down to the pond and there he was right near the surface. *(10-07-74)*

The enclosed check for 5 bucks is your share of the winning lottery ticket. *(02-13-77)*

I had a call the other night from a guy who wanted to sell me a farm in Accident, Maryland. Since I had already seen a place in Mistake, Virginia I wonder if there's a hidden message in these possible addresses. *(10-03-76)*

Good start to this week. Took the Mercedes over to New Canaan for a long overdue overhaul, and the muffler fell off on the Jeep as Mom was following me. We arrived home to find water in Andrew's room, just minutes before an engineer representing a prospective buyer arrived to check out the house. *(10-25-76)*

We went out for breakfast on Sunday. Yep. After church, we went to the dairy place for their special 99 cent breakfast. *(02-22-77)*

Among the major events of last week was the purchase of a new washing machine. The old one had been around since Far Hills (1966?) and had seen quite a bit of action and was just plain worn out. The dryer may be next – and it dates back to Cunningham Road (1960?). *(12-04-77)*

Finally, concerning the weather, I forgot to mention that last week's high wind brought down the soccer ball that Andrew had lodged high in one of the pine trees. (02-05-78)

In my original schedule for this morning, I should be toodling down some interstate on my way to NYC. But every once in a while, I manage for some reason to have a night of thinking, planning, worrying, dreaming and just plain staring at the ceiling. I got home last night from a very pleasant dinner at the Blodgetts, fell asleep, and then awoke shortly after midnight – and that was the end of sleeping. It was also a new record for "awakeness" – and who needs that? So, I called Mr. Rahr and cancelled myself out of the meeting and will try to find some time today to recoup some z-z-z-z's. *(10-23-78)*

Add to those events, the normal list of trips to the dump, the stores, the gas station etc.; and the morning walk, and the noontime snooze, and the knitting and needlepoint, and the reading, and the backgammon, and the nice quiet moments of chatting – and you have a very good week in old Pumpkin Center. *(10-29-78)*

Wednesday, Mom went to a church meeting, and that evening brought a fair amount of snow. It also brought an accident or two on the hill. One car sheared off a telephone pole, and the electric and telephone company trucks were out there until 3 AM, with blinking lights and much noise. *(02-11-79)*

We read, we needlepoint, we knit, we tend fires in the shop, and we run to the mailbox looking for mail. It's a good life! *(02-27-79)*

Among the other highlights of this weekend was Pop leaving Mom behind as he drove off to church. I didn't realize that she was planning to go, and I drove off leaving her to wave and try to stop me. *(10-22-79)*

Here's a quote from Mark Twain – "Always do right; this will gratify some people and astonish the rest." *(07-07-80)*

Most of the days were spent reading or chatting, and in the evening, we played a new card game called Uno. It is lots of fun and a pleasant departure from pinochle. Since it's each person for himself, the issue of Pop's awful bidding is avoided. *(08-11-80)*

However, it is clear that the days are filled with many important events and crises. Last week this included: going to the dump, getting a haircut, taking a morning walk, making a swing for Matthew, filling the bird feeder every other day, fixing the screen where Charlie had plunged through, and a happy couple hours watching the young man who mows the lawn try to fix a belt on his broken mower. The last brought back many memories – some of which I probably should forget. *(07-14-80)*

Also, one of the pleasures of last week was a breakfast ritual of a piece of Paula's super apple pie with coffee. What a way to start the day! *(10-20-80)*

On a numerical note, the new car passed the 10,000-mile mark, and the van went past 43,434.3 miles. *(12-08-80)*

Also, while cleaning out old papers, I ran across the hospital bill for Andrew's birth and the daily room rate was 21 bucks. *(01-19-81)*

Among other major events last week was a trip to Spags, a trip to the dump and a trip to the barbershop. The excitement can be unbearable. *(01-26-81)*

I did participate in the church bell ringing last week for the welcome to the hostages, and we also had a bright yellow ribbon on the mailbox. *(02-03-81)*

Have you heard about the father who has doubts about solar energy – because he says his teenagers have spent most of their lives on the beach and they have less energy than anyone he knows. *(07-27-81)*

I drove home on Tuesday via Gladstone in order to deliver Mrs. Casendino's present and discovered to my horror that someone in the NYC garage had opened her present and left torn wrappings all over the back seat. Ah, honesty in the big city. *(12-14-81)*

It really rained, and the fairly substantial snow piles disappeared. I went to the dump that day and almost stayed as part of the landscape – stuck. *(01-11-82)*

Life these days seems to center around wood fires, carrying wood, filling bird seed feeders, and checking the daily paper for signs of winter's progress. For example, and this has puzzled me, I have noticed that the sun rose for five successive days at 7:19 AM. I thought it changed every day. *(01-19-82)*

Last week had some notable events. I went to Spags. I went to the dump. The car turned 33333.3 miles – and I think it important to watch for these milestones. *(01-25-82)*

Pomfrog Center was the address on the bill at the Ritz in Boston – where Mom and I spent a pleasant couple of days last week. *(02-14-83)*

I saw a bumper sticker: No more missiles until we use what we've got. *(06-27-83)*

Speaking of the future, I ran across a quote from Casey Stengel: "I never make predictions – particularly about the future." *(03-19-84)*

One of the questions that eternally haunts a guy like me is the refrain from old friends and others – "What do you do with yourself?" Well, as I sit here in these early hours, I can recall things from last week such as sanding shutters (they won't fit in the new room after all, and so I have sold them), weeding, putting the leaf mulch into the garden, getting the Woodie started, going to Spag's and to the dump, making an antique sign, painting some new windows, cleaning up after the carpenters, taking ticks from the dogs (a real plague this year), putting up a new swing, fund raising for Princeton, smoke bombing a woodchuck hole, trying to catch up on reading (I failed), needlepoint and of course the morning walk and the noonday nap. Not very productive, I guess, but when I think back to some of the days in big biz at RCA and other places, there may still be a favorable comparison for useful days. *(07-30-84)*

I wrote a check on October 12 – and the check number was 1492. *(10-15-84)*

On Tuesday, we headed for Boston where the day was spent shopping. As I sat in the Mall while Mom added to her Christmas bundles, I came to some heavy sociological conclusions. First, people actually wear some of those weird clothes we see in the Sunday Times; second, most women seem to have sore feet; and finally, the saddest creatures are the obviously retired men being led around by busy wives. They look lost and I suspect some of them are. *(12-03-84)*

I just got back from Worcester where I checked in at Filene's basement store, for today was their annual Brooks Brothers sale. I picked up a few things. It's kind of dumb for me to buy such fancy things when my uniform is basically dungarees and old shirts. *(02-04-85)*

Here's a question from Andrew: what is big, yellow (or orange) and sleeps three? Answer on the other side. [*A state highway truck.*] *(09-23-85)*

Mom had an argument with a gas station attendant claiming that he shortchanged her by ten bucks. Wonder of wonders – he called later and said she was right. *(07-14-86)*

We heard a loud noise the other day and looked up and saw the Goodyear blimp. It was very low and weaving around the tops of trees. Mucho excitement. *(10-26-86)*

Big news? One morning last week, Pop went back to bed about 6:30 and went to sleep. Until 8:05AM! *(12-15-86)*

Last night, we went to a church Christmas supper. Pop was the bartender in my new apron that reads . . . Peas on Earth, Good Will Tomatoes. *(12-22-86)*

It's snowing. The forecast is for a bad storm. Pop is out of gin. *(2-09-87)*

Pop was a winner in a Ford sweepstakes – a 12-volt air compressor for getting air into a flat tire. I hope it never gets used. *(05-04-87)*

There is a Pumpkin Center. I saw it on a map of California. *(02-08-88)*

There is good and bad economic news. The good is that we got our tax refund. The bad is that Mom discovered that I had registered one large deposit twice in the checkbook. So, it's back to poverty. *(05-09-88)*

Since I write the Weekly Letter, I decide what's important from the preceding week. And last week was some week. The Big 65 was celebrated in proper style, and I want to thank you all for the cards, gifts, calls and everything. One of the best wisdoms was from Uncle Bob's card . . . "Your birthday is a good time to look back and see where you've been, to look ahead and see where you are going, but most importantly, to look down and see what you are eating." *(06-12-88)*

Mom is furious. She sent in some coupons for a rebate – and the check came made out to Donald P Dickson. *(11-21-88)*

I drove into Putnam the other day, hit the curb while parking, and slashed a tire. I was right next to the Goodyear place. The irony is that I was going to the bank to deposit a Goodyear dividend check.

And so, I bought a-Goodyear tire. *(03-26-89)*

My calendar says: With a small boy, cleanliness is not next to godliness, it's next to impossible. *(08-06-89)*

Another failed experiment: I bought unsalted pretzels. Not good. *(12-04-89)*

A new Law from Pop. Don't ever stay at a place with a buffet. I gained five pounds. *(07-22-90)*

New Year's Eve was very quiet here. But we went to a New Year's Day luncheon. My lunch partner was a young woman who lived in various homes in London, Singapore and Buenos Aires. I didn't have much to talk about except Pomfret, Putnam and Dayville. *(01-07-91)*

A house divided. We are of different views as to whether Pete Rose should be on the ballot for the Hall of Fame. Your view? *(02-10-91)*

We have bulbs coming up! And on my afternoon walk up the hill with Mac, I go through a wooded area, and there yesterday was a golf ball. I have been walking this stretch for a dozen years. Where the heck did the ball come from? Fallout of a tree? *(03-04-91)*

Surprising news! I went to Spag's, and they had a sale on dungaree jackets, and I now have a replacement for the old tattered one. *(03-11-91)*

Quote of the week: I hate housework. You wash the dishes, make the beds, and six months later you have to do it all over again. *(06-30-91)*

When Mom came up with the idea for the extension of the dining room, she may have not realized what a great spot it would be, especially in wintertime. We spend many hours each day with books, magazines, needlepoint . . . and just watching the birds on the feeders in the trees just a few feet away. To the long list of types, we added finches last week, and we saw a dozen robins in the field! *(02-14-91)*

Mom surprised me with a handsome piece of needlepoint on a footstool that will help with snoozes at the easy chair. *(01-12-92)*

Perhaps it was the early hour, but the announcer on the news the other morning meant to say 'the latest news' and instead said 'the newdist lays.' Did I spell it right?
Walmart is coming to Putnam!
I got a handsome certificate from the Cancer Society. What does one do with such things? *(07-12-92)*

We have new mattresses in the front guest room. I have tested them at nap time – and they pass. *(09-13-92)*

Since I have some space, I will report what my 'inspirational calendar' says for today. "Use what talents you possess. The woods would be very silent if no birds sang there except those that sang best." Good advice. *(10-11-92)*

A long letter from Uncle Bob included this: "Last night we went to a concert in Lancaster, wherein the piano-soloist was a high school senior from Manheim. He played a Bach Concerto, a Sonata by Mozart, and a long and varied Carnaval by Schumann. This lad was tremendous, and the unbelievable factor was that he has been blind since the age of two. . . . I rather think that none of us in the audience will gripe about our personal circumstances for a long time to come." Amen. *(10-25-92)*

A sign of the times . . . the local school had two open teaching jobs.

And 354 applicants. *(11-01-92)*

I also found a bunch of menus that I had collected over the years, most of them from expense account meals. For example, Christmas dinner at the Hotel Washington Canal Zone in 1943 at $1.50; a ham dinner at the King's Arms in Williamsburg at $3.75; lamb chops at the Chez Paul in Chicago at $4.25; filet mignon at Alfred's in San Francisco at $4.75; and swordfish in the Cape Cod room of the Drake Hotel in Chicago at $2.65. These were all for complete dinners! *(01-11-93)*

And some time ask Mom how I told her to get to East End Avenue – when the affair was at West End Avenue. But I'd wait a while. *(02-21-93)*

Do you know what happens when you play a country-western song backwards? You get back your girlfriend, your job, your house . . . but you lose your horse. *(03-19-93)*

Also, last fall, on October 22, we purchased a bed and two rockers at a place called the Vermont Store in Middlebury. Well, they delivered the bed some months ago – wrong color. We shipped it back, and it arrived again last week – right color. But the rockers have been painted wrong. *(03-28-93)*

They don't make things like they used to department. When we lived in Indian Hill (which house?), Mom knitted me a pair of gray woolen socks. During these many years I have worn them once every week or so, and they are wearing in the sole. If Mom was in the sock business, she would have gone broke a long time ago. *(05-09-93)*

The film mystery has been solved. Unhappily. I apparently sent a blank film for processing and put another film back into the camera. Thus, we have Easter Sunday egg hunt on top of ranch pictures, and Matthew's graduation on top of the egg hunt. Sorry. *(06-27-93)*

Speaking of the camper, I finally got the hole in the rear of the camper repaired. That hole had been caused by my backing into Will Ludwig's mailbox. Well, then, you guessed it; when I brought it home and was backing it into the space at the barn (with Mom watching and screaming), I backed into the mailbox by the gas pump. Happily, no damage. *(08-15-93)*

If we have a stagnant economy, it's hard to tell on the highways. Trucks, trucks, trucks. I find it difficult to understand the economics of trash hauling. An endless stream of large trailers from New Jersey and Pennsylvania are on the highways in Ohio and Indiana. *(10-03-93)*

And so, I was in NYC on Friday evening. How do people live in that city? My parking fees for overnight were $43.00 a day and a bagel and a coffee at the airport cost $2.83. Life is very different in Pumpkin Center. *(11-07-93)*

Some time ago, I wrote some post-Christmas letters. One of them was to Al Lemaire, a friend from Scout days. Another was to my cousin Dickie who lives in South Carolina. She called last night and among other things said, Who the hell is Lemaire? What had happened is that I took a newspaper clipping about a hockey player named Lemaire, and put it in the wrong envelope. But I got a call from a cousin out of it. *(02-08-94)*

Are you looking for a vacation idea? An ad in the New Yorker says: "Restored Hacienda in the bottom of the Canyon. Hidden in the misty reaches of the Mexican Sierra Madres. At the end of an 8-hour cliff hanging dirt road." Should I go further? *(02-20-94)*

I said goodbye to an old friend last week. A heavy sweater from L.L. Bean, with big holes in the elbows, finally was discarded, and with heavy heart. *(05-08-94)*

It is so nice to have all this technical wizardry in the automobiles. But, when some device goes awry, hold on to your wallet. The wagon had such a problem, and the bill was 250 bucks. *(05-15-94)*

I took many walks along the Charles River on some beautiful days. From early morning on, there were walkers, joggers, bikers, roller bladers . . . who was working? Also, I was the only person wearing shoes, everybody had some fancy footwear. *(08-28-94)*

Local tragedy department: We moved the mailbox from roadside to a spot on the driveway, but some guy backed into the driveway and broke it. Then, yesterday, a 25 foot plus part of the large evergreen in front of the house just collapsed. Finally, while digging, I dug into a huge toad, and ripped him open. He crawled away, trailing blood. It has bothered me since. *(08-21-94)*

They just don't make things right anymore department. I took a pair of shoes to the shoemaker last week for repair, and he said "they couldn't be fixed." Those shoes were good for 30 years. Too bad. *(12-04-94)*

The other night, I put a 'used martini' in the refrigerator for overnight parking. The next day, I found a dead fly in the martini. Very dead. But he looked happy. *(01-29-95)*

I bought a frozen Green Giant entree called Veggie Burger, and the instructions included the phrase "load on, catsup, mustard, onions etc." I know why. Zero taste. *(03-05-95)*

Do you listen to Car Talk? It comes on Saturday mornings at 10 AM on Public Radio. Two lunatics talking about car problems. But great. *(04-02-95)*

Lucky Pop. The man from the gas station in Massachusetts called the other day to say that a credit card had been found there. It had fallen from my wallet. There are good people out there. *(06-11-95)*

On Father's Day, I must tell you about a Charlie Brown card that said on its cover: "You're the kind of Dad who would scale the highest mountain and cross the hottest desert to make his family happy! And on the inside, it said "Vacations might have been easier if you'd asked directions." *(06-18-95)*

On your next call here, you may be greeted by an answering machine. With great reluctance, we have installed one. During the past month or so, we have been badgered by childish calls (adult inspired?), especially in the wee hours of the morning. The machine at least lets us screen the calls. *(08-06-95)*

My calendar on the desk has this thought: Worry is interest paid on trouble before it comes due. *(11-05-95)*

Mom has been reading some of Aunt Flo's letters and cards from the 30's and 40's. One item raised my interest: "we are sending you a chicken." By mail? *(11-19-95)*

When we were in Scotland some years ago, I picked up the morning paper at the Inn, and guffawed at an article that said that oatmeal reduced the risks of heart attacks. How self-serving of the Scots that have oats as a national product! But today, there was a full page in the Times from Quaker Oats announcing that the FDA was about to issue a statement that confirmed that finding. Tomorrow morning, it's oatmeal. *(01-14-96)*

I did some filing work and some filing cleaning out. Among the items I found were trade-up certificates for American Airlines. I bought these some years ago for a planned vacation flight, and when it came time to leave, I couldn't find them. I found them last week. They expired in 1992. *(01-21-96)*

Message of the week – don't play cards. A Jersey man went to Atlantic City to play cards in a tournament but quit the cards because he had lost his glasses and had difficulty seeing the cards. So, he wandered into the slot machine area, played once, and won 4.4 million bucks. *(02-11-96)*

Finally, on Saturday morning, I started for Spag's, but the snow of the previous day had been preceded by freezing rain – and I had a tough time opening the driver's door. But I did, and then I couldn't keep it closed. So, I locked it. When I stopped for the paper, I couldn't open the door, nor the other door. I climbed into the back seat, and neither door would open – and I panicked. There's no other word for it. I finally laid on the seat and pushed a door open with my feet. But I was really 'bushed.' And then I started again for Spag's, realized I was low on gas, and that the gas flap was probably frozen, too. I turned around and went to a friendly station with a mechanic, and sure enough, it was frozen, but they fixed it. It took me an hour to recover. Are you still with me? *(03-10-96)*

A mean thief: somewhere, sometime, someone opened the door of our car and removed the disability sticker. *(03-31-96)*

We had Greg Hannah, a temporary bachelor, for supper one evening. He borrowed an electric drill – one that I had purchased in Cincinnati at least 40 years ago. It blew four fuses, and I finally tossed it. So much for quality. *(03-31-96)*

Question of the week: "Why do you call her Mom when she's not your Mother?"
Story of the week: A 94-year-old man went to the doctor and said there was something wrong with his left knee. The doctor reminded

the man that he was 94. The man replied that his right knee was 94 years old and in good shape. True story. *(06-23-96)*

One afternoon, as I started my walk from the library, I noticed a camper from Oregon in the parking lot. I chatted with the owner, and learned that he was checking on his New England ancestors, and was heading for Taunton, Mass. His name? . . . Dean [*maiden name of our mother*]. Mom went up and they traded genealogy data. Small world? No. Tiny world. *(06-30-96)*

A newsletter listed a few sayings from Sunday School kids. To wit: The Fifth Commandment is humor thy father and mother; Solomon, one of David's sons, had 300 wives and 700 porcupines; the greatest miracle in the Bible is when Joshua told his son to stand still and he obeyed. *(08-05-96)*

Another record broken! After lunch today, I had a good nap (is there any other?), and then went to the chair by the greenhouse, read for an hour, and then went to the couch in the library and had another nap! Glorious. *(08-11-96)*

In my view, there are three kinds of naps. The first is the bed-nap, a serious and deliberate decision; then there is the couch-nap, usually a spontaneous and what-the-heck decision; and finally, the chair-nap, also known as the reading nap. I am happy to report that today I have enjoyed two of them, and the day ain't over yet. *(08-25-96)*

Milestones: I looked down at the odometer in the Escort and it said 56789.0. Also, the Earnings Report in the paper the other day had a list of companies with every letter in the alphabet. Rare. *(10-20-96)*

One of the gifts here was a package of wines, with the following words on the carton: A Latin Saying – It is well to remember there are five reasons for drinking: the arrival of a friend; one's present or future thirst; the excellence of the wine; or any other reason. *(12-30-96)*

Mom arrived, almost on time, at the Providence airport on Monday evening. Boy, was I glad to see her! Providence has a spectacular new airport. And it has Southwest Airlines . . . and the ticket prices for all the airlines have plunged. Mom flew to Phoenix for $174 round trip. As I waited and watched incoming and outgoing travelers, a thought surfaced, namely, where are the business suits? *(01-19-97)*

They just don't make them right anymore department: I showed Mom a bath towel that was frayed, and she advised me that it was purchased at Shillito's in Cincinnati about 35 years ago and was for use at the Indian Hill pool. *(03-16-97)*

I made a big decision last week. When returning the Reader's Digest Sweepstakes, I decided to take the payments on a monthly basis for 20 years, rather than a larger one each year. I like to receive checks each month. *(03-31-97)*

I saw a sign on a clothing store . . . Formal and Limousine wear. What the heck is Limousine wear? *(03-31-97)*

Research Department: I sat outside the mall while Mom and Aunt Ruth shopped. Results: Of some hundred shoppers, only six wore skirts; and only one man had a jacket and tie (and a fedora). *(04-06-97)*

The mundane department: On the way home, we stopped for a lunch on the turnpike. Two hot dogs and a coke cost $8.40. Good grief. *(4-20-97)*

Big Spender! To celebrate the final sale of the Camper, I told Mom we would splurge with a lunch at our new fine restaurant, the Harvest.

However, it was full (Secretary's Week). We went into Putnam to the Vine, but there was no place to park (too many antiquers). We had lunch at 233 Pomfret Street [*home*]. *(04-27-97)*

The Homestead Village Nursing Area is large (maybe 50 rooms) and seems to have complete facilities. But they have and do the same thing as the place Gil Ferguson was in. The 'command' area is like a large atrium, and they gather the wheelchairs in a large circle, and it is a depressing sight.

You look at these wheelchairs and realize that each of these persons (mostly women) was once an active child, parent, gardener, teacher etc., and here some are tied in a wheelchair, and some bent over asleep. But the reverse is, of course, if not here . . . where? *(04-27-97)*

There was an ad for a house in Peapack yesterday that sounded of interest. It has 25 fireplaces. *(05-11-97)*

What's in a name? Seen on a truck – As Soon As Possible Plumbing Co! *(08-03-97)*

We went to a memorial service for the mother of a selectman. It was in the old Meeting House in Brooklyn, and the benches were narrow and hard. How did people handle the long services in yesteryear? *(08-17-97)*

We are well. We are in love. And we wish the same for you. *(08-24-97)*

I dig and work for five or ten minutes, and then sit for the same time. During that sitting time, I watch the endless parade of silage trucks. I also watch a leaf here, a leaf there tumble down. There is a great Norway maple in the field in front of the house. And it is slowly turning red, orange and brown from the top down. The top half is now in great color. What a wonderful occupation . . . watching a tree change colors.

Speaking of color . . . the New York Times has added color! Good grief! *(09-21-97)*

I wore my new corduroys for the first time. Swish, swish. You can hear me coming. *(10-05-97)*

I'm rich! At least on the desk. I received a check of many thousands from the brokerage house. And I also received a phone call saying that a mistake had been made, and that the check had been 'stopped.' But it is fun to look at it. *(10-19-97)*

I need your advice. Many years ago, Mom knit me a glorious sweater. Now, the elbows are gone. She says, Toss. I say Keep. And you? *(11-16-97)*

An interesting item: With all the talk about 'Bible' churches, we learned that if you went to an Episcopal Church for one year, you would have been exposed to 80% of the Bible. *(12-01-97)*

Today is also the anniversary of my jumping up from the chair, tripping on the rug and breaking my wrist. *(02-14-98)*

When we lived in Wilton (23 years earlier), I bought or was given a pair of white Levi's. I am sorry to report that (with Mom's blessing) they are now in the rubbish. Things just don't last. *(08-08-99)*

We are having a debate about a new car. There are good reasons to trade in the Escort, and some reasons not to. It would clearly strain the budget, and we have already signed up for some budget breakers. When I took the car to the Ford dealer, he took it for a spin, and noted that the mileage was 77,777.7. A good omen? *(10-12-98)*

We have a new Escort car. It sure looks like the old one, but after 8 years and 80,000 miles it was time to change. Funny, buying a new car used to be an exciting event, but now I rather resent the diversion of dollars from other projects. *(03-07-99)*

We got a card from Wagon Trails in Door County about some special prices for the Fall. Any interest? The mailing was addressed to Comfort Center Ct. *(08/29/99)*